LEADERSHIP FOR AFRICA

IN HONOR OF OLUSEGUN OBASANJO
ON THE OCCASION OF HIS 60TH BIRTHDAY

LEADERSHIP FOR AFRICA

IN HONOR OF OLUSEGUN OBASANJO
ON THE OCCASION OF HIS 60TH BIRTHDAY

Edited by
Hans d'Orville

LEADERSHIP FOR AFRICA
In Honor of Olusegun Obasanjo
on the Occasion of His 60th Birthday
New York 1995
ISBN 1-885060-03-3
© by Hans d'Orville, New York 1995
Cover: Edjo Aton (Desert spirits) by Bruce Onobrakpeya
Art layout: Irene Connors, Collage Press
Design, formatting and production: Terencia Leon-Joseph
Printed in the United States, 1995

Table of Contents

FOREWORD by Hans d'Orville 5
Bruce Onobrakpeya 11
    EDJO ATON (Desert spirits)
Lord Callaghan of Cardiff 13
    MILITARY TRIALS IN NIGERIA

I. Personal Tributes

Joaquim Alberto Chissano 19
    CONSEQUENT WITH HIS WORDS
Jimmy Carter 23
    TO GENERAL OLUSEGUN OBASANJO
King Moshoeshoe II 25
    WE NEED HIS WIDE EXPERIENCE
Mohammadu Buhari 29
    A SALUTE TO GENERAL OBASANJO
Chief Mangosuthu Buthelezi 31
    FATHER OF THE CONTINENT
Flora Lewis 33
    THE FUTURE WILL BE ON HIS SIDE
    FOR NIGERIANS, A VOICE OF CONFIDENCE THAT MUSTN'T BE SILENCED . 35
Jonathan Power 37
    THEY'VE LOCKED UP AFRICA'S GREATEST POLITICAL FIGURE
Babacar N'Diaye 39
    TRIBUTE TO A VISIONARY LEADER
Boubakar Diaby-Ouattara 41
    LETTER TO GENERAL OBASANJO
Layashi Yaker 45
    AN ARDENT LEADER
Mario Graça do Machungo 49
    WISHES FOR A LONG LIFE AND SUCCESS
Ted Turner 47
    LETTER TO GENERAL OBASANJO
Shridath S. Ramphal 53
    HOMAGE TO GENERAL OLUSEGUN OBASANJO
Roelof F. (Pik) Botha 55
    HIS SOUTH AFRICAN CONNECTION

Jeremy Pope 71
    IMAGES OF A NIGERIAN IN APARTHEID SOUTH AFRICA
Colin Eglin 75
    A GREAT HUMAN BEING AND A TRUE DEMOCRAT
Robert von Lucius 79
    "ARCHAIC ROCK"—MEDIATOR FOR A BETTER SOUTH AFRICA
URGESTEIN 83
Emmanuel A. Erskine 85
    MY HEARTIEST CONGRATULATIONS
Ad'Obe Obe 87
    A COMMITTED OPTIMIST
Carol Lancaster 91
    A LEADER FOR AFRICA AND THE WORLD
Bona Malwal 93
    AFRICA'S BEST KNOWN SOLDIER, DIPLOMAT AND STATESMAN
Eme Awa 97
    AMBASSADOR-EXTRAORDINARY FOR AFRICA
Chief Afe Babalola 101
    GENERAL OLUSEGUN OBASANJO AS AN EXEMPLAR
Onukaba Adinoyi Ojo 109
    THE CAUTIOUS REFORMER
Yohei Sasakawa 115
    DEAR GENERAL OBASANJO
Olatunji Dare 117
    THESIS ON GENERAL OLUSEGUN OBASANJO
Tunji Abayomi 119
    IN HONOUR OF A MAN OF MANY MEANINGS
Joan Holmes 125
    A GREAT SON OF AFRICA
Abul Maal A Muhith 127
    NO TIME TO WASTE, NO TIME TO REST
Tunji Lardner 131
    OUR GENERAL
François van Hoek 135
    LETTER
Chief Jonathan Adio Obafemi Olopade 137
    THE MAN OBASANJO—A DISCRETE NEGOTIATOR AND MEDIATOR
Ayodele Aderinwale 139
    THE ESSENCE OF OBASANJO
Terencia Leon-Joseph 145
    THE ABILITY TO RESPECT OTHERS
Mehri Madarshahi 147
    LETTER TO GENERAL OBASANJO
Magemeso Namungalu 151
    THE UNIQUE GENERAL

II. Africa's Leadership Challenge

Ali A. Mazrui 161
    POLITICAL LEADERSHIP IN AFRICA: SEVEN STYLES AND
    FOUR TRADITIONS

Reginald Herbold Green 165
    AFRICAN LEADERSHIP FOR AFRICAN AGENDAS
Francis M. Deng 171
    LEADERSHIP BEYOND POWER: THE OBASANJO MODEL
Oyeleye Oyediran 181
    THE MILITARY AND POLITICAL TRANSITION IN AFRICA:
    THE OBASANJO MODEL
Ibrahim Agboola Gambari 183
    THE SPECTRE OF MARGINALIZATION OF AFRICA IN THE EMERGING NEW
    WORLD ORDER: A PERSONAL REFLECTION
Gabriel O. Olusanya 187
    AFRICA: WHAT FUTURE?
Hans d'Orville 193
    THE NEW CHALLENGES OF GLOBAL COMMUNICATIONS
Dragoljub Najman 197
    DEMOCRACY AND GOVERNANCE IN AFRICA
Transparency International 203
    LETTER
Peter Eigen 205
    THE "MORAL RELATIVITY" OF CORRUPTION
Ednan Agaev 215
    NORTH-SOUTH: THE NEED FOR A CO-OPERATION STRATEGY
Peter Anyang' Nyong'o 219
    THE CHALLENGE OF NATIONAL LEADERSHIP AND DEMOCRATIC
    CHANGE IN KENYA

III. Africa's Development Challenge

Chief Emeka Anyaoku 229
    THE IMAGE OF AFRICA
Robert S. McNamara 235
    SUB-SAHARAN AFRICA'S DEVELOPMENT CRISIS
Per Pinstrup-Andersen 241
    FOOD SECURITY IN SUB-SAHARAN AFRICA
Ellen Johnson Sirleaf 247
    THE LEADERSHIP DIMENSION OF AFRICAN DEVELOPMENT
Babafemi A. Badejo 257
    THE ASSOCIATIVE SECTOR AND THE POOR IN AFRICA
Pierre Claver Damiba 271
    INTRODUCING CULTURAL FACTORS INTO DEVELOPMENT IN AFRICA
Thomas R. Odhiambo 281
    THE MILITARY DIMENSION OF THE AFRICAN SCIENCE ENTERPRISE
Jean F. Freymond 289
    AN AGENDA FOR THE COMING YEARS
LIST OF CONTRIBUTORS 295
CONTRIBUTING ARTISTS 297

FOREWORD

Almost six months ago, on 5 March 1995, I saw General Olusegun Obasanjo last. He had arrived in New York on his birthday—his 60th birthday—to attend a meeting called by the Carnegie Corporation of New York to discuss its future grant policies towards Africa. Heading to my home first, he didn't realize that we—a small group of his personal friends and close associates—wouldn't forget. We wouldn't forget that it was his jubilee birthday and so he arrived just in time for a surprise dinner party in his honor. Over the previous weeks, I had arranged clandestinely to assemble some 50 of his friends, partners, admirers and associates in various Africa-related undertakings to contribute to a book honoring this restless world leader on HIS day. Given the tight deadlines, I was only able to present him with a table of contents of the book to be—*Leadership for Africa*—accompanied by a personal letter which he asked me to include in the printed version of the book.

And *as we wouldn't forget him then, we will not forget him now*. In the space of a few short months, General Obasanjo—the former Head of State of Nigeria and the only military leader in Africa to surrender voluntarily power to civilians in an organised manner—sadly has become *the most prominent political prisoner in Africa, if not the entire world*, after the Burmese military regime has lifted unconditionally all sanctions on Aung San Suu Kyi . As I am writing this foreword he has not been seen for more than three weeks and all his friends are deeply concerned about his physical well-being, and his safety. Gratifyingly, many world leaders and governments share this trepidation and have sought to obtain his freedom through a variety of initiatives and interventions.

What has happened since that 5 March 1995?

Following his brief visit to New York, General Obasanjo proceeded to Copenhagen, where he attended the World Social Summit called by the United Nations, as a distinguished international guest and as a Human Development Ambassador of the United Nations Development Programme. While in Europe, newspapers reported that the Nigerian Government had uncovered a coup plot and arrested a number of military persons. Among those detained was, according to wire reports General Obasanjo's erstwhile number two while in Government, General Shehu Musa Yar'Adua. Before heading home from Copenhagen, General Obasanjo called me and mentioned that he had been told of rumours that he would also be arrested upon his return to Lagos. He told me "You know, I did nothing unlawful and I have nothing to fear" and no one was able to convince him from spending a few extra days in Europe to assess the unfolding situation in Nigeria. His place was in Nigeria, his beloved country, for which he has more than once put his life on the line. And then, one should not forget the notion of "Not My Will", the title of his memoirs which describe how he literally had to be forced to become Head of State of Nigeria succeeding his friend and associate General Murtala Muhammed who had been assassinated in a coup attempt. "Not My Will" is a motto which certainly would best characterise the General's attitude and ambitions—nationally or internationally. He would never seek office or glory, he would make himself only available if and when he were asked—and even then he would have to be pushed sufficiently hard to comply. Whoever knows him can attest to this basic trait of this unassuming, unpretentious and unambitious personality.

He was arrested a day after his return to Nigeria, on 12 March 1995. The outside world did never learn precisely of what crime or transgression he was being accused or tried for. By now, the long drawn out process has become a charade.

With Obasanjo's detention, Nigeria and Africa are deprived of one of their most illustrious, vocal and worldwide respected sons, whose political judgement, intervention and mediation was solicited worldwide and he has been made a pawn in a political struggle.

His sterling service and leadership "beyond power" for over more than a decade on behalf of Africa, should qualify him to be nominated as the first ever black African outside South Africa for the Nobel Peace Prize. Indeed *General Olusegun Obasanjo should be proposed for the Nobel Peace Prize*. And the occasion of his unjustified detention and imprisonment as well as his 60th birthday may serve to focus once more on his unique accomplishments, for which this book provides ample testimony: a leading and effective crusader for the abolition of apartheid and racial discrimination in South Africa. Zimbabwe and Rhodesia; a successful mediator and conflict manager in the wars besetting Angola, Mozambique and the Sudan; a democrat who organised without pressure free elections in his own country and handed over power to the democratically elected victor; a farmer setting an example of the importance of agricultural development for the future well-being of African countries; a former general determined to imbue the spirit of democratic governance, accountability, the rule of law and the proper role of the military in African governance; a fighter for clean government and elimination of corruption in business and government; a promoter for effective regional cooperation, as in the case of ECOWAS; an interlocutor in crisis management ranging from Sudan, Zaire, Kenya, Burundi, Rwanda to Mali; the founder of the Africa Leadership Forum and an indefatigable fighter to bring to fruition the Conference on Security, Stability, Development and Cooperation in Africa (CSSDCA); an advocate for sustainable human development and women's rights; an articulate and effective spokesman for Africa, its woes and aspirations in international fora. And and and.

His lifetime accomplishments deserve the highest recognition the world community can bestow. It would be the only adequate response to the cruel treatment meted out to him at this moment!

This book, *Leadership for Africa*, shall therefore serve not only as one other birthday contribution to a unique leader, but as a testimonial to the abilities and historic contribution of "the General", as he is widely known. General, we all miss you and we hope to see you soon again in the midst of the myriad of efforts that have coined your life since retirement!

And in this spirit, let me conclude with adding the text of the letter I presented to General Obasanjo on his birthday, 5 March 1995:

"Dear General,
"From the bottom of my heart, please accept my most sincere congratulations on your jubilee 60th birthday. In the seas of many other—considerably more senior—jubilees, this milestone in your distinguished life looks almost like belonging to the "junior league", as it were. Yet, in your life time, you have established through your career and your devotion to many causes—local, national, regional and international—a track record and a reputation second to none. I was almost incredulous when it was intimated to me recently that your 60th birthday was just around the corner. You may even remember that I cautiously asked you during your last visit to New York, when you would turn 60. Characteristically you replied, that "no matter what my passport says, I know that I will be 60 on 5 March 1995—and if you want, I will spend my birthday in New York at a meeting dealing with US policy formulation devoted to Africa". Here you go again—I was almost tempted to say, because you placed the public cause ahead of personal interests or, let alone, even the idea of private celebrations at home.

"And so I succumbed, virtually at the last minute, to urging by an unnamed friend of yours, to arrange for a special birthday salute and presentation to you. Over the past few years, some observers came to like some of the publications I had arranged and edited on various occasions—and they, as I, felt that the only true tribute commensurate to your personality and spirit, to your very intellectual faculties and presence and—yes—to your subtle and open domination would be to assemble this uniquely European, scholarly-clad publication called *liber amicorum* or, in my own language, *Festschrift*. Such a book, as it is dryly called in the English language, is a special salute by friends, collaborators, associates, admirers and family friends to celebrate and honor both the person—in all his dimensions—and his life time achievements thus far.

"I took on the challenge and within a time-frame of barely a month, I was able to organise a unique collection. True, the selection of the invitees was mine and thus, some who might have wanted to contribute might not have been asked to do so. *Mea culpa*, *mea maxima culpa*—but no ill will or discrimination was intended. To the contrary, from heads of states to younger individuals, who are at the threshold of their careers, this book represents a virtual microcosm of your interests, commitments and personal-political relationships. It is thus with humility and deep emotion that I wish to present you herewith with the table of contents for YOUR book, which has the working title "Leadership for Africa": some 50 contributors from many countries attest to the respect and love that you have acquired and nurtured and which you are commanding worldwide. In a real sense, as some of us used to call you during a particular exciting and challenging episode in your life during 1991: *The Great Commander*.

"Unfortunately, for technical reasons it may be a while until the book itself will be published. So, the suspense will be there, and the intellectual celebration is willy-nilly bound to be stretched out.

"Let me add that this project was for me, in a way, the apotheosis of our association, collaboration and friendship, coinciding as it does with the termination of activities of the InterAction Council, which was the forum where we first met in November 1983. My respect and dedication to you and to our various causes was and is limitless. You have taught me a lot in words and deeds and you have been a central and exciting part of my life over the last decade, to the point that I sometimes used to characterise you affectionately as either my "brotherly father" or my "fatherly brother" who imparted in me the Yoruba art of "*eni suru*" (have patience). Whoever you were, our association was exceedingly rewarding and I want to take this jubilee anniversary to say a very warm and sincere "thank you".

"I could not think of any better tribute to you as latter-day *Cincinnatus Africanus*, but the poetic verse of a chapter of Norman Corwin's *On a Note of Triumph* published 1945 in the wake of World War II.

> Lord God of trajectory and blast
> Whose terrible sword has laid open the serpent
> So it withers in the sun for the just to see,
> Sheathe now the swift avenging blade with the names
>   of nations writ on it,
> And assist in the preparation of the ploughshare.
>
> Lord God of fresh bread and tranquil mornings,
> Who walks in the circuit of heaven among the worthy,
> Deliver notice to the fallen young men
> That tokens of orange juice and a whole egg appear
>   now before the hungry children;

That night again falls cooling on the earth as quietly
    as when it leaves your hand;
That Freedom has withstood the tyrant like a Malta in
    a hostile sea,
And that the soul of man is surely a Sevastopol which
    goes down hard and leaps from ruin quickly.

Lord God of the topcoat and the living wage
Who has furred the fox against the time of winter
And stored provender of bees in summer's brightest places,
Do bring sweet influences to bear upon the assembly line:
Accept the smoke of the milltown among the accredited
    clouds of the sky:
Fend from the wind with a house and a hedge, him
    whom you made in your image,
And permit him to pick of the tree and the flock
That he may eat today without fear of tomorrow
And clothe himself with dignity in December.

Lord God of test-tube and blueprint
Who jointed molecules of dust and shook them till
    their name was Adam,
Who taught worms and stars how they could live together,
Appear now among the parliaments of conquerors and
    give instructions to their schemes:
Measure out new liberties so none shall suffer for his
    father's color or the credo of his choice:
Post proofs that brotherhood is not so wild a dream as
    those who profit by postponing it pretend:
Sit at the treaty table and convoy the hopes of little
    peoples through expected straits,
And press into the final seal a sign that peace will
    come for longer than posterities can see ahead,
That man unto his fellow man shall be a friend forever."

In conclusion, let me thank sincerely all contributors to this book who all presented their text in their personal capacities. They have thus expressed their faith in, gratitude for and friendship with General Obasanjo. My special thanks goes to the renowned international artists whose artwork is gracing this volume: Bruce Onobrakpeya and Twins Seven-Seven of Nigeria, Elimo P. Njau of Kenya, A.R. Penck, Pina + Via Lewandowsky, Thomas Florschütz, Clemens Weiss and Werner Bartsch of Germany.

Their mastery and art add a special touch and express in artistic terms the call to "Free Obasanjo". My personal thanks go to Terencia Leon-Joseph who assisted me, as in many other undertakings, in this project which was so close to our both hearts. Her husband, Peter Joseph, graciously gave of his time and skills to facilitate and ensure production of this volume. Finally, I am grateful to Irene Connors of Collage Press in New York for her advice, artistic layout and all printing arrangements.

New York, 31 July 1995   Hans d'Orville

Bruce Onobrakpeya

EDJO ATON[1]
(Desert spirits)

Two in one,
Androgynous
Mysterious Forms
Etched by time
Towering above all turbulence,
Stand as beacon of light
To travellers
in the arid plane.

Agbogidi, devine mediator
Radiates endless energy
From God the supreme intelligence.

Ariuwevwi in traditional garb,
A magnet and catalyst
of progressive forces,
Gives identity

And a hope for the future.

Irhigbedowara inspires
Diligence, hard work
And self-sufficiency.

Ejiro'gba bequeaths
Valour, courage and conquest.

Odiri imbues with patience
To live in harmony
with nature.

May these spirits
Guide continuously
in our endless struggle
For Survival.

---

[1] This poem appeared first in "Bruce Onobrakpeya, Poems and Lithographs—Print notes and Comments № 9", Ovuomaroro Gallery, Lagos, 1989. It is reprinted here with the gracious permission of the author.

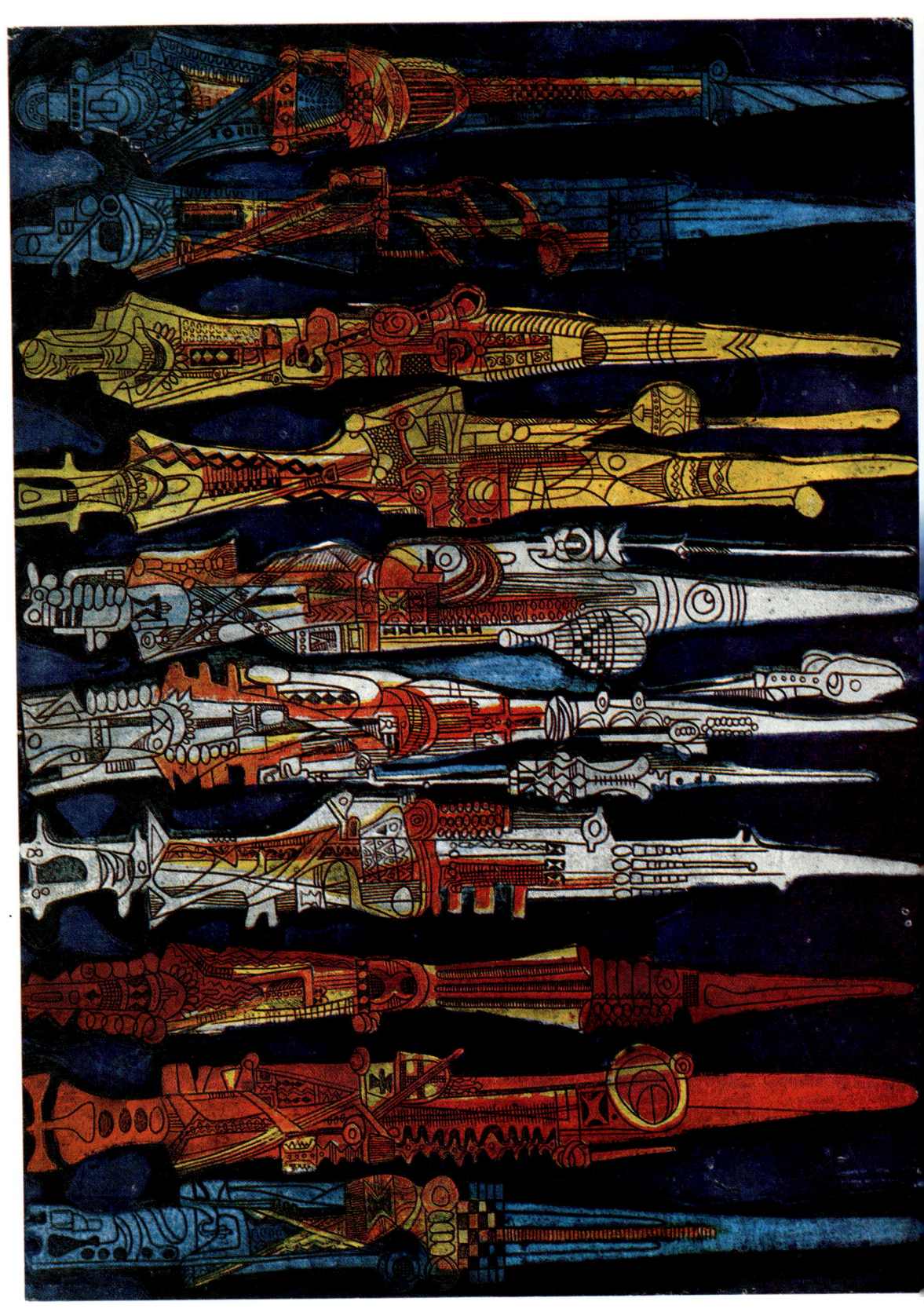

Bruce Onobrakpeya
"EDJO ATON"
(Desert Spirits)

Bruce Onobrakpeya
"UNITY"

Lord Callaghan of Cardiff

MILITARY TRIALS IN NIGERIA[1]

Once again, the miserable consequences of army rule in parts of Africa have been shown up by the news this week that a Military Tribunal in Nigeria has found guilty a number of people accused of plotting against the regime. Twenty-three alleged conspirators have been convicted and at present await the passing of sentences, which can run from twenty-five years' imprisonment to death by firing squad.

Nigeria is the largest country in Africa, with a population approaching one hundred millions, with rich oil reserves and with the potential to be one of the "Big Three" in Africa. Once it was proud to be known as the champion of the African continent, but during the last two decades, it has languished under the rule of a self-perpetuating group of army officers, the latest being General Sani Abacha. Before he came to power, Abacha had a hand in at least two previous coups, and it is alleged, took power himself by forcing the retirement of the former Head of State at gunpoint in November 1993.

Earlier that year, the army had annulled the result of a national election to fill the office of President. Despite the verdict of the international observers that the election had been the fairest and most free and peaceful in Nigeria's history, the army refused to acknowledge the victor, Moshood Abiola, as President. Instead, they placed him under military detention and so he continues until today.

Under army rule, the once robust economy of Nigeria has been raped by personal greed and by incompetence. Inflation is rampant; the country is heavily in debt; manufacturing output has seriously declined because of an overvalued currency; its oil revenues have been frittered away; corruption is widespread; a number of Nigeria's highly educated and professional workforce is leaving the country in face of the alarming increase of threats to life and property. The country has become notorious for the level of fraud and drug-running.

The present military trials, which have highlighted the country's plight and brought upon the regime the condemnation of governments and leaders in many parts of the world, have taken place following the supposed discovery by General Abacha of an alleged plot against his regime by forty or fifty civilians and soldiers, among them a former State Governor, a former Director of the Army's Legal Service, the head of the Campaign for Democracy—a so-called "unlawful society". The most prominent of those arrested and tried is former President Olusegun Obasanjo and a retired Major-General Shehu Musa Yar'Adua.

Little information about these military trials has been disclosed. It is known that the accused were not permitted their own lawyers but instead had to accept representation by army lawyers. The exact charges levelled against former President Obasanjo are unclear, but for those of us who have worked with him for twenty years, it is simply not believable, until direct evidence is produced, that he would have any part in an attempted coup—if indeed there was one. He is deeply respected on the international scene, a constant spokesman for African needs, a strong opponent of apartheid, a consistent advocate of democracy and the developing countries. He is also the only military officer—he is a four-star General—who, when Head of State, freely handed back Nigeria to civilian rule.

His last engagement prior to his detention last March was a conference in Denmark on ways of relieving world poverty. Whilst there, he was warned by friends that he might be arrested if he returned to Nigeria. This was a threat he had lived under for some time and he had told me more than a year ago that he felt that his life was in constant danger because of his calls for a democratic government and his opposition to the army regime. At the same time, he told me that he would always face his accusers conscious of his innocence. So despite the warnings, he travelled back to Nigeria. Since then, no-one has heard anything directly from him and all attempts at communication have been rebuffed by the authorities.

Shortly after his arrest I had a long telephone conversation with General Abacha who undertook at that time to ensure Obasanjo's safety and said that he would hope to release him after he had been questioned.

Obasanjo's detention and arrest, the secret trial by the military, the exclusion of the public, the refusal to allow access to him or to the other twenty-three accused, has aroused serious protest around the world from many governments and from those who admire his work and know his personal standing.

This is not the only rebuff. A short while ago, President Mandela of South Africa sent Archbishop Tutu to Nigeria to secure the release of President Abiola. His mission was rejected. In the case of the present trials, the American, Canadian, German, Ghanaian and Zimbabwean governments, among others, have expressed their concern and objections. The British Government, through the Minister for Overseas Development Lynda Chalker, has stated that if those detained were to be subject to summary justice or capital sentences, it would be incomprehensible and totally without justification. With the same intention, South Africa's Vice-President, Mr. Thabo Mbeki, has also visited General Abacha, with what result is not yet known.

Among others, former President Carter, Prime Minister Trudeau of Canada, Chancellor Schmidt of Germany, together with three former British Prime Ministers, have all made representations expressing publicly our concern and urging General Abacha to show restraint, to promote political reconciliation and to lay the foundation for a return to civilian democratic rule.

Perhaps as a result of this sustained international pressure, and also in the knowledge that a meeting of fifty-one Commonwealth countries will take place in New Zealand next November, General Abacha is reported to have told a Nigerian constitutional conference (of which, incidentally, one of the accused, Major-General Yar'Adua was a member) that he will be ready to make certain commitments about the future. The Nigerian High Commissioner in London, Alhaji Abubakar Alhaji, The Sardauna of Sokoto, recently informed me that General Abacha will announce a timetable on 1st October for the handover of power to a democratic civilian government. he has further said that the ban on political activities is to be lifted and that an electoral commission will be established to review the electoral register and supervise the formation and registration of political parties.

This ought to be good news, but in the light of the army's broken promises, these statements will be treated with a certain reserve. Nevertheless, if carried through and a reasonable timetable is met, a new phase of political process would begin. It will be up to the Commonwealth Conference at its meeting next November to hold the Nigerian delegation to General Abacha's undertakings and if they are not kept, to take steps, for example a temporary oil embargo, to force the army's hand.

The opposition to General Abacha is divided and it will need a combined effort at working together and a higher degree of responsibility than has been shown heretofore on all sides, civilian and military, if political reconciliation is to be effected, and the foundations laid for a transition to a civilian government and to democratic rule.

But before this step is taken and if it is to have any chance of success, General Abacha must use his power to set aside the verdicts of "guilty" by the army court and either hold a fresh trial in public with proper civilian legal representation, or else release those charged forthwith. Nothing else will satisfy those who believe that the accused are guilty of nothing more than working for civilian democratic rule in their own country.

---

[1] Lord Callaghan wrote this article for the New York Times Syndication Sales Corporation at the end of July 1995. It is reprinted here with the kind permission of the author and the Corporation.

I. Personal Tributes

Joaquim Alberto Chissano

CONSEQUENT WITH HIS WORDS

Olusegun Obasanjo is a name that struck our minds in 1970 when suddenly and in a dramatic way the Nigerian civil war come to an end.

Colonel Obasanjo, then General Officer commanding the 3rd Marine Commando Division of the Nigerian Army Unit hit the front pages of the news when on 13 January 1970, in the field, he accepted the Biafran Surrender.

The way he performed his duties in this particular case indicated that General Obasanjo was a man of the future, not only in Nigeria but in the world at large.

Magnanimous in victory, General Obasanjo viewed that event as a real opportunity to keep Nigeria together as a country and at peace with itself. He exemplarily applied in that act the policy followed by the Nigerian government after the war: "No victors, no vanquished".

General Obasanjo's association with important events in his country was, to a large extent, due to a mixture of luck and a great sense of opportunity.

He had months, earlier taken over from Colonel B. A. M. Adekule as General Officer commanding the 3rd Marine Commando Division when he was a few months later selected to initial the surrender papers, thus becoming one of the most outspoken officers during the war.

The change of government in July 1975 made General Obasanjo the second in Command to General Murtala Muhammed, the Head of State. His becoming himself Head of State following the death of General Murtala Muhammed on 13 February 1976 was just a natural and logical consequence. This again attracted to him fame, name and sympathy, also out of Nigeria.

But what makes the difference in all this is that General Obasanjo is a particularly very active man who impressed special dynamics to the governance in Nigeria and tried to do the best for his country by implementing what he felt was good and correct for the people of Nigeria without any particular intention to be original.

Honest, consequent with himself and faithful to his colleagues and friends, General Obasanjo had this to say when he assumed office as Head of State after the death of General Murtala Muhammed: "I can pay no better tribute (to him) than to continue in the way with which he had led the country."

Those were not just words from an emerging General Obasanjo. Those words became the main thrust of his administration which became known as the Murtala/Obasanjo regime. That is how consequent Obasanjo could be with his friends and with himself.

As outsiders and leaders who in our own country had just taken over the governance of Mozambique from the colonial administration, we could not but follow very closely the way an African leader was governing the most populous country in our continent. Amazingly, General Obasanjo pursued, step after step the policies enunciated by the late Murtala Muhammed by implementing thorough reform of local government and by paying greater attention to agriculture in order to diversify the basis of the Nigerian economy which had then become a monoculture economy deriving most of its revenue from oil.

The popular catch phrase by General Obasanjo "Operation Feed the Nation" was spread in many countries of our continent which had inherited monoculture economies based on the production of one or two agricultural crops.

General Obasanjo made history when he became the first African head of a military regime to freely and peacefully relinquish power and hand over to a democratically elected civilian administration.

This is particularly remarkable for General Obasanjo, who was once again consequent with his word. He did prepare this by reviving the constitutional drafting committee and have it complete its work.

He then made sure that elections were held at the promised date and power was smoothly transferred to a civilian President.

But the area in which we were more familiar with General Obasanjo was foreign policy. Under General Obasanjo's regime Nigeria pursued a vigorous foreign policy with Africa as its centrepiece. In this connection, Nigeria became particularly notable in its role in enforcing sanctions against the rebel Rhodesian minority regime and the South African racist regime.

Apart from nationalising major British companies as a way to force Britain to stop breaking sanctions against Rhodesia, Nigeria hosted the World Conference for Action against Apartheid in 1977 where further commitment for the vigorous fight against racism, apartheid and colonialism was taken.

The African National Congress (ANC), the Pan-Africanist Congress of Azania (PAC) and the South-West African People's Organisation (SWAPO) were during General Obasanjo's regime allowed to open offices in Lagos.

For us, the former Portuguese colonies, General Obasanjo will be particularly remembered for his firm stand following the steps taken by General Murtala in support of the recognition of the MPLA-led government in Angola by the OAU when many countries vigorously campaigned against that recognition.

After retirement from office, General Obasanjo is still very active. His struggle to foster democracy, peace, justice and understanding amongst human beings has made him member of many international bodies throughout the world in pursuance of this ideal.

A man of exceptional leadership qualities, a man of action, a man whose size can not be compressed to just fit in Nigeria, General Obasanjo has made himself a Nigerian and an international figure of the highest caliber. He is a good friend of Mozambique, a country that he has visited a considerable number of times, a country where he is very cherished.

JIMMY CARTER

March 5, 1995

To General Olusegun Obasanjo

It is with pleasure that I join your friends and colleagues in congratulating you on your 60th birthday. This testimonial book is a well deserved tribute to your outstanding contributions to Africa and, indeed, throughout the world.

You have dedicated your considerable talents to serving the people of your nation. As President of the United States, I had the honor of welcoming you to the White House. Later, I became the first president in my country's history to visit sub-Saharan Africa when you hosted me in Lagos. I was inspired by your leadership and your vision for your own government in meeting the challenges of an emerging democracy. You showed great faith in the judgment of Nigerian citizens and set an example for other African leaders who sought to restore peace and stability to that great continent.

There have been many occasions in the ensuing years when I have had the privilege of calling on you, as well as responding to your calls, to collaborate on matters of mutual concern. You have been very helpful to us at The Carter Center and have been quite generous with your time and counsel.

Your longtime friendship means a great deal to me personally. Rosalynn joins me in expressing our warm best wishes for continued health and happiness.

Sincerely,

Jimmy Carter

THE CARTER CENTER · ONE COPENHILL · ATLANTA, GEORGIA 30307

King Moshoeshoe II

WE NEED HIS WIDE EXPERIENCE

Over the last twenty years, very many people all over the world have come to associate the name of General Olusegun Obasanjo with a deep personal commitment to action in the cause of Africa's quest for that basic need of all nations, namely good governance as the only base on which to build a culture of genuine democracy and respect for the human rights of every African citizen on the basis of an authentic African definition.

On the occasion of General Obasanjo's 60th birthday, all of us who have had the privilege of knowing him, sharing with him some of his aspirations, and benefiting from his wide experiences, are happy to celebrate with him and convey our best wishes for his well-being, good health and happy future. We are happy to celebrate with him in recognition of his enormous personal contribution to Africa's development and his tireless efforts in promoting the ethic of good governance and democracy in Africa, coupled with his achievement beyond the borders of Africa.

From 1976 to 1979, General Olusegun Obasanjo, as Head of the Military Government of Nigeria, worked tirelessly to restore a civilian elected government to his country, and succeeded.

From the very beginning of his time in office, as Head of State and Government, General Obasanjo saw the central importance of local government systems and structures, in his recognition that local people understand local needs better, and that decision-making, at local level, is an invaluable exercise in the preparation for effective national participatory democracy. Such local government reform was also seen, by the General, as the natural first step towards the creation of a new democratic constitution centred on a vision of consensus, consent and participation. Both these first steps were achieved, not without difficulty, with remarkable success.

At the same time, General Obasanjo recommitted and firmly allied Nigeria to the cause of the freedom struggle in Southern Africa. Under his leadership, Nigeria assumed a front line position among those nations which were committed to the just cause of the freedom movement both in Rhodesia then — now Zimbabwe — and in South Africa. The increased international support such a commitment engendered, made a very significant contribution to the outcome of that freedom struggle.

General Obasanjo also encouraged the ethic of both self-reliance and the indiginisation of industry, in his recognition of the importance of establishing durable local and national infrastructures in the new nations of Africa, as an essential national economic base, without which no nation can be truly independent.

As we know, after the elections of 1979 in Nigeria, and the restoration of civilian rule, General Obasanjo concentrated his enormous energies on the international promotion of good governance in Africa, and founded the now well known Africa Leadership Forum.

From his own direct experience, the General is well aware that the search for an African-defined and African-entrenched democracy has proved to be difficult and often elusive, bedeviled by external pressures, prescriptions and conditionalities on one side, and, on the other, by those who merely use the concept of democracy in the name of promoting their own narrow self interests, while still excluding the majorities in whose name they claim to be promoting "democracy".

It has become increasingly clear that the road to genuine democracy, linked to economic recovery and equity as it must be, will be a long and hard one, strewn with difficulties and dangers. Africa's fragile and often deteriorating economics expose African nations to ever increasing degrees of dependence, and thus to external prescriptions based on the self-interests of those external forces. The interdependence of economic progress and any genuine democratic process presents its own problems and dangers, making the task ahead more urgent. Few people will be more aware of these realities than General Obasanjo.

As we celebrate his 60th birthday, congratulating him and thanking him for his outstanding service to Africa, and to the wider world, we shall also express our awareness of the need for him to continue his work for the well being of Africa and her citizens. We are in need of his wide experience, his insight, and his vision of what constitutes good governance for Africa.

We owe him a debt of gratitude which, hopefully, will be repaid by progress, within Africa's nations, towards the entrenchment of those democratic values and processes on which General Obasanjo has spent so much of his time and energies in promoting.

There is still a long way to go. The international forum he has provided for Africa's leaders and for those sympathetic to Africa's enormous political, social and economic problems, has been and will continue to be invaluable to our search for the means of economic recovery and social stability, without which true democracy will continue to be elusive. The interdependence of economic progress and democracy is still in need of further exploration and realisation in terms of Africa's need to find both the means and the will to actuate African defined solutions to our own considerable problems.

We look to the Africa Leadership Forum, under the guidance of General Olusegun Obasanjo, for the further extension of opportunities to come together and explore these vital issues as matters of increasing urgency.

God Bless.

Mohammadu Buhari

A SALUTE TO GENERAL OBASANJO

It is remarkable that at sixty, General Olusegun Obasanjo is already a political has-been. Not at all a politician, General Obasanjo is a soldier, an administrator and a statesman of repute. His record of achievement is astonishing: a soldier who rose to be Inspector of Engineers, General Officer Commanding a Division, playing a vital role in winning the Nigerian Civil War, Minister, Chief of Staff and finally Head of State. To cap all these achievements, he is a world statesman.

I have served under General Obasanjo and he is one the very few Officers who inspired his subordinate by example; never shirked a challenge, never declined a responsibility and never deliberately let his fellows down. In point of hard work, dedication, commitment to the army and the nation, he stood above all the military officers of time. His energy was proverbial. He was the vital clog of the wheel of the famous Murtala-Obasanjo Government. Minutes of frequent meetings of Senior Chiefs were supposed to have been taken by some junior officers, but Obasanjo in rank, title and substance No. 2 took down the minutes, distributed them and gave everyone present and absent their marching orders.

I had the privilege of working closely under him as Minister for Petroleum in 1976-79 when he was Head of State. He has never one day disappointed me on a point of principle, never once gave me an instruction which I felt was contrary to the interest of Nigeria and though occasionally given to impulse he would immediately see reason and change his mind if confronted with superior professional argument.

His role as the only military leader to pilot a successful transition programme which restored power to elected representatives of the people entitles him to be counted among Nigeria's very great men. Leaving office, he has shown appetite and dedication to international causes which came close to securing for him a major role in international affairs. He may yet reach those summits as his energy shows no sign of diminishing, yet his perception and judgement have sharpened and matured. I wish him many happy returns of the day.

Kaduna, 23 February 1995

Chief Mangosuthu Buthelezi

FATHER OF THE CONTINENT

I feel humbled by the very idea of trying to pay tribute to this great son of Africa because I feel incompetent to do this adequately. I first heard of General Olusegun Obasanjo when he took over the governing of the State of Nigeria after the tragic assassination of General Murtala Mohammed.

In 1976 General Obasanjo as the Head of State of Nigeria did something I can never forget. It was in October 1976, when Transkei was taking its so-called "independence". The General feared that I might somehow be compelled to attend such a farce. General Obasanjo instead made sure that I was invited to speak at the Nigerian Institute of International Affairs on the same day as Transkei was celebrating its 'circus'. So in fact, when that travesty of justice took place and Transkei was declared "an independent State" through the grandiose apartheid plan I was in Lagos speaking at the Nigerian Institute of International Affairs.

The second reason for the General to invite me to Nigeria was in order to arrange a meeting between me and the President of the African National Congress (ANC), Mr. Oliver Tambo. I stayed in Lagos waiting for Mr. Tambo longer than my visit was scheduled for. Unfortunately I had to leave before Mr. Tambo arrived but we met at the Lagos Airport. Just as I was leaving he was arriving.

It is ironic that a military General such as General Obasanjo should be such a devotee of peace. General Obasanjo wanted to encourage me and Mr. Tambo to stand together in our common fight against apartheid and the oppression of our people by the Apartheid regime. When differences between the ANC and the Inkatha Freedom Party (IFP) escalated into violent attacks he continued to try and bring about peace between us.

The man is big in every sense. To him we were all his brothers and his duty as he saw it was to engineer a spirit of brotherhood between the ANC and the IFP members and to ensure that bloodshed stopped.

In everything that General Obasanjo has done it has always been prompted by his desire to ensure that peace prevailed and that Africa thrived economically and becomes a success story. I know of no other single leader who has done this more than General Obasanjo.

The very manner in which he voluntarily abdicated as the Head of State of Nigeria in order to pave the way for a civil government is so typical of the man. It demonstrated his commitment to peace, democracy and justice.

General Obasanjo is still doing a lot for Africa and we wish him well as he reaches the prime age of 60 years. Those of us who know him and admire his talents know that there is still a lot that he will yet do for Africa.

He is a man who deserves the title of Father of the Continent. We thank God for many Blessings in our time and all of us who have had the privilege of knowing General Obasanjo know that one of the Blessings of Africa in our times is General Olusegun Obasanjo.

May the Lord give him many more years for I cannot imagine Africa without this great warrior of peace and stability in Africa at this crucial time, when Africa is struggling so hard to come into her own, like other continents in the world.

Flora Lewis

THE FUTURE WILL BE ON HIS SIDE

The conference was being held in Cologne, Germany, in a handsomely restored municipal building which gave an air of gravity and formality. Most of the delegates were Africans, from a wide variety of countries, some of them angry, all of them eager to be head and to be noticed. I don't remember the precise title of the meeting, it was another of those big seminars on whither Africa, what's gone wrong, what's to be done. General Obasanjo, in his inevitable pastel robe and matching cap that make him look even bigger and more serene than life, was presiding. The talk wandered endlessly, sometimes in a drone, sometimes in sharp outbursts of indignation. A European or an American chairman, I thought, would have pounded the table, cut off the blatherers, called for order. But Obasanjo let them carry on, intervening gently from time to time to nudge the orators back to the subject, express a mild doubt. No consensus seemed possible. And then he summed it all up, with such subtle and unmistakable authority, such conviction and assurance of what had been on his mind all along that everyone agreed to agree, satisfied they'd had a fair hearing. It was a masterful performance, a demonstration of the secret skills of an African chief, it seemed to me.

He is a conciliator, but not a compromiser. Instead of lecturing or propounding, he puts questions that push people to recognize they may not own the whole truth. The questions strip away the self-serving arguments, the cliches, the evasions that always find someone else to blame and reject responsibility. Maybe they don't really change much. But they show Obasanjo's patient determination that they should, his persistent hope that they could, his faith that they will. They reveal his honest awareness and anguish at how badly Africa has used its hard-won opportunities in the first generation or two after colonialism, and the intensity of his search to find the tools and techniques for doing better.

Tools and techniques and ideas, not theories, because Obasanjo is a practical man who measures by actual results and disdains illusion. His chicken farm is an example, zillions of chickens, chicken for breakfast, lunch and dinner if you are a guest, so tuck a tin of sardines in your suitcase if your palate craves variety. His chicken farm works, and its purpose is to prove that mundane, concrete, unpretentious enterprise can work and make a real difference. But it also serves as an intellectual retreat, a place accessible but far enough away from the devilish frenzy of Lagos to convoke people for serious discussion of Africa's needs.

Quite rightly, in my opinion, Obasanjo has identified the critical, decisive need as leadership, informed, intelligent, competent people honestly dedicated to improving their countries' lot. So he runs seminars, collecting youngish people who have already shown capacity and interest who need support and a sense of not being alone in their efforts. That is not a spectacular approach, but it has the best chances of being sound. It rests on the conviction that it is up to Africans themselves to fix what ails Africa, and that until they are prepared and willing to try, outside help won't achieve what's needed. It is at once a diagnosis and a prescription for cure, for it brings the essential momentum of self-confidence.

At this time, Obasanjo's great candor and lucidity don't seem to be protecting his own country from devastating regression that only makes the road ahead steeper and bumpier, his vision more important and less needed. I feel sympathy and sadness, though I have never heard him ask for that. There is a sturdiness and wisdom in him that makes him carry on and keeps alive the sense that whatever the obstacles, the future will be on his side.

For Nigerians, a Voice of Confidence That Mustn't Be Silenced

By Flora Lewis

TORONTO — Word has reached here that Olusegun Obasanjo has been put under house arrest at his farm in Nigeria. It is a bad sign in a country already wracked by the destruction and despair of military dictatorship.

General Obasanjo, who became president after a military coup in 1976, pledged that he would hold elections under a new constitution and then turn power over to a civilian government. Amazingly, he did, in 1979, sparking hopes of a change of course in African politics.

The hopes were not realized. The military seized control again in 1983 and since then there has been one coup after another in Nigeria. Promised elections were held in 1994, but annulled before results were announced. The evident victor was jailed, political activity and labor unions were banned, and the independent press was shut down by an increasingly severe military dictatorship.

Now, having announced that it had crushed an attempted coup, and manifestly unable to cope with the country's steadily deteriorating economic and social disorders, the dictatorship is trying to crack down even more.

Since he left office, General Obasanjo has become a leading voice both on his continent and among world statesmen wherever there is an effort to end the recurrent bloody conflicts and promote democracy in Africa. He is not an accuser, always seeking to mediate and to reconcile in the style of a traditional African chief.

But he hides neither his anguish nor his blunt acknowledgment that what has gone wrong can no longer be attributed to the legacy of colonialism and tribalism, to the outside world's interference or to its indifference or lack of help. He has focused on leadership as the critical gap that keeps Africa down, and organized a group of educated young men from many countries in the African Leadership Forum to help each other promote the ideas and skills needed to turn the tide.

"The bald fact is that Africa is a continent in dereliction and decay," he told the forum's inaugural session in 1988. It was held at his big chicken farm an hour's drive from Lagos where he demonstrates with commercial success that Africa can do a great deal more to feed itself and end starvation.

"We are moving backward as the rest of the world is forging ahead," he said. "In the last resort, only we ourselves know what is really amiss with us, and what is more, only we as Africans can tell it as it is to ourselves. Our destiny ultimately lies in our own hands."

The troubles, he said, "stem from human failure" to establish institutions which "make for a humane society," and the cause was "our false political start."

He travels widely, receiving international honors to encourage others to hold such views. It was just after his return from the United Nations social summit in Copenhagen earlier this month that police went to his farm. It is evident that the intent is to stifle even moderate criticism.

General Obasanjo, 58, is an imposing figure in flowing, pastel-colored robes and matching cap, a big man with a lively sense of humor and the natural poise that confers authority. As he celebrated "freedom in South Africa," he warned last year of the "darkening night of barbarism" threatening many countries in the wake of "the senseless and shameful carnage in Rwanda that diminishes for us t the sense of accomplishment."

Even before his arrest, an unprec dented campaign was launched in Ame ica by the powerful black lobby Tran Africa calling for sanctions against t Nigerian dictatorship. Its leader, Randa Robinson, says, "We must isolate Nig ria politically, socially and economicall in the same way we were able to isola South Africa and Haiti."

For too long the tyrants of black Afr ca have been indulged as the world ta geted the racist regime in Pretoria. But is another form of racism to treat Afri as an exception where, for reasons of hi tory or culture or whatever, human righ and emergence from poverty are not to expected — a kind of nature preser where the evil of which all men are cap ble is to be left untamed by the will to d good of which all men are also capabl

General Obasanjo often expressed h refusal to believe that Africa, with i immense resources, was somehow co genitally unable to join the world econ my and produce decent societies. H must not be silenced. His fate is a test.

© *Flora Lewis.*

A.R. PENCK
Free Obasanjo, 1995

Jonathan Power

THEY'VE LOCKED UP AFRICA'S GREATEST POLITICAL FIGURE

There is a man in Africa who had been a military ruler for four years who decided at the age of 42 to walk away from the Presidential palace of the continent's most populous, and potentially richest, country, put on a pair of blue jeans and start a chicken and vegetable farm. No, this is not some surreal tale from a sequel to John Updike's "Coup". This is Olusegun Obasanjo, the man responsible for engineering Nigeria's transition to democracy in the late 1970s and the man arrested two weeks ago by members of the same self-perpetuating clique of self-besotted officers who overthrew a functioning democracy in January 1984.

General Obasanjo was so obsessed by his countrymen's refusal to come to terms with Nigeria's economic chaos, not least the run down of the country's precious agricultural base, that he decided to show what could be done with the land. He does not have a private palace tucked away. He has a sizeable, but modestly furnished house in Abeokuta and a farm in nearby Ota. He used to often sleep rough in the farm's makeshift buildings still under construction, watching over every detail with the same tenacity that made him a successful officer during the civil war, brought him to the top of the army and the country when he was in his late 30s and led him to modernize the constitution.

He was principled but he was also tough. When Prime Minister Margaret Thatcher refused to move to restore British authority in Rhodesia after it was usurped by the country's whites, Obasanjo nationalized British Petroleum's interests in Nigeria and threatened to boycott British exports. Mrs. Thatcher later changed tack and began the process that led to free elections and majority rule in what is now Zimbabwe. Without a free Zimbabwe we can be sure that there would have been no free South Africa.

Democracy, farming and disarmament are Obasanjo's passions and he has relentlessly promulgated them. As President he once accused his countrymen of "callousness and sadism". Today he speaks frankly of the disequilibrium in a society that has been propelled so suddenly from ancient to modern. "We got caught up in the conflicts of culture, of trying to graft the so-called sophistication of Europe onto our African society. The result so far has been abysmal failure. We are betwixt and between."

Once when I arrived to interview him at his home he apologized for being five hours late. Driving home from his farm he had come on a long line of traffic halted by an accident. He went to investigate and found six bodies on the ground. There was a crowd of onlookers and two policemen standing idly by. No one was helping.

The policemen claimed that it was not their responsibility; they were en route to "other business". Obasanjo ordered the crowd to help him move the bodies to the roadside and commandeered a car to rush one of the dead women, who was obviously pregnant, to the hospital in the hope of saving the baby. He then directed traffic for three hours until the police finally arrived.

I met him again the next day. He had just learnt that the hospital had refused admission to the woman because there was no police certificate recording the accident. I should have done a Caesarian myself, by the roadside", was his only comment.

I have talked at length with him many times about this conflict between the old and the new. Nigeria, after South Africa, is black Africa's most developed and wealthy nation yet at the same time it struggles, not very successfully, to transform the values of centuries-old village life to the impersonality of the four-lane highway.

He sees a three- or four-generation timetable. "The improvement of having standards and the wealth of nations are more of a journey and less of a destination", he told me in one conversation. "Within our traditional society there are lots of things that we can pick, improve and develop into our own political concept. What for example is wrong with our traditional society which respects age, experience and authority? Or the norm that everybody is his brother's keeper? Or the practice of stigmatizing and ostracizing evildoers and the indolent?"

It is an immense and almost overwhelming struggle to achieve transition. When asked to predict which way the scales will tip Obasanjo is cautious. He has hope for the future, but at the same time he is awed by the demands put upon the average Nigerian. He does not believe oil has helped. Much of its wealth has been wasted and "the people put in a pressure cooker".

When will the pressure cooker burst? When indeed will the people rise up and say they have had enough and perhaps propel Obasanjo back into the presidential palace to sort things out?

The generals by locking this man up and then detaining him may well have turned up the heat so high that this time they get cooked in their own juice. If this should happen my only comment would be, at last.

Babacar N'Diaye

TRIBUTE TO A VISIONARY LEADER

It is a great pleasure for one to join other friends and associates of General Olusegun Obasanjo from various stages of his life, career and activities in contributing to this book which has been commissioned to mark his 60th birthday.

There is no doubt that General Obasanjo's first sixty years were full of achievements. From an infantry soldier, he rose to become a general as well as head of a military government of Nigeria. To most Nigerians, General Obasanjo is usually remembered for making and honouring a pledge to end military rule and return his country to democracy. By keeping that promise, General Obasanjo has joined the ranks of world statesmen who have shaped the course of events during their lifetime.

But to the rest of the world and indeed to Africa, General Obasanjo is remembered as a military man with a democratic vision. Although democracy became a worldwide phenomenon with the collapse of Communism in the former Soviet Bloc in 1989, General Obasanjo was a convinced democrat prior to that time. Even though he is a career soldier, he was convinced long ago, that military involvement in politics, if it takes place at all, should be an aberration that should be terminated as soon as possible. his is because the military, by nature and tradition, is not well suited to the governance of civil societies. General Obasanjo realised along with earlier thinkers on the subject that sustainable development cannot occur without good governance and the involvement of the people in that process. Thus, his handing over of power in 1979 was the actualization of his vision as a democrat. To him, democracy and good governance are not ends in themselves but instruments of social and economic engineering. Thus, the current wave of democracy in Africa has been partly influenced by the democratic ideals which underpinned his handing over power in 1979.

But as a great African statesman that he is, General Obasanjo's vision goes beyond Nigeria. As a retired Head of State, he established the Africa Leadership Forum as a centre of reflection on African problems. The establishment of the Forum is derived from General Obasanjo's realization that Africa needs to develop indigenous capacity in governance. Since its establishment, the Forum has attracted the attention and participation of African leaders, policy makers as well as outsiders interested in African development issues.

General Obasanjo will also be remembered for spearheading the crusade for an African Security Conference, along the lines of the European Security Conference. When fully established the Conference, which would be part of the Organization of African Unity, would have responsibility for peace-making efforts in Africa.

Beyond all these, General Obasanjo will also be remembered for his writings and contributions to public debate in and outside Africa. Through these writings, he has tried to articulate his views on governance, democracy, African development issues and world policies, to name a few. These writings will remain a testimony to posterity by a great African statesman.

On the occasion of his 60th birthday, I join others in wishing this great and visionary son of Africa, many more years of active service to the Continent and indeed to the world. While saluting this soldier of noble cause, I would like to remind him that a lot still remains to be accomplished on Africa's development agenda. I therefore urge him to carry on with the struggle as a good soldier that he is.

Boubakar Diaby-Ouattara

LETTER TO GENERAL OBASANJO

Dear General,

It gives me great pleasure to wish you all the best on the occasion of your 60th birthday. I am particularly happy that you celebrate your 20th birthday, for the third time stronger than even the first time. This augurs well for your continued leadership in your country, in Africa, and in the world.

I want to focus this birthday tribute on both my personal experience in working with you, and on an issue which I think is of central importance to Africa—leadership.

For over two decades now your leadership has inspired those of us who have been privileged to work with you in demanding circumstances to achieve critical developmental goals in Africa and outside the African continent. Yours has always been true leadership by example. As a successful General and a respected Head of State who presided over a period of considerable political, economic and social development, you had ample opportunity and popular support to continue to lead your country. Nonetheless you kept your promise and successfully managed a smooth and well-programmed transition to a democratically elected civilian government.

As Chief Executive of ECOWAS, I had a first hand opportunity to witness the immense difference your leadership made at the regional and continental level. Successful regional integration depends on dedicated and effective individual and country leadership. As Head of Government you provided both in West Africa. In 1979, ECOWAS' 16 Heads of State signed, ratified, and effectively implemented—at all the border posts in West Africa and in less than 60 days—the Community's historic Protocol instituting the total freedom of movement of people without visa requirements.

This was achieved against the background of intensely troubled interstate political and diplomatic circumstances in West Africa at that time. Not only did many countries not have diplomatic relations, but in several instances the movement of people between countries was forbidden outright.

The credit for the speed and effectiveness of this landmark Protocol, unmatched in the history of regional cooperation in Africa, goes exclusively to you. All the 15 other Heads of State took their cue from your example as the leading country in the organization. I recall that exactly 21 days after the signing of the Protocol by the Heads of State, the instruments of ratification by your Government were received in the ECOWAS Secretariat. Largely due to this action and example, the ECOWAS Secretariat received the required number of ratifications within one month to enforce the Protocol throughout the whole region. It is revealing that it seems as if significant progress toward effective regional integration in West Africa has eluded the region since the end of your stewardship of your great country.

Your leadership and foresight have been demonstrated many times since the ratification of the ECOWAS Protocol, and in equally far-reaching ways. As an internationally respected statesman you have not only tirelessly championed Africa's cause, but have provided an outstanding example of African leadership. You clearly identified the importance of political pluralism, good governance, and effective conflict management to Africa's sustainable development at a time when this was not widely recognized, either in Africa or elsewhere. As with regional integration, your leadership in this area has been both influential and practical. You have demonstrated your commitment to peace and development by your willingness to devote considerable time and attention to preventive diplomacy and conflict negotiation, despite many other pressing obligations.

As the Executive Secretary of the Global Coalition for Africa (GCA), I have been privileged once again to work with you, and once again to witness your commitment to Africa. The GCA has called upon your unique experience and leadership in almost all aspects of its priority agenda, and has benefited immensely from your dedicated and active participation, particularly in its work on governance and conflict management. With characteristic good grace, you have always been ready to assist, both intellectually and practically.

Africa's development crisis is first and foremost a leadership crisis. I remember discussing this subject with you the first time in Turkey on the shores of the Bosphorus, and thereafter in Abeokuta in Nigeria. Your subsequent establishment of the Africa Leadership Forum was a timely initiative, focussing on the most critical aspect of development in Africa and yet the least analyzed; leadership as a major determinant of development, especially in the case of latecomer countries (all of Africa) which need to design and implement effective, rapid, industrialization strategies. Except in very rare cases, throughout most of Africa's contemporary history leadership has invariably been part of the continent's predicament.

All those who believe in and admire your example and relentless dedication to promoting human progress in Africa should spare no effort in joining your crusade to underline the key role of dedicated, enlightened, and competent leadership for the realization of Africa's development aspirations. And so we shall.

Happy birthday, General!

Layashi Yaker

AN ARDENT LEADER

On the occasion of his sixtieth birthday, it is a pleasure for me to contribute a few thoughts on the eventful life, career and accomplishments of General Olusegun Obasanjo. It goes without saying that statesmen like him, who are concerned not only with the management of current problems but also with long-term issues of a continental or global nature, are an inspiration. This is the case of my friend General Obasanjo, retired soldier, former Head of State and Commander-in-Chief of the Nigerian Armed Forces, and currently a steadfast farmer, writer and intellectual and an ardent Africanist and internationalist.

General Obasanjo offered distinguished services to the Nigerian army and earned well deserved promotions, raising to the rank of Commander, 3rd Marine Commando Division in the South-Eastern State. He was the one to whom the Biafran rebels surrendered to in 1970 bringing an end to the Nigerian civil war.

Even though a soldier by profession, he was a democrat at heart. During his tenure as Head of State and Commander-in-Chief of the Nigerian Armed Forces from 1976 to 1979, having been Chief of Staff, Supreme Headquarters between 1975 to 1976, he was the first military ruler to voluntarily hand over power to a democratically elected civilian regime in October 1979 at a time when democratic governance was not yet in vogue. In Nigeria, he has been an outspoken advocate of good governance and democracy. No one had a better background than he to offer counsel—his service in the army and in conflict situations, his charismatic military career, and the firm decision to quit government and introduce democracy.

Equipped, with the experiences of his own country, he quickly realized the prebendal tendencies and dangers that were at the door steps of post-independence African leadership. The lack of a political culture, the weakness of national integration, widespread poverty, the predominance of the peasantry and the limited development of a class society, all made for factors that would strain central institutions and encourage leaders to lord it over their own people. His commitment to Africa has been unwavering for over three decades causing him to lead very activist African policy. From his early days in the army, he served in the Nigerian contingent of the United Nations Force in the Congo (now Zaire) in 1960. It was during his tenure as Head of State that Nigeria nationalized the British Petroleum (BP) company because of its recalcitrant stance and violation of sanctions against the white minority regime in Rhodesia (now Zimbabwe) and South Africa.

Since leaving office in 1979, he has been actively involved in national, regional and international affairs. He succeeded through his extraordinary analytical ability and the integrity of his personality to continue making significant contributions to meeting many of the African and global challenges. Unlike most of his colleagues who had tasted the sweetness of power the African way, he quickly realized that the challenges facing his country, Africa and the world should and must be tackled at the grassroots. In 1979, he established himself as a farmer in Ota, Ogun State, Nigeria and since then he has accepted the higher function of giving advice, and expanding his vision and interests into other areas and comments.

As an African farmer, he believes in self-sufficiency, that is the notion that our salvation lies in our own hands and no where else. Only we can be the architects of our own fortune; as we have been the architects of our misfortune by and large for the past three and a half decades. According to him, it is, therefore, the responsibility of Africans to develop Africa, to resolve to make their world a relevant and important part of the rest of the world. Africans must climb the steep development hill by their own efforts before seeking for external assistance. Symbolic to his commitment towards helping poor and debt-laden African countries, he established the Nigerian Trust Fund at the African Development Bank (ADB), a lending window from which resources were to be made available to African countries at concessional terms.

Wary of the authoritarian populism of the military and unpersuaded by the promises of a liberal-democratic model as a means of reviving stagnant African economies, General Obasanjo founded the Africa Leadership Forum in 1988.

Unfortunately, there are no private institutions in Africa devoted to preparing potential leaders with a global outlook, leaders who will be able to cooperate within and across national, regional and institutional boundaries. Nor are there possibilities to foster, in an informal setting, the exchange of experience and reflection among current leaders and to seek responses to emerging challenges. Furthermore, in most African countries, it is difficult, if not impossible to get relevant and timely information on most national, regional and global issues. The mandate of the Forum is therefore dedicated to the enhancement of leadership performance and qualities at all levels and in all walks of life in Africa.

More specifically, the Forum aims at diagnosing, understanding and searching for concrete solutions to local, regional and global problems by involving both current and future potential leaders. It will generate greater understanding and enhance the knowledge and awareness of development and social problems within a global context while fostering close and enduring relationships and promoting lifelong association and cooperation among leaders. To be more effective, the Forum sensitizes incumbent leaders and policy-makers, the media and the public at large—both in and outside Africa—on national, regional and global problems of development, strategy, environment and management so as to solicit their effective contributions to solutions. It believes that the establishment of democracy is essential to Africa's development and therefore will undertake all actions and measures that will sustain democratic practice and culture in the region. To achieve these noble objectives, the Africa Leadership Forum maintains a close network, outreach and cooperation with organizations, institutions and individuals inside and outside Africa, with a view to mobilizing and coordinating efforts and resources.

His experience at home and the international arena had prepared him well. Armed with these objectives, General Obasanjo set out to organize national and international conferences from 1988 through to 1992 with themes that included "The Challenge of Leadership" (1988); "The Impact of Europe in 1992 on West Africa" (1989); "Challenges of Agricultural Production and Food Security in Africa" (1989); "Leadership Challenges of Economic Reforms in Africa" (1990); and "Population, Environment and Climatic Changes: Their Impact on Development" (1990).

A major initiative of the Africa Leadership Forum was the convening, in cooperation with the United Nations Economic Commission for Africa (UNECA) and the Organization of African Unity (OAU), in 1991 of the Kampala Conference on "Co-operation, Security, Stability and Development in Africa". Writing in the editorial of *Africa Forum* on the above conference, Obasanjo observed that "the time has come for the fundamental obstacles facing the African continent to be grasped in their priority context for a continental consensus and a collective systematic action". He emphasized that the concept of security must transcend orthodox definition and perception of security in military terms. To be effective, it has to be all embracing, all encompassing and ramifying so as to include personal security, food security, economic security and social security. His recommendation was simple. "We need a regional security based on common and collective security rather than one-sided national security." He is convinced that with the right mixture of strategy, commitment and leadership, Africa should get out of the doldrums within a generation and regain a place of honour and respect within the international community and move into the mainstream of the world.

At the national level, a bimonthly Farm House Dialogue has been held at the Forum Office in Ota, Nigeria which discusses contextual issues relevant to the country. More than two dozen dialogues on development have been held so far: Leadership for Development; Education for Development and Youth; Communication and Development; Labour and Development; Culture and Development; Rural Development; Management and Development; Food and Development; and Technology and Development—to name but a few.

General Obasanjo has played other important roles, both nationally and internationally since leaving government service. As from 1979, he became a fellow at the Institute of African Studies, University of Ibadan and between 1981-1986 he was a member of the UNESCO Commission for Peace in the Minds of Men; and a member of the Independent (Palme) Commission on Disarmament and Security Issues since 1983. When the InterAction Council was formed in 1983, General Obasanjo became a founding member of this group comprising some thirty former Heads of State and Government committed to the same honourable purpose of protecting mankind from nuclear or ecological conflict, from the chaos of unbridled population growth, and from the ever greater gulf between the developed and the impoverished parts of the world. Similar questions as those treated by the Forum (peace and security, development and reviving the world economy) are fields which the Council has tried to identify. In 1985, he was member of and Co-Chairman of the Commonwealth Eminent Persons Group on South Africa and was nominated by Commonwealth leaders to assess the security needs of the Commonwealth Frontline States and Mozambique; later he became a member of the UN Secretary-General's High Level Panel on Africa.

Borne in a family of educators and an environment of hard work, General Obasanjo has been able to exhibit in six decades remarkable virtues like organizational skills, efficient management combined with an analytical and a brilliant mind. These qualities elevated him in Nigeria where he was honoured as a Grand Commander of the Order of the Federal Republic of Nigeria in 1980. The same qualities place him in a unique position to extend his knowledge and experience as a special adviser to the International Institute for Tropical Agriculture and earned him several honourary degrees in Nigeria and the United States of America. He is an erudite writer with several books and numerous articles on national and international issues.

I cannot end this tribute without saluting General Obasanjo as an ardent leader and visionary, dedicated to Africa and the world. His claim to fame based on contributions to the enrichment of the African world is well documented by the publication of the present book. My final wish is that his continuous generous legacy of contributions will continue to provide viable solutions to existing challenges facing Africa.

Mario Graça do Machungo

WISHES FOR A LONG LIFE AND SUCCESS

Maputo, 28th February 1995

It is indeed with pleasure that I acknowledge the celebration of the 60th birthday of our beloved and respected friend, General Olusegun Obasanjo, on 5 March 1995 and it is for me a pleasant duty and a privilege to join the initiative to celebrate the occasion.

I first met General Obasanjo when he was Head of State, during a short visit to Nigeria by our late President Samora Moises Machel.

I was part of the Presidential delegation as Minister of Planning. It was since then that I learned to admire and respect General Obasanjo. During the talks held with President Obasanjo he revealed his exceptional qualities as military chief and statesman fully devoted to his people, with a deep knowledge of the problems of Africa and actively committed to the search for its solutions.

I had the opportunity to get to know General Obasanjo better as Chairman of the Africa Leadership Forum. Within this Forum, the General masterly develops his qualities as statesman and a perspicacious analyst of the political problems of our continent.

During the 1990 Conference held in Paris on "The Impact of Changes in Eastern Europe on Africa" his foresight of the evolution of the events in Southern Africa proved to be very accurate:

> *"In Southern Africa, the "Mandela factor", which at long last has become a reality, is a result of new thinking and perestroika of its own by the South African Government. It may soon lead to the emergence of a nonracial, democratic and united South Africa. If accomplished through a peaceful transition, it would be striking.*

> *There must be democracy with its fundamental factors of freedom and choice in Africa. My own experience with the organization of free elections and the peaceful transfer of power from a military to a freely elected civilian government not only attests to my personal commitment but also to the fact that such events can take place without external pressures on the country or its leadership. But today's reality is that the majority of African countries have neither freely elected Governments nor a system based on democratic principles. We also should acknowledge that the democratization process might take more time in some African countries than in others. Nondemocratic regimes in Africa should be encouraged and assisted to attain true democracy. But in doing so we must exercise patience and tolerance and make allowance for African cultural peculiarities.*
>
> *Let me set forth some interrelated preconditions for responsive governance—"strategic imperatives", as it were—that must be instituted and institutionalized in African countries to meet the litmus test of our own peoples' aspirations and of people and governments in industrialized countries so as to re-attract their interest in, and support for African development efforts:*
> 1. *Responsiveness and efficiency in governance;*
> 2. *Trust creation and confidence-building which must be between the governor and the governed;*
> 3. *Decentralization of political power to grassroots;*
> 4. *Pluralism and decentralization of the economy;*
> 5. *Political communication;*
> 6. *Education and political education;*
> 7. *Promotion and defence of human rights;*
> 8. *Creation of appropriate political machinery;*
> 9. *Renewal of mandate and succession programme;*
> 10. *Popular participation in all aspects of the development process."*

I believe that the preconditions above mentioned for Africa to experiment with a process of irreversible transformation leading to the solution of the major problems afflicting the continent, lay down the foundations for a new era of progress and development. They produce successful results in the countries that managed to adapt and adjust to their objective and specific cultural and economic conditions.

I am sure that the Copenhagen Summit on Social Development will benefit from the contribution of General Obasanjo and from the Africa Leadership Forum he chairs in what concerns Africa and its future.

Lastly, I would like to warmly congratulate General Obasanjo on his jubilee birthday and express my wishes for long live and success in his work devoted to the development challenges facing the continent.

BROADCASTING SYSTEM, INC.
ONE CNN CENTER
BOX 105366
ATLANTA, GEORGIA 30348-5366

R. E. TURNER
CHAIRMAN OF THE BOARD

NORTH TOWER
(404) 827-1717

March, 1995

General Olusegun Obasanjo
c/o Mr. Hans d'Orville
1255 Fifth Avenue, Apt. 7K
New York, New York 10029

Dear General Obasanjo:

Happy 60th Birthday! It is my pleasure to take the opportunity of this special occasion to convey my heartiest congratulations. My colleagues and I at Turner Broadcasting System/CNN have enjoyed our association with you through your esteemed positions with the State of Nigeria and the Africa Leadership Forum, and look forward to additional cooperation.

Best wishes for continued success and happiness.

Very truly yours,

R. E. Turner

Shridath S. Ramphal

HOMAGE TO GENERAL OLUSEGUN OBASANJO

General Obasanjo became head of the Government of Nigeria in 1976—not long after I had left Guyana to take up the office of Commonwealth Secretary-General in London. Over the next three years Olu was one of the many Heads of Government with whom I worked closely to advance Commonwealth objectives—the defeat of apartheid prominent among them. His withdrawal from political office, making way for the restoration of constitutional processes in his country, did not, however, mean an end to our contacts. The manner of his going did him great credit, and released him for service in the wider world. Our paths continued to cross.

The Independent Commission on Disarmament and Security Issues chaired by Sweden's Olof Palme, which functioned from 1980 to 1982, provided an early opportunity for Olu to make the kind of thoughtful contribution to the consideration of global issues that we were to come to associate with him. As a former soldier, who had himself taken part in a United Nations peacekeeping operation—in the Congo in 1960—he had the specialized knowledge to make a distinctive input to the deliberations of that Commission. Its sessions enabled us to meet every few months during that period, and there have been occasional reunions of its members since.

But it was the struggle against apartheid that brought us into closest contact, and for which I remember him best. At their meeting in Nassau, the Bahamas, in October 1985, the leaders of Commonwealth countries came to an *Accord on Southern Africa* under which they agreed to appoint a group of eminent persons to encourage a process of peaceful change towards the dismantling of apartheid and establishment of democratic structures in South Africa. This was breaking entirely new ground; it was to be the beginning of the final international push complementing the national struggle.

I worked with the Heads of Government of seven member countries in developing the modalities of this exercise, and looked to these leaders to nominate persons—not necessarily from their own countries—to form the group. President Kaunda of Zambia and Prime Minister Mugabe of Zimbabwe jointly suggested Olu as a member.

I was glad that they did so and that Olu accepted my invitation to be a co-chairman, along with Australia's Malcolm Fraser, of the seven-member group. The Report "Mission to South Africa" came to be an event of significance in global efforts to nudge movement towards freedom in South Africa. Olu and Malcolm had both been prominent Commonwealth activists in the campaign for freedom and human dignity in Southern Africa. I know this helped to make them an effective pair at the head of the Commonwealth's Eminent Persons Group.

Olu made a major personal contribution to the work of the Commonwealth Eminent Persons Group. He took part with Malcolm and another member (Dame Nita Barrow of Barbados) in a preliminary visit to South Africa and to its neighbouring states to lay the groundwork for the team's mission. After the whole group had made its first visit to South Africa, covering all the key centres, Olu with another member (Tanzania's John Malacela) visited the Frontline States of Zambia and Zimbabwe as well as Nigeria on behalf of the Group.

The value of the Group's mission at that critical moment in the struggle against apartheid was greatly enhanced by the fact that it was able to have detailed discussions with Nelson Mandela himself, in Pollsmoor prison. Olu was the first member of the Group to be able to see him, on the preliminary visit to South Africa which prepared the ground for the later conversations.

Olu has made many other contributions to the cause of freedom in Southern Africa and to other worthy causes. Other friends and colleagues will document these. In saluting him on his 60th birthday I am happy to recall those endeavours in which we were able to work very closely together—and to hope that the future may bring further opportunities for his very considerable talents to be used by Nigeria, by Africa and by the entire global community in the cause of the highest human values for which he has always resolutely stood.

Roelof F. (Pik) Botha[1]

HIS SOUTH AFRICAN CONNECTION

General Olusegun Obasanjo was a Co-Chairman, with Mr. Malcolm Fraser, of the Commonwealth Eminent Persons Group on Southern Africa which in 1986, at the behest of the Commonwealth Heads of Government Meeting at Nassau in 1985, grasped the South African nettle and attempted to forge a solution to that country's seemingly intractable dilemma. In June 1986 it published its Report entitled *Mission to South Africa*. After writing my tribute to General Obasanjo I read through *Mission to South Africa*. I was struck by the counterpoint which it provided to much of what I had written. Significant portions of the Report are therefore interpolated in the text in italics and between asterisks. These extracts are to a large extent General Obasanjo talking.

He is not a man you would overlook in a crowd. Even from a distance, he is conspicuous and prominent. His large frame complements his largeness of vision and his breadth of understanding. Anyone who has conversed with him or encountered his speeches, if not live at least in transcript as in *Africa Embattled* for example, can testify to the dimension of his thought.

I never saw him in a suit. He always wore his traditional *agbada* Nigerian robe and headgear, often in light green with a touch of embroidery.

I met him on several occasions and enjoyed hours of discussions with him, both official and personal, in South Africa. He came on various missions, which demonstrated the esteem of many world leaders which he clearly commanded, an esteem that even outlasts his 1976 to 1979 achievements as Head of State.

This has been demonstrated *inter alia* by his membership of the *Independent Commission on Disarmament and Security Issues* (the Palme Commission), the *InterAction Council of Former Heads of Government* and the *United Nations Panel of Eminent Persons on the Relationship between Disarmament and Development*.

It was also demonstrated in March 1987 when he became the first African invited to deliver the *Leffingwell Lectures* sponsored by the US Council on Foreign Relations. Cyrus Vance's tribute to him as being one of "a new breed of senior statesmen… committed to serving their countries as disinterested counsellors rather than active aspirants for power" is an apt one. The lectures themselves, reproduced in the book *Africa in Perspective: Myths and Realities*, are thought-provoking and profound, particularly for an African like myself.

I remember him expressing to me quite often the fundamental truth that violence and conflict is always the worst option to enforce peace. There is nothing worse because it does not produce progress. It deepens passions, widens divisions and obstructs the process of national reconciliation. "It is well known," he has said, "that in the absence of peace, there can be no meaningful development".

The General was a consensus man. He wanted commitment and agreement from opposing forces to be reached in such a way that neither felt themselves to be the loser. I myself applied this strategy in the protracted negotiations leading up to the agreement between Angola, Cuba and South Africa signed at the United Nations in December 1988, on the 40-year-old dispute surrounding South West Africa. After a heated meeting with Cubans and Angolans in Cairo in June of that year, I said to a Cuban delegate, "We could both retire as winners from the Angola-Namibian conflict if we were prepared to understand the sensitivities which both sides have to face at home. South Africa agrees to Namibian independence. Cuba withdraws her troops from Angola. I can tell the South Africans that the Cuban troops are going back to Cuba. You tell your people that Namibia's independence has been achieved."

I will always remember my first meeting with General Obasanjo. I did not meet him on his arrival at the airport but instead arranged a helicopter flight for him over the Pretoria-Witwatersrand-Vereeniging industrial complex. With Johannesburg as its core, this area is the financial, economic and industrial hub of South Africa. Highways, factories, skyscrapers, shopping complexes and a sea of residential areas of all kinds testify to the dynamic and pulsating activity that is visible from the air.

After his trip, we met and I asked him how he was. "I'm suffering from shock, severe shock," was the reply. I was taken aback for a moment. But then he put my mind to rest by saying, "I did not know a place like this existed on the African continent. There is such a high level of development, of roads, industries, houses and buildings. It is as good as anything in America or Europe. This is part of Africa and all of us in Africa must be proud of it and preserve it and improve it. This is the hope of Africa."

In the *Leffingwell Lectures*, which I mentioned above, he says, "What struck me on my first visit to South Africa was the natural beauty of the country, its economic achievement, and its crying human tragedy. Such a beautiful and economically strong country in Africa must be preserved for all South Africans, all Africans and all citizens of the world."

His task as Cochairmen of the Eminent Persons Group on South Africa set up by the Commonwealth in 1985, and presenting its Report in June 1986, must have been one of the most exacting challenges he faced subsequent to his retirement as Head of State of Nigeria. He would be one of a few leaders to engage both sides of the South African divide in penetrative, challenging and solution-orientated dialogue.

Certainly and to start with, a strong test of his perseverance and tolerance would have been his Cochairmen, the Right Honourable Malcolm Fraser, Prime Minister of Australia from 1975 to 1983. Mr. Fraser was not what I would call the easiest of men with whom to get along.

General Obasanjo had to save more than one situation when discussions with the South African Government threatened to shipwreck. The Eminent Persons Group (EPG) arrived in South Africa at a critical stage in South Africa's contemporary history. The idea of the EPG was part of a worldwide effort to ward off what seemed to be inevitable: a bloody conflict. Its task was to try and mediate to see whether a peaceful solution was not possible, whether the two main opposing forces, the National Party Government and the African National Congress, could not somehow sit around the negotiating table to pursue a peaceful option instead of the devastating alternative.

Looking back, 1985 stands out as a dark year in our history. The South West Africa issue was far from being resolved. South African troops were fighting in Angola. The high hopes raised by the 1984 Nkomati Accord between Moçambique and South Africa had dissipated.

In August 1985 President P. W. Botha had delivered what has become known as his Rubicon speech, in Durban. The world had been waiting for good news: important announcements on dismantling apartheid and releasing Mr. Nelson Mandela. I myself drafted that part of the speech in which the phrase "today we have crossed the Rubicon" appeared. President Botha retained the sentence but removed what had preceded it: the release of Nelson Mandela and the Government's intention to dismantle apartheid. The effect of the speech on the world, and on many South Africans, was that of a bucket of iced water in the face.

Relations with our neighbouring states were characterised by animosity, suspicion, resentment and mistrust. There were acrimonious exchanges and cross border military operations. Within South Africa, bombs were exploding. Pressure for Nelson Mandela's release mounted inexorably.

Against the gloomy background of South Africa's situation in 1985, the Commonwealth took the initiative at a meeting of Heads of Government at Nassau in October of that year to appoint a Group of Eminent Persons (EPG) to see whether they could help us break out of this impasse, this looming threat of escalating conflict, not only internally in South Africa but also in the region as a whole. It was certainly a formidable task.

The Commonwealth Accord agreed to in Nassau was terse in its language. It said that "the growing crisis and intensified repression in South Africa mean that apartheid must be dismantled now if a greater tragedy is to be averted and that concerted pressure must be brought to bear to achieve that end."

The Accord called upon the South African Government to take the following steps as a matter of urgency:

"*(a) Declare that the system of apartheid will be dismantled and specific and meaningful action taken in fulfillment of that intent.*

(b) Terminate the existing state of emergency.

(c) Release immediately and unconditionally Nelson Mandela and all others imprisoned and detained for their opposition to apartheid.

(d) Establish political freedom and specifically lift the existing ban on the African National Congress and other political parties.

(e) Initiate, in the context of a suspension of violence on all sides, a process of dialogue across lines of politics, colour and religion, with a view to establishing a nonracial and representative government."

As Foreign Minister since 1977, I inherited the apartheid issue at the United Nations as well as the Rhodesian and South West African problems. For decades, successive South African Governments took refuge behind Article 2 (7) of the United Nations Charter, which prohibited intervention in the domestic affairs of member states.

I knew from experience that attitude merely infuriated the country's opponents and only made them more determined to isolate the South African Government. It also implied that we were guilty of all the accusations levelled against us and had no credible response to them, even though they were often exaggerated. I circumvented this petrified policy by, yes, continuing to repeat the Article 2 (7) objection in every communication with the UN, but then at least proceeding to give the facts to contradict the prevarications.

I felt strongly about the inherent immorality of apartheid. But I believed that the equivocations which characterised many of the UN actions against South Africa were counterproductive. It did not assist me and others who shared my views to persuade our colleagues to move faster in eradicating apartheid. At times I really thought that certain antiapartheid organisations would hate the day apartheid was removed.

I knew that apartheid had to go. I said so as South Africa's Ambassador to the UN in a statement to the Security Council in 1974. The question was how to bring it about without plunging the country into chaos and destruction. My strategy was to assail the distortions and fabrications about the country and at the same time warn the white voters that discrimination based on the colour of a person's skin could not be defended.

In similar vein, I reacted to the Nassau Accord by ignoring the peremptory tone of the demands made and instead interpreted the terms of the statement as an effort to bring the opposing forces together without attempting to prescribe. This prompted General Obasanjo and Mr. Fraser to write to President P W Botha in which they noted with appreciation the statement by the South African Foreign Minister. Their letter in turn enabled me to draft a reply for President Botha in which we warned that the Commonwealth Group could do incalculable harm if it saw itself as a pressure group charged with the task of extracting concessions from the Government and generally engaged in prescribing solutions to problems which were the sole responsibility of South Africans to solve. If on the other hand the EPG wished to be informed of the situation in South Africa and confined itself to promoting peaceful political dialogue and if, moreover, it could be seen to be unbiased in this respect, a useful purpose could be served.

The ANC leadership told the EPG that their immediate reaction to the setting up of the Group had been one of disappointment. According to the EPG Report, their hopes had been raised by the debate in Nassau and the prospect of increased international pressure on the Government through sanctions against Pretoria. Instead, the Group had been established and, in their view, it would assist in relieving the pressures on the South African Government which had been building up in the period before Nassau. The EPG was nevertheless warmly welcomed as the ANC had a keen interest in hearing what the Group felt it might be able to do.

The ANC expressed great interest in the South African Government's response to the EPG's mandate because only then would it be able to make its own contribution. If the Government was prepared to shift its ground and indicate its readiness for fundamental change this would impact on the ANC view. Their assessment was, however, that nothing had changed and nothing would change. If that proved to be the case, then the conditions for negotiation did not exist.

The ANC placed much emphasis on the release of Mr. Nelson Mandela, a crucial step which recognised that it was not possible for negotiations to take place in the absence of the people's authentic leaders. A prerequisite for talking to the Government was that it should be through the people's recognised leaders, not through the ones the Government chose to identify. Without this essential first step the conflict would continue.

Denis Worrall, our Ambassador in London at the time, played a major role in preparing the EPG for their visit to South Africa. Both of us saw in the visit a real chance to make progress in ending the turmoil in our country.

What was not often understood or known to the outside world was that the National Party was not a monolithic party. Although it had by 1986 made important progress in dismantling petty apartheid, membership of the Party was still restricted to whites. All of that has ended and today the Party is a new Party with black National Party Members of Parliament sitting side by side with their white compatriots.

It was however clear to me long before 1986 that South Africa would not come to peace with itself unless all our citizens could vote on an equal basis for the government of their choice.

Hence my response to a question at a media conference in Cape Town on 6 February 1986 to the effect that there would be a black President and that I would be willing to serve under him.

I knew that my statement would cause a flutter and arouse antagonism in my Party, but I did not expect the ensuing fury and furor. A special Cabinet meeting was called the next morning. President P W Botha bluntly told me that I would not survive. Apparently some colleagues in the Cabinet and in the Party at large warned him that there would be a split unless disciplinary steps were taken against me. The

President's choice was either to fire me or thrash me publicly in Parliament.

The President took the latter course that same afternoon. In a speech to a packed Parliament, under the glare of a full press and public gallery, President P W Botha administered a solemn and severe rebuke. For a few days I considered resigning, tempted by the idea of forming my own party. Messages and telegrams poured in from all over the country supporting me and urging me to hang in there. I did just that.

I mention these events because of their relevance to the EPG mission. General Obasanjo and Mr. Fraser arrived in South Africa on a preliminary visit a few days later. They had a meeting with me on 17 February 1986. Had it not been for my black President remark I would probably have been in a stronger position to influence the discussions more positively. As things turned out, my room to manoeuvre was restricted.

I could however give advice to General Obasanjo on the sensitivities on both sides. He understood my position. A strong personal bond of friendship began to grow between us. We could say to each other whatever was in our minds, openly and without inhibition.

During February and until 13 March 1986, the EPG held meetings with South African leaders across the full spectrum of opinion: the Government; the ANC and all other political parties; church leaders; business leaders; academics; women's organisations; even governments of South Africa's neighbouring states. By 13 March 1986 the EPG had developed its *Possible Negotiating Concept* which evolved out of their consultations and their judgement of what might be possible.

In formulating the *Concept*, the EPG juxtaposed the South African Government's own assurances to the Group alongside the demands of the black community. Both parties, the South African Government and the ANC, said they wanted a peaceful solution, but each had a different view of what a democratic solution would be.

The position of the South African Government was summarised as follows:
- *It is the conviction of the Government that any future constitutional dispensation providing for participation by all South African citizens should be the result of negotiations with the leaders of all communities.*
- *The Government will not prescribe who may represent black communities in negotiations on a new constitution for South Africa.*
- *The only condition is that those who participate in the discussions and negotiations should foreswear violence as a means of achieving political objectives.*
- *The agenda for political reform is open. In the process of negotiation the Government will not prescribe and will not demand. Give and take will be the guiding principle.*
- *On the part of the Government, negotiations will be based on the following premises: the principle of a united South Africa, one citizenship and a universal franchise within democratic structures;*
- *political participation of all communities at all levels on matters of national concern;*
- *co-responsibility and power-sharing between these communities on matters of national concern;*
- *the devolution of power as far as possible;*

- *the protection of minority rights, without one group dominating the other;*
- *the sovereignty of the law as the basis for the protection of the fundamental rights of individuals as well as groups;*
- *equality before the law; and*
- *the protection of human dignity, life, liberty and property of all, regardless of colour, race, creed or religion.*
- *The South African Government also confirms that the situation of detainees or prisoners will be reviewed as violence recedes and normality returns; and*
- *it is positively committed to and actively involved in contributing to the peace, stability and development of the Southern African region.*

The EPG's reaction to this was that "*the South African Government's position defies succinct summary. It has perfected a specialised political vocabulary which, while saying one thing, means quite another. Thus the stated approach to negotiations was qualified by a number of provisos, which were repeatedly underlined during the course of our discussions. While apartheid was declared 'outmoded', 'finished' and, indeed, 'dead', the Government's objective was the exercise of political rights and freedoms within the structures of 'groups' or 'communities'. South Africa was a 'nation of minorities' and future constitutional arrangements would give expression to individual aspirations only within the confines of their ethnic groups. Group rights were to take precedence over individual rights, with built-in assurances of no one group being dominated by others. Western democratic practice had no relevance to South African conditions.*"

At the time I urged General Obasanjo to explain to his colleagues that the South African position represented progress. What we needed was to start the talks with the ANC. I negotiated the Nkomati Accord with Moçambique in 1983-4 which involved equally intractable obstacles in an atmosphere of severe suspicion and animosity. Written positions only change when you sit down with your opponent and ask him face to face what his words mean. General Obasanjo agreed with me but said that he had difficulties with some members of the Group. He reminded me that "obduracy was not confined to certain members of the South African Government".

The EPG came closer to success than most people realise, or at least suspected at the time. I saw in the EPG a real chance of achieving a breakthrough. This was a smaller and less emotional forum than the United Nations. It was able to draw closer to the protagonists. Also, General Obasanjo was not only an African leader but a realist. He had gone through severe and troubled times in his own country, he had been a witness of the havoc conflict brings.

It was his dogged and courageous realism which, for instance, enabled him to launch what must surely have been an unpopular plea to the European Parliament in Strasbourg on 17 February 1987. He asked the then European Economic Community to "sponsor and finance a scheme to assist white South Africans who cannot live with the inevitable change, to emigrate ... If some black South Africans similarly so wish and choose, the scheme should not exclude them".

In my discussions with General Obasanjo, he displayed a ready willingness to understand the Government's difficulties without surrendering the objective of achieving a solution based on a full democracy, which in effect meant a one-person-one-vote election at the end of the day.

He knew our history and had a deep understanding of the position of the Afrikaner. He accepted the Afrikaner's anticolonial stance. He used to say, "the Afrikaner is an inherent part of Africa. Consequently," he would continue, "other Africans should acknowledge this to a greater extent and by so doing diminish the Afrikaner's fear of being overwhelmed."

He has said, for instance, "The Afrikaner mentality is reported to thrive in isolation and be prone to rigidity under pressure. Yet my limited contact with the Afrikaner does not suggest that he is suicidal."

The EPG Report comments:

"*Clearly, a number of Afrikaners, including some who trace their roots back over three hundred years to the original Dutch Colony, feel their whole future threatened and see no country which might match up to their 'fatherland'. Some of them are turning to the misguided notion that their power to subdue blacks by using the full power of the security forces renders them sufficiently strong to resist fundamental change. They close their eyes to the simple fact, acknowledged by Government and business alike, that both whites and blacks separately have it within their power to destroy the country.*

"*... In recent months the country has witnessed the emergence of a growing and increasingly assertive extreme right wing as Afrikanerdom begins to fragment under the cumulative weight of the pressures we have described. This phenomenon is not altogether surprising. For two generations, whites in South Africa have lived as beneficiaries of apartheid in a system engineered by a political party which constantly asserted white supremacy. When they witness an apparent change in Government theology, with the rhetoric of total white control giving way to talk of power-sharing, a backlash of some description is inevitable. But just as the far right is a creation of the National Party, so too it must accept responsibility for dealing with it. The need for courageous leadership has never been greater. Certainly, whatever the threat from the extreme right, the Government can still rely on carrying the majority of the white community if it takes bold decisions to bring peace and prosperity to the country as a whole.*

"*We recognise the huge difficulties of adjustment facing the white community. As the Editor of one leading English daily put it recently: 'It will not be easy for many whites to settle down to what is their inevitable destiny in a multiracial country where the population is three-quarters black'.*

"*...Many whites genuinely entertain fears about their future in any new dispensation. We found a keen awareness of this among responsible black leaders, together with an acknowledgement of a need to allay them.*"

The talks centred heavily on the issue of violence as a means of achieving political objectives. The Government insisted that the ANC should abandon it, while the ANC were adamant that certain conditions had to be fulfilled before they could make such a commitment. The EPG responded by seeking to persuade the ANC to enter negotiations and suspend violence.

The EPG reported as follows on this issue:

"Throughout our work in South Africa, the issue of violence cropped up again and again. It is, in a way, central to the political debate in the country. The Government demands of its opponents a renunciation of violence—or a 'commitment to nonviolence'—as a precondition to negotiation; its opponents say their violence is reactive, and call upon the Government to abandon its violence first. Where does the truth lie?"

The question of violence was inextricably interwoven with Mr. Mandela's release. General Obasanjo met with Mr. Mandela in Pollsmoor Prison on 21 February 1986. Thereafter the full Group met with him on two occasions although not with other detainees. I had great difficulty in persuading my colleague, the Minister of Justice, to allow these meetings.

The EPG reported extensively on Mr. Mandela's views. The following extracts are particularly significant in the light of the events which commenced four years later when he was released:

"...Nelson Mandela is also a symbol for blacks not only of their lack of political freedom but also of their struggle to attain it. He is a potent inspiration for much of the political activity of black South Africans. His role in the management of the Defiance Campaign of 1952 and his leadership of Umkhonto we Sizwe (Spear of the Nation) for which he remains imprisoned, together with the manner in which he has borne his fate, has established him as a legend in his own lifetime. His suffering is seen as the suffering of all who are the victims of apartheid. The campaign for his release has been the galvanising spur for rising black political consciousness across South Africa. His name is emblazoned across the length and breadth of South Africa.

"In particular, the call for his freedom has developed into the centrepiece of the demand for a political settlement. It is the shorthand for the proposition that, as his daughter Zinzi conveyed it, 'There is an alternative to the inevitable bloodbath'.

"But we also recognise that, for some whites, he represents something rather different. Their fears, if unfounded, are real nonetheless. They include the belief that Nelson Mandela is a man of violence and that violence could not be contained on his release; the fear that, as one of the principal black nationalists, his sole aim is to achieve a hand-over of state power from white to black; and the fear that his release would be the signal for chaos and destruction. Most of these fears have been fuelled by the Government's own campaign against Mr. Mandela and the ANC. To that extent, they are self-induced, but they are real for all that and cannot be ignored.

"We accept that the release of Nelson Mandela presents the South African Government with a difficult dilemma. Having held him too long in prison, there is a growing realisation in Government circles that any benefits of incarceration are outweighed by the disadvantages which daily become more apparent. Yet to release him now, as some in Government say is their wish, would be to do so into conditions much changed from ten, or even five, years ago. In a mood of unrest and upheaval, with growing black awareness and political protest being matched by increasing anxiety among whites and the rise of white extremism, the Government has expressed the fear that his release might result in an uncontrollable explosion of violence.

"We do not hold this view. Provided the negotiating process were agreed, Mr. Mandela's own voice would appeal for calm. We believe his authority would secure it.

"In our discussions with the ANC, it has become clear that they, along with every black group within South Africa, see the unconditional release of Nelson Mandela and other political prisoners and detainees as a necessary and crucial step towards a settlement. Negotiations cannot take place in the absence of the people's authentic leaders. The release into South African society of these leaders would lead logically to negotiations, through a process of normal political activity, on behalf of legally recognised organisations. No other equation is possible. No piecemeal or more limited approach can possibly succeed.

"Without this first step, linked to a wider package, the ANC and others will have no basis for believing in the state violence of the apartheid system ever abating and will not be persuaded to suspend violence themselves. The struggle and the killing will continue with greater intensity. The cycle of violence will remain unbroken.

"To disregard Nelson Mandela by continuing his imprisonment would be to discard an essential and heroic figure in any political settlement in South Africa. His freedom is a key component in any hope of a peaceful resolution of a conflict which otherwise will prove all-consuming.

"We questioned Nelson Mandela extensively about his views on violence. The ANC, he said, had for many years operated as a nonviolent organisation and had been forced into armed struggle only because it became the unavoidable response to the violence of apartheid. He stressed that violence could never be an ultimate solution and that the nature of human relationships required negotiation. He was not in a position to renounce the use of violence as a condition of his release, and we recognised that in the circumstances currently prevailing in South Africa it would be unreasonable to expect that of him or anyone else."

General Obasanjo emphatically denied that Mr. Mandela was ever a communist or anything else except an African nationalist leader. He identified the South African conflict as being between two nationalisms both wishing the best for their country, but fighting each other for power.

The EPG reported as follows on this aspect:

"In our discussions, Nelson Mandela also took care to emphasise his desire for reconciliation across the divide of colour. He described himself as a deeply committed South African nationalist but added that South African nationalists came in more than one colour—there were white people, coloured people and indian people who were also deeply committed South African nationalists. He pledged himself anew to work for a multiracial society in which all would have a secure place.

"...We were impressed by the consistency of his beliefs. He emphasised that he was a nationalist, not a communist, and that his principles were unchanged from those to which he subscribed when the Freedom Charter was drawn up in 1955."

General Obasanjo repeatedly reminded both sides that they were in one ship. He said: "If you could set a common course for this ship and continued to sail towards a shared goal, stability and progress would be assured and minorities would feel secure".

In their Report the EPG said they were forcibly struck by the overwhelming desire in South Africa for a nonviolent negotiated settlement. By 12 March 1986 the EPG had developed a _Possible Negotiating Concept_, based on five elements, which on 13 March 1986 was transmitted to my colleague Mr. J. C. Heunis, Minister of Constitutional Development and Planning, and to myself:

"The first related to the negotiating agenda in its broadest sense. What were negotiations to be about or designed to achieve? Despite the Government's various statements that apartheid was outmoded, the ANC and black opinion within the country was looking for a more positive declaration of intent and some specific and meaningful steps in regard to the dismantling of the apartheid system. The reforms implemented so far had not impressed the black community. There was thus a need for the Government to make a firmer and more categorical statement of intent.

"The second major element would need to be confidence-building measures to allay suspicions and fears and to demonstrate the Government's good faith.

"The third element would be a link between the release of political prisoners, and the parties to which they belonged, and the initiation of a political process.

"The fourth element would need to be a moratorium on violence—by both the Government and its opponents.

"The fifth element would need to be synchronisation. The Government and the ANC were each looking to the other to make the first move. We believed the only way this problem could be resolved would be through prior agreement between both to act simultaneously in fulfillment of their respective commitments.

"It was on this basis that we developed what we described as a 'Possible Negotiating Concept'. It embodied the 'package' approach which we believed to be necessary. Its preamble constituted a firm statement of intent that apartheid would be ended; its operative paragraph set out measures that were needed to create a climate of confidence and enable all concerned to turn to the task of constructing a new South Africa; and the postscript embodied statements made by the South African Government which we hoped would facilitate the negotiating process."

General Obasanjo and I were in close contact with each other as the *Concept* took shape. I made sure that he was under no illusion as to the difficulties that lay ahead of us. My purpose was to get down to talks with the ANC. He fully shared this objective. Accordingly I urged him all along to avoid words and phrases which recalcitrant elements in both the Government and the ANC could use to block progress and prevent dialogue.

I knew from experience how difficult it was to get opposing forces to talk to each other. Even the venue of a meeting would often become controversial and could delay that meeting endlessly, leaving the door wide open for unforeseen events to intervene. These in turn would eventually result in a rejection of holding the meeting at all. I call it the cave withdrawal syndrome, inherited from *homo habilis*.

I also knew that Mr. Mandela personally was prepared to accept the *Negotiating Concept* on the understanding that his colleagues in the ANC be consulted in order to obtain their acceptance as well.

The EPG told Minister Heunis and myself at a meeting on 12 March 1986 that if the South African Government saw no merit in their proposals, little purpose would be served by taking them to the other relevant parties inside and outside South Africa.

Although the efforts of the EPG did not succeed, the *Negotiating Concept* was a prophetic document. It embodied all the elements which formed the basis of the negotiations between the South African Government and the ANC four years later. Those negotiations led to the new era in South Africa's history. For that reason, and because of the major contribution General Obasanjo made to it, I reproduce it here in full:

"**The South African Government** has declared its commitment to dismantling the system of apartheid, to ending racial discrimination and to broad-based negotiations leading to new constitutional arrangements for power-sharing by all the people of South Africa. In the light of preliminary and as yet incomplete discussions with representatives of various organisations and groups, within and outside South Africa, we believe that in the context of specific and meaningful steps being taken towards ending apartheid, the following additional action might ensure negotiations and a break in the cycle of violence.

"**On the part of the Government**:
(a) removal of the military from the townships, providing for freedom of assembly and discussion and suspension of detention without trial.
(b) the release of Nelson Mandela and other political prisoners and detainees.
(c) the unbanning of the ANC and PAC and the permitting of normal political activity.

"**On the part of the ANC and others**:
˄ entering negotiations and suspending violence.

"**It is our view** that simultaneous announcements incorporating these ideas might be negotiated if the Government were to be interested in pursuing this broad approach.

"**In the light of the Government's indication** to us that it:
(i) is not in principle against the release of Nelson Mandela and similar prisoners;
(ii) is not opposed in principle to the unbanning of any organisations;
(iii) is prepared to enter into negotiations with the acknowledged leaders of the people of South Africa;
(iv) is committed to the removal of discrimination, not only from the statute books but also from South African society as a whole;
(v) is committed to the ending of white domination;
(vi) will not prescribe who may represent black communities in negotiations on a new constitution for South Africa;
(vii) is prepared to negotiate on an open agenda;
the South African Government may wish to give serious consideration to the approach outlined in this note."

Even a cursory comparison of the text of this document with the language of the Nassau Accord will show a vast difference. The *Negotiation Concept* was a balanced document couched in inoffensive language inviting the two opposing forces to start talking and to stop fighting about the country's future. General Obasanjo's hand was all over the document.

I drafted the postscript points (i) to (vii). I was naturally pleased that it was used prominently in the *Concept*. Eyebrows were lifted on our side but I was not shot down. I explained to my colleagues that I could substantiate each point from statements made by several Government members over the past year even if they may have been made in a different context.

The *Possible Negotiating Concept* of the EPG will in my opinion come to be regarded as one of the most remarkable documents to emerge from the seemingly interminable negotiation processes which had to be passed through over the years in order to arrive at the South African solution. I am sure this will be confirmed when historians write our history of the past decade. General Obasanjo played an important if not decisive role in drafting this intuitively incisive document.

Our discussions with the EPG floundered on the issue as to whether the ANC should merely *suspend* violence or instead *terminate* it. There were also a few other questions of concern to us but the main problem was that if *"suspending violence"* meant only discontinuing violence for as long as negotiations continued, then the threat of a resumption of violence would become a bargaining counter. In other words: "Keep talking... or else".

Significantly this same issue again formed the major stumbling block in getting the negotiations going four years later. It was eventually resolved at the end of 1990. The irony is that today few South Africans would even know what the fuss was about. In such a way it is that history moves us past some of our most earnest issues.

On 19 May 1986, I formally responded to the EPG's *Negotiating Concept* in a letter to General Obasanjo and Mr. Fraser. It was the culmination of intense debate and argumentation amongst my colleagues and myself. It was the best I could do. I expressed the Government's concerns on the issue of violence and three other points, but ended by saying:

"The South African Government would welcome further discussions which could accommodate the Government's concerns. I would like to thank you and your colleagues for the spirit in which we have been able to conduct our discussions."

I should have added a postscript: *"My particular thanks to Olusegun Obasanjo"*.

On 5 June 1986, the Co-chairmen responded. They did not agree with the South African Government's points of concern and reiterated their belief that their *Negotiating Concept* would assist in achieving negotiations in a nonviolent atmosphere. They concluded by saying that in the absence both of movement on the part of the Government on the major points and a positive response to the *Concept* as a whole, they were unable to see merit in further discussions. They came to the conclusion that there was no prospect of setting in motion a dialogue with a view to establishing a nonracial and representative government.

I like to believe that General Obasanjo himself did not share this view. He was the kingpin in the drive shaft, but also a member of a team. One day I shall ask him what he really thought at that time. And I know that he will tell me. But that is not the only reason why I recently conveyed a personal message to the President of Nigeria, General Sani Abacha, appealing for clemency for my friend and his fellow Nigerians.

Or perhaps he will tell me that, yes, he had still thought there was a good prospect of getting talks off the ground. But in the early morning of 19 May 1986 the South African Defence Force launched attacks on Harare, Lusaka and Gaborone. Each was a Commonwealth capital which the EPG had recently visited in the course of their search for a South African solution. He will probably tell me it was just one provocation too much. If so, I understand him. I felt very much the same.

General Obasanjo was only too aware of the disastrous consequences of misconceptions and notional perceptions. He warned that they should not be underestimated. Instead, they needed to be removed. The mind-sets of both black and white had to be changed. Both had to come to realise that only one country, South Africa, would have to be shared for both to survive and live in peace.

He remained optimistic of success in South Africa. "I have confidence in the inevitability of victory ... and believe that we can bring it about without revenge, recrimination and bitterness," he once said.

The fatefully critical divergence of views between the South African Government and the ANC on the issue of *terminating* or *suspending* violence in 1986 is a classic illustration of an innate human trait which has been haunting humanity for centuries. I call it the revocability fear. It emerges in our daily lives every time an individual has to decide whether to enter into a contract or commitment. Will the other party renege, repeal, revoke, reverse? Worse: the other party's offer is a ruse intended to obtain my commitment to do something which will make it impossible for me to retrieve my original position and the moment I take the irrevocable plunge, the other party will renounce his liabilities.

In chemistry and physics the word "irrevocability" means the capability of changing or producing change in one direction only.

The ANC suspected that the Government's design to get them to agree to the termination of all violence on their part was to gain time to consolidate its position internally and externally. The Government could then enter into protracted negotiations, producing proposals which might seem reasonable and acceptable to the outside world but which would rob the ANC of a strong bargaining counter in exacting concessions from the Government. In short the ANC believed that the Government would not voluntarily relinquish power come what may.

The Government in turn believed that the ANC's willingness to *suspend* violence was their strategy to get the talks going with total world support and then to make demands under the threat of a resumption of violence if their demands were not met. They would then exploit antiapartheid world opinion to support their resumption of violence.

What I had in mind in making my ultimate appeal on 19 May 1986 to the EPG for further discussions on the issue of violence was to explore the feasibility of an international or Commonwealth guarantee or pledge to the effect that the international community would expect both parties to implement their commitments in good faith and would monitor the process. In the new world order which is emerging in the wake of the cessation of the Cold War, the world is going to need an instrument or structure which can allay the fear of reversibility in international dispute and conflict resolution. It will have to be a new institution divorced from any of the existing international structures because to be successful it will require unfettered imagination and unencumbered mental resourcefulness.

I can say today that the lack of success of the EPG was certainly not due to any shortcoming on the part of General Obasanjo. That *ons kon nie die knoop deurhak nie,* as we say in Afrikaans—we couldn't cut the Gordian knot with the EPG—was the greatest disappointment in my 16-year career as Minister of Foreign Affairs. So many hopes were raised by their mission. It could and would have saved South Africa a lot of pain, a lot of wounds, a lot of agony. Nevertheless, it was an important trial run for the breakthrough that was to come four years later.

General Obasanjo stood out as the dynamic kernel of the EPG, its heart and its brain. There was a quiet authority about him. He spoke in a conciliatory tone, avoiding petulance. He reacted to tension with composure. He was mild without being weak, relaxed but by no means lacking in concentration. He was self-possessed, unruffled, striving to soothe heated discussions and able by his presence and manner to do so. He discreetly explored every possible avenue of reconciliation in attempting to bring opposing views together.

I will remember General Obasanjo's role as that of a leader, a statesman, a man who could talk to you as someone who had gone through the vortex of more than one storm. He had experienced at first hand the futility of using violence as a means of resolving problems. He could speak with legitimacy and credibility and carry it with an inner force of persuasion.

Here is an African statesman that deserves prominent mention in the annals of history, a place of honour in any tribute to world leaders.

I agree with General Obasanjo's adaptation of a well-known book title in saying that Africa's situation is serious but not hopeless. I share his vision that "Africa can enter the next millennium more politically stable and united, more economically self-reliant, self-assertive and self-sustaining" provided we "abandon the narrow and myopic tribalism and nationalism of the past".

He is convinced that "in the long run, Africa's solution to her problems remains in her own hands". I am similarly convinced.

---

[1] This contribution has been adapted from a chapter of the author's Memoirs which are in preparation; it is published here for the first time. The manuscript was finished on 31 July 1995.

TWINS SEVEN – SEVEN
I Will Keep This Heavy Chain On Me
Until Real Democracy Is Established All Over Africa, 1995

Jeremy Pope

IMAGES OF A NIGERIAN IN APARTHEID SOUTH AFRICA

He was just off a plane and so his sleeping through the meeting seemed excusable. He sat, head bowed and his voluptuous robes flowing about him, as the meeting droned on in the antique surroundings of a British royal palace.

Who should sign the letter?, the officials asked earnestly.

Who indeed?

Uninvited, Commonwealth heads of government had decided that a group should mediate in a non-Commonwealth country. But surely no Nigerian—let alone a former Nigerian head of state—could possibly write a formal letter to President P.W. Botha, custodian of apartheid, of all people. The more so one couched in civil terms, suggesting a meeting, and least of all could he do so in December 1985, as war raged in the townships and there were scenes of carnage nightly on the world's television screens. It would be one thing for a former Prime Minister of Australia, Malcolm Fraser, to do so as Co-Chairman, but quite another—surely—for Olusegun Obasanjo.

The discussion circled and then, after about 20 minutes, seemed to stall. At last, the General opened a single eye. "Tell me," he asked quietly, "What am I?" Could he possibly be so jet-lagged as not to know?

"The Co-Chairman", the officials hastily assured him, the Co-Chairman of the Commonwealth Group of Eminent Persons.

"If I am Co-Chairman, then we both sign," he said, and slumped back into what was quite clearly a deceptive guise.

Right from the start Olusegun Obasanjo had established his credentials—and not just as an equal as Co-Chairman of the group whose work Oliver Tambo would come to describe as "the watershed" in the breakthrough for a negotiated end to apartheid. He had established himself, too, as intensely practical, adroit and pragmatic.

The next six months, on and off the road with the General and his cavalcade, were too extraordinary to attempt to summarise here. His ability to mesmerise South African cabinet ministers and the captains of South Africa's industry alike, adopting always a cool, careful and considered line. A General, indeed, who chose the ground on which he would fight, and who did not needlessly flirt skirmishes with the enemy.

He was completely relaxed when arrested with others of us, as battle raged in Alexandra, and no-one in the Carlton Hotel in Johannesburg could possibly forget how he passed himself off as being "just a hotel waiter" when a journalist succeeded in getting through to our office on the telephone at a time when we had decided to work quietly. In the office at the time there was a General answering the telephone, an Archbishop operating the photocopier and a Tanzanian-Prime Minister-to-be dispensing coffee to all.

One particular moment I will always personally treasure was walking hand-in-hand with the General, the two of us, alone in the main streets of Cape Town. Just what Capetonians could have made of the sight of a West African in flowing robes walking in this way with one all-too-conspicuously white is anyone's guess—the more so as the ban on sex between the races (let alone sex within the genders) had not then been lifted.

Yet if for General Obasanjo the pinnacle was when he became the first non-South African African to meet with Nelson Mandela, for others of us it was reached a little earlier, late on a hot and dusty day in the middle of the Karoo Desert.

The day had been a long one. The activists we had met with in De Aar for breakfast had been arrested by mid-morning, and the General was on the phone to Pik Botha. By early afternoon, he was standing in the pulpit of a crowded church in Graff-Reinet, where boys danced in the sanctuary with wooden AK-47s and the General preached a sermon on liberation theology of which any Latin American Jesuit would have been proud. So, too, would any Southern Baptist of the Martin Luther King school of oratory.

"We have come to see apartheid!" His eyes squinted and a low growl rose from the congregation. "We have come to smell apartheid!" He screwed his nose up theatrically and the growl grew louder. "We have come to touch apartheid!" his pointed finger leapt as though electrocuted as the growl became a shout. "And we have come to taste apartheid." His face contorted and gagged, as if by a mouthful of salt and the audience erupted in a full-throated roar. This, too, from a speaker taken completely by surprise when the parish priest offered him the pulpit. It was an effort worthy of Alan Boesak at his best.

By late afternoon we had flown in our charter plane to a township where the taste of tear-gas soured the air and (with outdoor meetings banned) the hall we were to meet with residents was crowded to at least three times its capacity—and had been since early morning. A little distance away the hated *casspirs* lurked, barring our way. Impassively, the metal-grey soldiers they carried eyed us with suspicion and disdain. Who were we? What were we? And what were we doing there? The General negotiated passage as the rank-and-file amused themselves by aiming their rifles at us in the yellow light of the dying day.

Smelling like a rugby changing-room, the hall was dank, dark and gloomy. As the General led our little party in through a back door and up on to a stage about 400 people, each one of them exploding with rage, jubilation and every emotion in between. Hysteria fed hysteria and the sound spiralled ever on upwards. In the bedlam, communication was impossible. The General took Canadian Archbishop Ted Scott by the arm and pulled him back down the steps and outside.

"No liberation theology here, Ted" he suggested. "The slightest provocation and they'll try to take the casspirs apart...."

They returned inside and after about 15 minutes the bedlam subsided to a roar. The General imposed silence and said, as quietly as the noise would allow:

"We have come here to help you, and you can help us. I am going to ask the Archbishop of Canada to say a prayer, and then I want you all to go home quietly. And without any trouble. That is how you can help us. If there is trouble, our ability to help will be reduced."

After Ted's prayer—a little longer than he might have wished but stretched to maximise its calming effects—the crowd emerged, subdued and obviously surprised. A few minutes ago they had been ready to rush outside and throw bricks and themselves into the muzzles of the waiting guns. Now the *casspirs* loomed between themselves and their homes, but the mood was subdued.

"Come on, General," one of us shouted. "We've got twenty minutes to get to the airstrip and get airborne, or it will be night and the plane won't be able to take off."

But it made no difference. The General, seeing the fight give way to fear in the eyes of our audience, and the menace that emanated palpably from the *casspirs*, walked swiftly to the front of the crowd.

"Come with me", he gestured, and, placing himself squarely in the line of fire, he walked the first fifteen or so safely past the waiting guns and tear-gas cannon. He returned for another group. Another. And then another.

"Come on, General!" the cry went up with increasing urgency. We knew the pilot was waiting and the sun was sinking fast. We had an evening appointment, too, in Port Elizabeth. But he would not stop until every single member of our audience was safely on their way home.

It was the mark of a most remarkable man, and is perhaps the most courageous and principled act I have ever witnessed. It is something I have seen again and again: an ability to empathise with any one and everyone. A willingness to help, no matter who. From the highest to the most humble, General Olusegun Obasanjo exemplifies that quality which the poet Kipling captured when he wrote:

To walk with kings, nor lose the common touch.

I can think only of one failure—if, indeed, it can be so described.

We were in Soweto on our first day in South Africa, in a combi van. Our driver was on edge. Glaring at me he muttered, "One word of Afrikaans and you're dead!" It was doubtless good advice, but of greater utility to someone who knows what the words are one should avoid uttering.

We stopped at a set of traffic lights and a car careered round the corner towards us, in reverse, its doors flailing open. A police van followed, also in reverse. The vehicles slalomed past us before the car finally veered off the roadway and slammed into a tree.

The driver rolled out and sprinted away, zig-zagging into the distance, seemingly aware that the policeman would jump from his van and shoot at him. Which is precisely what he did.

But he missed. The man disappeared into a line of huts, and the policeman returned to his van and drove off quietly in the opposite direction.

The General insisted that we get out of the van and try to find out what happened. Quietly he questioned the dozen or more bystanders.

Chase? What chase? Policeman? What policeman...? A shot? Was there a shot?

In the police state no-one, not even an eyewitness, sees a thing. Yet even there they recognised him. Greeted him cheerfully. But no, they'd seen nothing...

Once our report was done, the General was on the road—this time throughout Europe and the USA, promoting the findings of intransigence, of a white supremacist government which was simply not prepared to negotiate. And that the ANC and Nelson Mandela were indeed people the world could do business with, that they were slaves to no-one's philosophy.

The sanctions unleashed by the United States Congress throughout the late 1980s were due in no small measure to the General's quiet powers of persuasion—sanctions that ultimately unlocked the process of negotiation.

Back in South Africa with him again in December, again it was the irrepressible General at his effervescent best. Passersby, total strangers, would accost him, welcoming him back. Ministers would break out the last of treasured Irish whiskey. Everywhere his advice and guidance would be sought, but invariably only offered quietly and with a humility that rendered his words all the more telling.

Those who do not know him see only the contradiction: the only Nigerian General who, as Head of State, handed the governance of his country back to the people. Those who do, see the committed democrat. An intensely human person. One who suffers with the oppressed just as he can exult with the victorious.

Others are better placed than I am to write of his quiet diplomacy. Of helping Fidel Castro find an honourable way for his troops to leave Angola. Of helping to sustain the coherence of the elections in Mozambique. Of mediating in differences between Mandela and de Klerk at critical junctures of the negotiation process. Of his continuing personal and physical courage in opposing the dictatorship in his own country against the advice of well-meaning friends who urge him to take sanctuary abroad. And of his tireless work promoting democracy, human rights and integrity throughout the continent through the Africa Leadership Forum.

But the General is one whose qualities of humility and clear-mindedness, and whose depth of wisdom are all too often lacking in today's world. These will always be needed, and we—and most of all, Africa—are lucky, indeed, to have him.

Colin Eglin

A GREAT HUMAN BEING
AND A TRUE DEMOCRAT

General Obasanjo's and my paths met tangentially when, in January 1979, one of the security officers of the General's Federal Military Government detained me for a few hours at Lagos' Murtala Muhammed International Airport.

I had come from South Africa to observe and discuss the progress that was being made in the drafting of a new Constitution that was to bring Nigeria back to democracy and civil rule. In due course the Chef de Protocol resolved my entry visa problem and I was driven down to the VIP Guest House on Victoria Island where for a few days I was to stay as the guest of the Federal Military Government.

In Lagos I soon learned that the driving force behind the drafting of Nigeria's new democratic Constitution and the return of civilian rule was the head of Nigeria's military government, General Olusegun Obasanjo.

Although it was still 9 months before the October presidential elections the process of democratisation was already in place.

Five political parties had been registered. The Military Government was phasing itself out. The army was being reduced from 230,000 to 100,000. At local and state levels, military commissions were giving way to civilian functionaries. The future voters were being prepared for their new responsibilities. Civil servants were attending training courses to help them to carry out their tasks under a civilian government.

It was clear that under the leadership of General Olusegun Obasanjo—a military man with a passionate commitment to democracy—there could be no turning back!

I did not meet the General on that visit to Nigeria, yet in a powerful way I felt his presence and came to appreciate his commitment to development and democracy

My first face-to-face meeting with the General was in June 1986 when he was in South Africa as a Co-Chairman of the Commonwealth Eminent Persons Group (EPG). The EPG had come to South Africa in an attempt to find a process that would break the deadlock between the Liberation Movement led by the ANC and President PW Botha's National Party Government.

Sadly, at the very moment that the EPG looked like achieving a breakthrough, the South African Government's military aeroplanes struck at targets in Gabarone, Lusaka and Harare. A few days later, President PW Botha clamped down on the growing resistance to his regime by declaring a nation wide "state of emergency".

In an extensive off-the-record discussion I was struck, not only by the General's commitment to democracy, but his understanding of the fact that democratisation was a process and not an instant ready-made solution.

To him it was important to recognise the human realities of the South African situation. It was essential to ensure that democratisation went hand in hand with a process of trust and confidence building.

Three months later, this time at his London hotel, I met a disappointed yet determined General Obasanjo. The EPG was meeting to complete its report, its mission had failed. President PW Botha had made sure of this. But the General was determined to stay involved, determined to try to play a part in helping South Africa to shed the shackles of apartheid and move to a united and democratic future.

The General, in a way which reflected his understanding personality, had warmed to the people of South Africa. And in addition to this, with his vision of a democratic developing Africa always in the background, the General was aware of the positive, contribution that a "new" South Africa could make towards the development in Africa.

General Obasanjo continued to come to South Africa—at times as an individual, at times as a member of the InterAction Council, at times as a key player in the Africa Leadership Forum. He remained involved and he remained positive. His wise counsel made an impact on the thinking of the leaders of all political parties.

It was in Kampala, Uganda, in May of 1991 that I met General Obasanjo, the African democrat at his creative best. Months of hard work, preliminary planning sessions, private lobbying and of truly creative thinking culminated in the Kampala Forum. 400 delegates from nearly all the states of Africa—presidents, prime ministers, government functionaries, academics, writers, economists and community leaders—assembled in the Ugandan capital.

Frank discussion, self critical analysis, the identification of goals helped along by the guiding hand and wise counsel of General Obasanjo culminated in the unanimous acceptance of the Kampala Declaration.

At Helsinki in 1975, Europe decided to have its Conference on Security and Cooperation in Europe (CSCE). At Kampala in 1991, Africa committed itself to strive for a Conference on Security, Stability, Development and Cooperation in Africa (CSSDCA) with its four "calabashes" of security, stability, development and cooperation.

As he celebrates being sixty years young, I salute Olusegun Obasanjo—a great human being, a true democrat, a distinguished African patriot, and a good friend of the people of my country, South Africa.

Thank you, Olusegun, for being just what you are.

Robert von Lucius

"ARCHAIC ROCK"—MEDIATOR FOR A BETTER SOUTH AFRICA

He commutes between New York, Berlin and Cape Town. In between, he holds court at his chicken farm in Ota near Lagos and occasionally sells a Christmas turkey to the German embassy. Olusegun Obasanjo is "archaic African rock". He is respected, as few others are on the continent. He mediates in conflicts all around Africa. Britons and French might by now regret that they foiled his election as Secretary-General of the United Nations in 1991. Since 1986 he had been named as a candidate with good prospects for that post. His friends Helmut Schmidt and Lord Callaghan of Cardiff had encouraged him to make himself available. With them, Obasanjo is a member of the InterAction Council, a group of former heads of state or government. Obasanjo is or was a member of around twenty international councils that dealt with disarmament, population policy, Africa, raw materials or simply "a better world". His advice is in demand. Thus he was able to occasionally influence events stronger than is easily visible.

Obasanjo, Nigeria's head of state from 1976 until 1979, is apparently the only African who as a military man returned power to civilians in an orderly manner and without any pressure. He has a vision for the African continent. Among his pet themes are an African security conference that is based on the model of the Conference on Security and Cooperation in Europe, and an axis of the four regional African powers Nigeria, Egypt, Kenya and South Africa. These should, he believes, harmonise their efforts and act as nodes for regional development.

Obasanjo does not mince his words, even among Africans. His speech as head of state at the fifteenth annual summit of the Organisation of African Unity in Khartoum in 1978 was widely regarded as the highlight of the session and roundly applauded in spite of him speaking, contrary to then OAU-tradition, about "our own failings". Nine years later in Addis Ababa, addressing African ministers, he was even sharper, mentioning the "tendency to always find ready-made scapegoats for our problems, or blame others for our own shortcomings". He also castigated "reckless" programs of state expansion and "the life-styles of the new rulership".

In his home country—some people regard him as Nigeria's "clandestine foreign minister"—Obasanjo does not live without danger. While Ibrahim Babangida was still president, Obasanjo called him a dictator who ruined the economy. Towards Babangida's successor, Sani Abacha, he does not harbour or utter friendlier feelings. The greatest danger for any leader is, he says, to surround himself with sycophants. For Nigerians of lesser stature such an honesty is dangerous as even the literature nobel prize winner Wole Soyinka, a fellow Yoruba, had to experience recently again. The former chief of staff and commander of the Nigerian army is aware of these dangers, but he just smiles them away mildly. Even Obasanjo's memoirs "Not My Will", published in Nigeria, contained enough dynamite to have their sale temporarily banned by a Nigerian High Court in 1990. While distinctly aware of human rights, he says one has to see them in their African environment: indicating that one should not measure them with letter scales.

He had been honored as the best student at military courses in Great Britain (Aldershot and Chatham—cited as "best ever student in the British Commonwealth") and India (Indian Defence College). In spite of this academic applause the civil engineer and General appreciates quick decisions. One shouldn't waste time, he believes. When neighbours, diplomats, politicians come to his farm, an hour's drive from Lagos, to request his advice, he will always have time for them: they just have to wait, he says. Perhaps his role as a local chief—and their special responsibility, as described by Nelson Mandela in his recent autobiography "Long Walk to Freedom"—impressed upon him this trait. He will have soothing words of advice, comfort, consolation: nobody should leave him, he believes, empty-handed. His sharing in the burden is born, as he sees it, out of the communal nature of living together. The multiple honorary doctor is, incidentally, one of few African leaders where there are no rumours about bank accounts in Switzerland. While he was Nigerian Vice-President, more than ten thousand civil servants had been dismissed in his fight against corruption.

Even when far away from home, Obasanjo wears traditional Nigerian garb. That, and his occasionally mumbling-grumpy voice, may contribute to the dignity he exudes. Even when "humanity"—a word he likes to use—has precedence for Obasanjo, he is very aware of where he is born. Whether that was in 1935 or in 1937, he does not know. He can reconstruct his year of birth from the building of the village church in 1934; his mother had married shortly afterwards. Olusegun Obasanjo has an intuitive mind rather than an analytical, a good instinct for the main emphasis and relative importance of things. With his mixture of wit and (some believe, quite forceful) decisiveness he tends to achieve his aims, among them, that four of his children are academically trained. In an answer to how his friends might describe him, he mentions, in this order: stern, strict, compassionate, gentle, kind. And just as revealing is what these friends have to say about him: they regard him as "egalitarian", as concerned for his friends and warmhearted.

Violence, sanctions, peaceful change

As head of state Obasanjo had, in a moderate tone, pursued African interests. He demanded the withdrawal of Soviet and Cuban troops and criticised European failures in Africa. Among his many roles as mediator—among them in Namibia, Angola, Western Sahara and Sudan—South Africa takes a prime place. Already in May 1986, the London "Times" headed an article on the Commonwealth Eminent Persons Group which he cochaired, with "Realist Obasanjo impresses Pretoria". He made, the Times remarks, "a big impact on both black and white South Africans" whom he met during two earlier visits to the republic that year. Members of the Pretoria cabinet regarded him, in the words of then Foreign Minister Roelof (Pik) Botha—who met Obasanjo frequently and occasionally secretly henceforth—as "someone who knows the realities of Africa". That remark might stem from Obasanjo's conviction that one had to take into account fears and hopes of white South Africans. After a series of visits in South Africa in 1986 he remarked that white South Africans were full of fear of survival, of losing their privileges, of having to face revenge, of the unknown.

Obasanjo was not always a proponent of peaceful change in South Africa; he has learned, too. In 1987 he wrote in the German journal "Vereinte Nationen" that he had believed only violence could change the South African minority regime. He saw apartheid as violence in its "most pure form". Obasanjo did not need to speak abstractly about war: he had experienced it in Biafra, where in 1970 he commanded troops and received the capitulation of the last rebel battalions, and while stationed in 1960 in the Congo. But he hoped the 1986-Commonwealth initiative might have a small chance for success. During the trips he met both then President P.W. Botha and his later successor Nelson Mandela, as one of very few people who had the privilege to visit him in jail, and (except in the closing days before the release) as the only black leader. At that time the Commonwealth, and he, came close to success, which was then thwarted by South Africa's security establishment.

During the Commonwealth initiative Obasanjo strongly pleaded in Western capitals for economic sanctions. Some of the businessmen he then met afterwards felt that he came as a "preacher", not as one prepared to listen. Still, he was always aware that it was "in nobody's interest to destroy South Africa's economy". Everything possible had to be done to "save and preserve" its economy. With this in mind, he wooed for "sanctions, retreat of foreign capital, international isolation and other forms of pressure to entice the South African government to peaceful negotiations". He feared that otherwise an "explosion and holocaust" might destroy the whole of southern Africa. Still, he put himself apart from the black American caucus and the antiapartheid movement by pleading against disinvestors "just walking away, or handing over to people who cared less about the welfare of workers."

Obasanjo, undaunted, continued his involvement in South Africa in the nineties.

Without his influence, the Inkatha Freedom Party leader Mangosuthu Buthelezi would not have attended the National Peace Convention in September 1991, which was considered a decisive step towards the miracle developments in the region. Obasanjo's way of dealing with this conflict was typical. Just before he was due to depart from Johannesburg airport he heard of Buthelezi's intended boycott and asked to phone him immediately. He then, in a veiled threat, said "Africa" would "hold him accountable" if he did not turn up. That, apparently, changed Buthelezi's plans.

When it was announced that Nelson Mandela would receive the Africa Peace Award from the African Centre for the Constructive Resolution of Disputes on 18 March 1995, a few days after Obasanjo's (presumed) sixtieth birthday, it seemed almost clear that among the invitees would be, besides the OAU Secretary-General Salim Ahmed Salim, also Olusegun Obasanjo. There he would again be able to assess whether his vision stated in Windhoek in 1991 bears fruits: that the "new South Africa may represent a turning point for Africa as it should mark the beginning of effective continental cooperation and integration".

Olusegun OBASANJO Foto Robert von Lucius

Urgestein

Er pendelt zwischen New York, Berlin und Kapstadt. Dazwischen hält er hof auf seiner Hühnerfarm nahe Lagos und verkauft schon mal Weihnachtstruthähne an die deutsche Botschaft. Olusegun Obasanjo ist afrikanisches Urgestein. Wie kaum ein anderer seines Kontinents wird er respektiert. Er vermittelt in Konflikten überall in Afrika. Daß Briten und Franzosen seine Wahl zum Generalsekretär der Vereinten Nationen verhindert haben, mögen sie inzwischen bereuen. Seit sieben Jahren wurde Obasanjo als aussichtsreicher Kandidat genannt; seine Freunde Helmut Schmidt und Lord Callaghan hatten ihn zur Bewerbung ermutigt. Mit ihnen gehört Obasanjo dem Interaktionsrat an, einer Gruppe ehemaliger Staats- und Regierungschefs. Er ist oder war Mitglied in zwanzig internationalen Ausschüssen, die sich mit Abrüstung, Bevölkerungspolitik, Afrika, Rohstoffen oder schlicht „einer besseren Welt" befassen. Dadurch beeinflußt er bisweilen Entwicklungen stärker als vordergründig sichtbar.

Der Rat des wohl einzigen Afrikaners, der als Militär ohne Druck die Macht an eine gewählte Zivilregierung geordnet übertrug, ist gefragt. Obasanjo, 1976 bis 1979 nigerianischer Staatschef, besitzt eine Vision vom Kontinent. Zu seinen Lieblingsthemen gehören eine der KSZE nachgebildete afrikanische Sicherheitskonferenz und eine Achse der vier afrikanischen Mittelmächte Nigeria, Ägypten, Kenia und Südafrika; Pretoria übernahm bereitwillig diese Idee. Mehrfach vermittelte Obasanjo am Kap. Ohne seine Einflußnahme hätte die Inkatha den Nationalen Friedensvertrag wohl nicht unterzeichnet. Man müsse, sagt Obasanjo, auf die Befürchtungen und Hoffnungen weißer Südafrikaner eingehen. In seiner Heimat lebt er nicht ungefährdet. Er nennt den amtierenden Präsidenten Babangida einen Diktator, der die Wirtschaft ruiniert habe. Die größte Gefahr jedes Führers sei es, sich mit Jasagern zu umgeben. Für Nigerianer von geringerer Statur wäre solche Offenheit gefährlich. Der frühere Stabschef und Oberkommandeur ist sich dessen bewußt, lächelt aber milde.

Obasanjo besitzt eher intuitiven denn analytischen Verstand, einen Instinkt für Schwerpunkte. Mit seiner Mischung aus Witz und (manche glauben: rabiater) Entschlossenheit setzt er sich durch. Der mehrfache Ehrendoktor gehört zu jenen wenigen afrikanischen Führern, bei denen nicht von Konten in der Schweiz gemunkelt wird. Der Ingenieur und General – bei Kursen in Großbritannien und Indien war er als der jeweils beste Student ausgezeichnet worden – schätzt rasche Entscheidungen. Doch nimmt er sich Zeit, wenn Nachbarn, Diplomaten, Politiker ihn auf seiner Farm um ein Gespräch bitten. Auch aus seinem Kapstädter Hotelzimmer ruft er dort mal rasch an. Bisweilen gilt er als heimlicher Außenminister Nigerias. Er versuche immer zu helfen, sei es mit Rat, Trost, Geld: Man sollte, sagt er mit bedächtiger, bisweilen brummelnder Stimme, niemanden „leer" fortschicken. Menschenrechte müsse man in ihrem afrikanischen Umfeld sehen; mit der Briefwaage mißt er sie also nicht. Ob er 1935 oder 1937 geboren wurde, wisse er nicht, er könne sein Geburtsdatum nur vom Bau der Dorfkirche rekonstruieren. Auch wenn „die Menschheit" für ihn Vorrang habe, wisse er genau, wo er geboren sei. Als Staatschef hatte er, in gemäßigter Tonlage, schwarzafrikanische Interessen in den Vordergrund gestellt. Er forderte den Abzug sowjetischer und kubanischer Militärs und kritisierte westliches Versagen in Afrika. Auch fern der Heimat zeigt er sich stets in traditioneller nigerianischer Tracht. Das mag beitragen zu der Würde, die Olusegun Obasanjo ausstrahlt.

ROBERT VON LUCIUS

Emmanuel A. Erskine

MY HEARTIEST CONGRATULATIONS

This is a rare and pleasant opportunity for me to pay my highest respects to my distinguished friend, brother and colleague, General Olusegun Obasanjo, whom I affectionately call, Oba. On the occasion of your 60th birthday, I say to you, Oba, my heartiest congratulations!

General Obasanjo, the former head of State of the largest black African country, Nigeria, commenced the journey which has led him to be one of the few highly respected and distinguished African statesmen of world repute, as an officer cadet at the regular officers special training school (ROSTS), Teschie, Accra, Ghana in March 1958. We shared a room together and we grew up to be intimate brothers. Oba was an extremely hard working, assiduous cadet who was among the few Nigerian cadets selected at the end of the course in September 1958 for further training at Mons, Aldershot, United Kingdom, where he was commissioned as a Lieutenant into the corps of engineers, Nigeria Army, in early 1959.

General Obasanjo was a dedicated officer who made his contribution towards the resolution of the Congo crisis by his active participation with Nigerian contingents in ONUC in the early 1960's. His effectiveness in command was proven further in the Nigerian civil war which engulfed the country in 1967. He was a committed and a highly disciplined officer, whose loyalty to authority was never in question. It was therefore not much of a surprise to me that he should be the most competent and favoured General to be chosen by his senior colleagues to assume the reins of government, power and authority, as the Head of State of Nigeria, following the assassination of his trusted boss, General Murtala Muhammed. That General Obasanjo was reluctant and had to be prevailed upon to accept the highest political office of the land demonstrates his genuine sense of modesty and loyalty, personal qualities that have endeared him to other heads of state and government, politicians, diplomats, the military and other international personalities who have had the good fortune to share his company.

The few years as the Head of State helped him grow and mature in wisdom and to have more profound appreciation on issues of international dimensions. Just a week after handing over power to a democratically elected civilian government, General Obasanjo went to his Ota Farm, which provides him and his family with their principal means of survival. But selfless Oba, as a repository of the vast leadership experiences strengthened by the precious exposure in the highest political office could not be contented with the Ota Farm alone; he had to explore viable avenues to share those rich experiences and knowledge with Africa. This was General Obasanjo's motivation for founding the Africa Leadership Forum whose efforts at endeavouring to improve the quality of life of the African and to bring peace to Africa are well documented. Africa Leadership Forum's promotion of security, stability, development and cooperation needs to be seriously studied and its principles applied to bring peace and development to Africa.

The international community acknowledges General Obasanjo as a great African statesman and a leader, whose wisdom and knowledge have to be fully exploited. When therefore there was the pressing demand to intervene diplomatically in the South African crisis, the international community found it expedient to choose General Obasanjo as a member of the group of world eminent personalities.

Because of his moral strength rooted in his total honesty, General Obasanjo, in our contemporary times, is the only African leaders and a statesman, of that political stature, who is openly championing the ideals of probity and accountability among Africa's political leadership. He is the only African former Head of State who is sharing his knowledge, experiences and wisdom with international institutions on world issues spanning from economics, philosophy and environment to peace. A few Obasanjos could change Africa but for the moment, we can only be contented with Olusegun.

I hope and pray that General Obasanjo, at 60, will maintain his course and relentlessly continue his drive into the hearts of Africa's political leaders, in the earnest hope that they will change and help to bring succour to the millions of suffering women and children of Africa. General Obasanjo has served his country with distinction and is serving Africa with high honours. Do continue with this honourable duty! I have always respected and admired you for this excellent role that you are playing to salvage Africa.

Oba, my heartiest congratulations, once again, on your 60th birthday, and may you live long enough to see peace and development in Africa!

Ad'Obe Obe

A COMMITTED OPTIMIST

I was at school when General Olusegun Obasanjo was making his name as Nigeria's war hero. That image of him remained intact for me until I personally met him more than twenty years later. He wanted me to work on a journal of leadership in Africa. Africa's problem turned around quality of leadership, he told me. "Too many African leaders come to power without being prepared for it", he said. And he included his own experience as Nigeria's Head of State.

Forthright intellectualism tinged with humility is general Obasanjo's hallmark. He never forgets the first principles of an argument, prompting anyone in discussion with him to continually retain the objective. He has limited tolerance for digressions. It has been observed that General Obasanjo chairing a meeting is like a military operation, participants have to be precise and stick to the point, and conclusions come out correspondingly incisive. The General is always a good source of inspiration for people around him, especially at conferences.

My personal association with General Obasanjo began in the late eighties when despondency charactirised the attitude of many Africans towards their continent. Expressions like 'continent without a future' was frequently heard from Africans lamenting The African Condition. Personally, being acquainted with the gory details of many African events, I too was inclined to be cynical about Africa. General Obasanjo talked me out of much of that cynicism. Rather than moan, he said, 'We must ask ourselves: what can WE do to salvage the situation?'. All Africans must ask themselves this question. But, most of all, African leaders should lead the way. For it is the leaders who have the ultimate responsibility for setting the agenda for change and managing the critical decisions to effective conclusions. Any African leader who did not show evidence of having started with this question was suspect in the General's eyes.

This perception is a major strand of the logic underpinned the establishment of the Africa Leadership Forum (ALF). A primary aim of the ALF was to prepare young Africans for leadership responsibilities. As an army officer, the General, or course, knew a few things about leadership training. But the leadership training he intended with ALF has a wider socio-political context, the same context about which he, in spite of military training, would later admit unpreparedness when he became Nigeria's Head of State. The admission was not so much about his own personal weakness as much as acknowledgment of the consequences of the rapid evolution of modern African societies and the institutions therein. With ALF, the General hoped to give younger people what he, with hindsight, felt he had missed: an institution that processed and passed back lessons learnt by experienced people.

As a Nigerian, I most admire General Obasanjo to be one of the few persons of his generation who deserved the attribute of patriotism. When the General says 'We fought to keep this country together', there was no mistaking the depth of passion. All those who have been privileged to participate in the famous Farmhouse Dialogue at his base in Ota will confirm this.

The Farmhouse Dialogues were, so to speak, specific application of the ALF concept to his own country. His tenure as Nigeria Head of State has the internationally and nationally recognised distinction of peaceful transition from military to civilian rule, long before pro-democracy activism became a trend in world politics. In the General's view, soldiers have no business being in politics, so a military regime is an aberration, which, if it becomes necessary, should perform its corrective service effectively and promptly make way for the wishes of the people.

The General deserves to be proud of his record in office. Many Nigerians now say that institution building Nigeria, a prerequisite for young nations, stopped in 1979 when the General handed over power. This equally applies to physical structures: most of the durable and impressive structures and landmarks in the country seem to be pre-1979. Nigerians bewildered by the bizarre phenomenon of multimillionaire generals managing a national economy crippled by debt in the last decade, have constantly referred to how General Obasanjo handed over power with billions of dollars in foreign reserve.

Quite naturally the General has to get involved in stopping the decay of a country he loves so much and to which he had given so much dedication. There was an instance when the General disagreed with a young Nigerian's business proposal on the grounds that they were inimical to national interest. The young said national interest was none of his business. The General was furious with this young Nigerian on a scale I had never before seen in him. But when he calmed down, he told me: 'That's what happens to young men when you have unpatriotic leaders who cannot lead by example".

Like the rest of Africa, the General refuses to accept that Nigeria's problems were insurmountable. He applies his criterion ('What can We do to improve?') of dedicated leadership to his compatriots and found them wanting. Nigeria's problems stem from the fact that leaders in the last decade have been role models for one thing only: pursuit of self-interest. The result, as he once wrote: "When the Nigerian political class gather to discuss Nigeria, one thing you can be sure is NOT on the agenda is 'Nigeria'".

Despairing Nigerians are notorious for the cry of Nigeria is ungovernable'. Or, as one minister put it, "Only God can govern Nigeria'. The General's response, in a private discussion, was "At least that means God believes in Nigeria". He went to stress that he too believed in Nigeria and he would rather stick to the belief that God helps those who help themselves. He extended that belief to the whole of black Africa.

Dynamic optimism is the essence of that quality which marks General Olusegun Obasanjo as a natural leader. He has and will continue to give everything to keep hope alive. May the Almighty God keep him alive—we need him!

Carol Lancaster

A LEADER FOR AFRICA AND THE WORLD

It must have been over a decade ago that I met General Obasanjo. Of course, as a scholar of African affairs, I had long followed the General's career. And he was frankly one of my heroes for his commitment to a transition from military to democratic rule in Nigeria in the late 1970s and—most extraordinarily—his carrying through on his commitment. He is still a hero and an almost unique model in the continent in this regard.

My real work with the General began after he became chairman of the Africa Leadership Forum. This Forum which has come alive under General Obasanjo's leadership, has proven invaluable as a meeting place for prominent and rising African leaders to discuss major issues, to network and, most importantly, to mentor and teach one another. But for me and many of my colleagues, both in government and in the scholarly community, the Africa Leadership Forum is an important interlocutor for us, an organization to which we can look for dialogue with Africans—not as representatives of their governments but as spokespersons for their peoples and their region.

But even more importantly for someone like me—a foreign expert—and sympathetic observer of Africa and now as a United States government official, a partner to many in the region in promoting development—I know I can look to General Obasanjo for wisdom and advice as I try to understand events in Africa and the individual shaping those events. I feel I can look to him as I would to a village elder and feel confident not only of his advice but of his concern and affection. He has made the world smaller and more secure for many like me. I am sure that many others feel, as I do, enormous gratitude and affection for him and wish him the best on the occasion of his 60th birthday and hope for many more years of health, happiness and productive partnerships together.

Bona Malwal

AFRICA'S BEST KNOWN SOLDIER, DIPLOMAT AND STATESMAN

I am pleased to be invited to make this contribution to a publication on the occasion of the sixtieth birthday of General Olusegun Obasanjo, the world-respected former Nigerian head of state who has been a close friend over the years. No one small piece like mine here, or even a whole publication like the one this piece will appear in, can do full justice to General Obasanjo. He has made history for his own country, Nigeria, has been the best example of Africa's good nationalist soldier and is arguably one of Africa's best roving ambassadors.

I shall take no space from the few pages I have to write about General Obasanjo's background. I am fully confident that those who have followed his career more closely than myself, many of whom I know are contributors to this publication, will do his illustrious background better justice than I can. I confine myself to my personal encounters, relationship and friendship with *the General* as I like to fondly call him.

I met General Obasanjo for the first time at an Organisation of African Unity (OAU) meeting in Mauritius in July 1976. I was Minister of Culture and Information of the Sudan at the time. Another general, Jaafar Mohamed Nimeiri, was the head of state of the Sudan. I had not known that an old colleague and a contemporary from Indiana University in the United States of America, Adediji Ayo, was General Obasanjo's Minister of Information.

General Obasanjo decided to call on General Nimeiri at his residence at the Summit Centre in Mauritius. Accompanying him was his Minister of Information, my colleague Ayo. General Nimeiri had asked me to be with him during his meeting with General Obasanjo. I never got to know whether the name of Ayo had been communicated to General Nimeiri in advance of the meeting and that this may have led him to ask me to be present as a counterpart to the Nigerian minister. General Nimeiri had often asked me anyway to do some work of the Minister of Foreign Affairs, even when the Minister was present, so I had no reason to be surprised by this particular move.

When the Nigerian head of state introduced my colleague to the Sudanese President as the Minister of Information of Nigeria and I was introduced to him as the Sudanese Minister of Information, and the sense of reunion between two colleagues Ayo and myself permeated the room, General Obasanjo's excellent sense of humour, which I came to enjoy for the many years of friendship that ensued, struck. He told General Nimeiri, "We have to be careful with these American educated civilians. They will want to take over from us generals in the name of democracy". At the time, of course, I did not suspect that General Obasanjo had plans for handing over power in Nigeria to a democratically elected civilian government.

From Mauritius to Angola, to Gabon, Cairo and Khartoum, I kept meeting General Obasanjo throughout the next few years, until he handed power to a civilian and democratically elected government. My years of knowing the General while he was in power were not particularly exciting in any sense. Our relationship was after all that between a subordinate me and a superior him. I was perhaps more conscious of this fact than the General, who always reaches out with simple but dignified friendship to anyone who knows him. Even though I felt a sense of friendship coming from him—and I believe I met that friendship with my own—it was not as full as it came to develop much later.

I lost touch with the General during the first few years after his handing over of power to an elected civilian government. He spent much of that time apparently organising his private life and deciding what his role in the world should be. He had retired from the army very young, in his forties. He was too vigorous and energetic a man to retire into oblivion on a farm somewhere in Nigeria. I knew I would see him again some time.

I myself had run into problems in my own country. General Nimeiri, through whom I had first come to meet General Obasanjo, had a dream from "Allah" that he should impose Islamic Sharia law on all of us in Sudan. He also decided to abrogate the 1972 Addis Ababa Agreement, which had ended the civil war between his government and Southern Sudan; an agreement which brought me into his government. I resigned my position from the Nimeiri government in protest. But, unlike General Obasanjo who had opted for a voluntary retirement, I was seized and sent into General Nimeiri's involuntary prison retirement for a long fourteen months.

I met General Obasanjo again in Sudan in 1987. He had got interested in peacemaking around Africa and the world and sought to mediate an end to the civil war in my country. He had teamed up with another close Sudanese friend, Francis Mading Deng. Dr. Deng was Sudan's Minister of State for Foreign Affairs at the same time I was a Minister and knew General Obasanjo even better than I did. They wanted to try their diplomatic skills on the resolution of the Sudanese conflict. I did not so much support them in their noble mission as simply encourage them. The two made extensive shuttle diplomacy between Khartoum and the capitals of the countries of the Horn of Africa.

The General did not succeed in negotiating peace for Sudan, but he has not given up his efforts to help bring about peace in my country. I was glad to see that General Obasanjo is now one of the friends of the Intergovernmental Authority for Drought and Development (IGADD) peace initiative, the peace process which is being undertaken by the four Horn of Africa countries of the IGADD. It was in this latest capacity that I met General Obasanjo in the Ethiopian capital of Addis Ababa in February 1995.

It is difficult to keep track of the numerous political and diplomatic initiatives that General Olusegun Obasanjo undertakes on behalf of his country, Nigeria, his continent, Africa, and the entire world. Since handing over political power to an elected government in Nigeria, General Obasanjo has established strong democratic and statesman credentials for himself that continue to shame all the generals in his country and Africa who continue to rape democracy by staging military coups. He has also shown the world that democracy still has a chance in Africa, even among its armies.

In the first decade of his retirement, General Olusegun Obasanjo has been a defender of human rights and an untiring advocate of open government and democracy for the African continent. He has inspired the establishment of a club of former African heads of state, who act as elderly wise men for the continent. He leads the Africa Leadership Forum, which brings together the continent's leadership of those in power and the younger African intellectual community to discuss common issues of concern. He has made his own private farm in Nigeria outside Lagos the headquarters and centre for some of these activities on behalf of Africa.

At the time of writing this piece, 15 March 1995, I had just learned that the present Nigerian dictatorship has arrested General Obasanjo, accusing him of being behind a coup attempt to overthrow the Abacha regime. It is incredibly sad that African despotism has not yet been fully eradicated and that the Nigerian dictatorship would dare arrest a leader who has given up power voluntarily, accusing him of a coup plot. Let us hope that celebrating the birthday of this great African will send a signal to the Nigerian despots to lay off him.

Eme Awa

AMBASSADOR-EXTRAORDINARY FOR AFRICA

It is a little upsetting to me to have to write about General Obasanjo beginning with a complaint. I was given virtually only one day in which to do the writing which would go into a publication to be presented on his 60th birthday. This came at a time when I was extremely busy, editing two books. If I do not do enough justice to the General, it is therefore not my fault.

General Obasanjo came into prominence during the civil war in Nigeria where he had a successful outing with his troops in the Port-Harcourt area and played an impressive role in the handling of the routines connected with the termination of the conflict. He appeared once or twice at seminars at the University of Nigeria, Nsukka (UNN), where he took a posturing which indicated that he might have acquired some knowledge of international relations. What impressed me deeply was his abrasiveness and a brazen presentation of his view on various issues at discussion in the seminars. At the time, the road from Nsukka to Enugu was a deathtrap. A contractor had been working on the road for some time but the company seemed to feel that it did not matter even if the job was completed as late as the year 2000. After General Obasanjo travelled through that road twice, he reorganised the contract and the job was completed with immediate effect. Nsukka gave him kudos for his concern and the achievements.

General Obasanjo appeared on my observatory again after he assumed office as the Head of State and Commander-in-Chief of the Armed Forces of Nigeria. I attended some of the leaders-of-thought conferences which he organised with a view to obtaining advice on various matters of policy from people who possessed some expertise on them. He carried himself very well before his guests and the abrasiveness did not show too much. All who attended the meetings derived considerable benefit from them.

Later General Obasanjo prepared a transition programme indicating when he would hand over power to civilians. When later he criticised his successor military leaders for preparing an unduly elaborate transition programme which, in any case, was running into murky waters, they chided him for not having devoted enough time and thought to his own programme. They implied that he had failed in his bid to reorganise Nigeria and that his criticism of their performance was a case of sour grapes. But we must note that Obasanjo assembled people of great intellectual competence into the Constituent Assembly and the Constitution Drafting Committee. The Constitution produced contained features which were novel and had great potential for integrating the country geopolitically and in socio-political terms. I refer to the noble statements in the preamble to the Constitution, the provision for the realisation of the federal character doctrine as well as the fundamental objectives and directive principles which set out seeming radical measures which could favour the lower classes, if implemented. Some of the provisions were said to be non-justiciable in a political, not in a judicial sense.

General Obasanjo worked for three short years and completed his assignment. In spite of the quibbling by politicians, he handed power back to them in 1979. That was remarkable as the most peaceful and smoothest succession that this nation has known in its development.

General Obasanjo does not possess a disposition of quietude and does not seem able to fold his hands and watch political events with resignation. In private life, he quickly established the Africa Leadership Forum and organised seminars and dialogues in his farm house at Ota, often inviting very important people from Nigeria and from abroad. A plethora of materials has been produced, covering many aspects of life in Nigeria and Africa: politics, education, agriculture, etc. When I was first introduced to all this in 1991, my first concern was how he could cause the materials to receive wide circulation in Nigeria and other African nations where they could conceivably influence policies. In my view, the General has achieved no remarkable success in this matter. But he has functioned reasonably successfully as an ambassador-extraordinary for Africa, being always on the move to give assistance of one kind or the other to African nations in distress and making a case with the West for assistance to be given to Africans.

General Obasanjo has run into serious difficulties in his pattern of participation in Nigerian politics in recent years. As I have indicated, he disapproved of then President Babangida's meandering and seemingly endless transition programme which was remarkable for the amount of money it gulped, with no tangible achievement to show for it. He played an important role in getting Babangida out of the way. By the time it was over, General Babangida did not know what had hit him and knocked him out.

These events also marked the beginning of General Obasanjo's agony. Although he helped to show Babangida the way out of Aso Rock, he has not unambiguously solicited the installation of Chief Abiola as the President. He does not seem to understand that 12 June 1993 is to Nigeria what 1688 is to England. In both cases, power shifted from a bumbling oligarchic group with ascribed powers (and in Nigeria also those with legitimacy based on coercion) to a broad grouping of people who derive power from the votes of the electorate. In our case, the oligarchy showed great incompetence and seemed to condone massive corruption and indiscipline as well as to manifest insensitivity to the needs and feelings of other classes of the people in and outside of their indigenous areas.

Since General Abacha came into power, it seems a pall of gloom enveloped the Nigerian political system again. Many Nigerians think that General Obasanjo is entirely capable of helping to ease him out of this position in as short a time as possible. General Obasanjo does not appear to show any great concern about this matter. It seems that he relegates 12 June to the background and seeks to discover ways of restructuring Nigeria without it. In the main he has tried to rally conservation forces together to join him in what he regards as a crusade to save Nigeria. His showing in these acts is entirely unimpressive. I think he has run into these difficulties because of the following problems:

(1) He is somewhat skeptical of democracy if it implies leaving immense power of the parties and of the government entirely in the hands of elected people. From this point of view, 12 June would to him be an open sesame to mobocracy.

(2) He does not seem to mind if the military, serving or retired, are installed in power provided that the individuals concerned are competent, patriotic and credible.

(3) He may have forgotten something in the State House which he would like to retrieve directly or indirectly. Or, it may be that he is engaged in delicate and devious strategy to rout the military. It will take some time for him to come out with something clear and unmistakable and he must live with the doubts which all these can create in the minds of many people.

But if eventually he is seen to have dug the ground from under his feet within Nigeria, it will not be long before the international community will take notice of the situation and react in its own way.

Chief Afe Babalola

GENERAL OLUSEGUN OBASANJO AS AN EXEMPLAR

Introduction

The coming and the making of the exemplar, otherwise known as General Olusegun Obasanjo, was unannounced and little was known about him until he took over the command of the 3rd Marine Commando of the Nigerian Army which operated in the South Eastern front of Biafra. The brave and the gallant efforts of the exemplar contributed in large measure to the surrender of the Biafran Army. He later served as Federal Commissioner for Works in 1973.

But it was the military coup in July 1975 that brought the genius of this soldier into the limelight. In October 1974 General Yakubu Gowon stunned many Nigeria when he said:

"Four years ago when I gave 1976 as the target date for returning the country to normal constitutional government, both myself and the military hierarchy honestly believed that by that date, especially after a bloody Civil War ... there would have developed an atmosphere of sufficient stability... 1976 is unrealistic, it would indeed amount to a betrayal of trust to adhere rigidly to that target date."

Not long after, General Gowon was ousted in a bloodless coup on 29 July 1975 and the mantle of leadership fell on Brigadier Murtala Mohammed with Obasanjo as his number two. However, in February 1976 a clique led by Dimka wickedly assassinated General Murtala Mohammed. It is to the credit of General Obasanjo that it is recorded that he had no ambition of succeeding Murtala Mohammed as Head of State. The unsolicited and providentially ordained headship of the most populous black country in the world bequeathed to him the grave responsibility at the age of 38 of solving the myriad of problems afflicting the country after the devastating civil war.

I was a keen observer of his activities during the tenure of his leadership of Nigeria from 1976 to 1979. The political programme which started with his predecessor, the late General Murtala Mohammed, was prosecuted with religious vigour, unbending determination and impressive consistency.

He set up the Constitutional Assembly and Presidential system of government. He carried out reforms in the Local Government System. He introduced measures to curb inflation; he lay the foundation for the Green Revolution through *Operation Feed The Nation* (O.F.N.) and established numerous River Basin Development Authorities to expand and develop agriculture and industry; he launched the Ajaokuta Steel Complex—an imperative for industrial takeoff; he widened external trade and indiginised enterprises operating in Nigeria; he promulgated the Land Use Decree to ensure fair and meaningful distribution of land; he waged war against the greatest malady in Nigeria—indiscipline; and he injected a sense of moderation in the display of wealth or power through a policy of low profile.

It was not until he engaged my services in defending a libel suit instituted against him following the publication of his controversial book *"Not My Will"* that I had a personal relationship with the General. I have since then held several meetings with the General at different times and places including his office at Abeokuta, his farm at Ota, and my office and home at Ibadan. We both participated in the West African subregional meeting of Transparency International in Cotonou, Benin.

I have therefore been privileged to see him at work and at play. He has boundless energy which I dare say is visible in his robust profile. He has inflexible purpose and empirical approach to every problem. His fertile imagination is reflected in his numerous speeches. He is a statesman of impressive range with a wide knowledge and understanding of international politics. He is a fascinating and good-humoured man. He combines attractive native intellect and traditional background with modern education and inundates his speeches with impressive and witty metaphorical expressions with which he sends his message home compellingly.

My aim in this little contribution, is to highlight some of his imperishable and enduring contributions to Nigeria's cause in particular and Africa and international causes in general. These contributions warrant his being described as an exemplar and merit his jubilee birthday to be celebrated with pomp and pageantry.

I have, for the purpose of simplicity, decided to discuss General Obasanjo's enviable and indelible contributions under various headings below.

Fidelity to the execution of Nigeria's transition to civil rule in 1979

It is now axiomatic that the typical African Head of State has a neurotic desire to perpetuate himself in power. Some have even nursed and/or are still nursing the politically catastrophic ambition of being the longest serving Head of State in Africa. This obsession with power has informed the chicanery, subterfuge and gimmickry that have become endemic features of the transition to civil rule.

The transition programme

The satanic obsession with power has culminated in the subversion of the electoral processes by many African leaders while there are instances of transition programmes being designed to end in fiasco by its planners. The above profoundly disturbing and depressing features no doubt blight the political stability of the African continent. At the risk of repetition, General Yakubu Gowon was the first Head of State to renege on his programme to hand over power to a democratically elected government in 1976 as he had earlier promised. He was deservedly disgraced out of power in 1975 in the putsch led by General Murtala Mohammed. It is to General Olusegun Obasanjo's eternal glory that his administration faithfully implemented its transition programme and peaceful handed over power to an elected civilian government on 1 October 1979. That was, and still is, a rare occurrence in the African continent that is characterised by many sit-tight leaders such as Abdou Diouf of Senegal, the late Felix Houphouet-Boigny of Cote d'Ivoire, Dr. Hastings Banda of Malawi, Mobutu Sese Seko of Zaire and General Ibrahim Babangida of Nigeria, to mention a few. General's Obasanjo's fidelity to the transition programme of his administration could be contrasted with the transition programme of many African leaders which were subverted by the very people that designed it.

A quintessential case of a perfidious transition programme is General Babangida's eight year transition programme in Nigeria. It was a transition programme that was deliberately subverted and aborted by its chief midwife, President Babangida. It is my firm believe that General Obasanjo has by the singular act of voluntarily relinquishing power to civilians in Nigeria performed a rare feat that is worthy of admiration and emulation.

Nigeria's agricultural policies

It is an unshakable belief of General Obasanjo that a hungry population poses an insuperable obstacle to the development of any country be it economic, political or social.

There could no faulting that belief. A Yoruba saying holds that *"the mind of a hungry man is not receptive to any idea"*. The above belief of the General resulted in the launching of the *Operation Feed The Nation* by his administration on 21 May 1979 with a view to mobilising the nation towards self-sufficiency and self-reliance on food and encouraging the nation towards self-agriculture so that the various sectors of the population would participate more actively in growing their own food. In spite of the failures and inadequacies of the succeeding governments, some of the Rivers Basin Development Authorities established by him are still operating credibly and have boosted agricultural production in their areas of jurisdiction.

The promotion of democracy and good governance in Nigeria

The African continent had been plagued by military dictatorships and misrule in an unsurpassable proportion. Thus, the continent with a surfeit of natural and human resources continues to wallow in excruciating and debilitating poverty principally because of the aberrant and abhorrent despotic leadership that is prevalent in

Africa. General Obasanjo's preoccupation with the promotion of democracy and governance must have started from his belief that the abundance of natural and human resources in any country would not necessarily bring about development if the country is wanting in democracy and good governance.

In a paper entitled "Democracy and Good Governance: Basis for Socio-Economic Development" delivered in Dakar, Senegal in 1991, the General stated:

"There is a strong link between democracy, good governance and development. The days when kings and emperors built castles and developed nations as private estates are gone.

If what we are advocating for Africa is democracy and not disaster, then we must strive for a democratic structure, system and practice that is based on responsive government."

It is no wonder then that General Obasanjo had been an undaunting advocate and champion of democracy and good governance in Nigeria in particular and Africa in general. Realising the herculean nature of the task of institutionlising democracy and good governance in Africa, the General resorted to enlisting the support of well-meaning and like-minded people so as to ease and quicken the actualisation of his dream of a democratic and well-governed Africa.

Charity, it is said, begins at home. General Obasanjo's pro-democracy activities are focused principally on Nigeria.

It is now public knowledge that General Obasanjo boldly and patriotically commented on the actions and deeds of successive governments, particular the Babangida administration at a time when many people could not so comment for fear of harassment at the hands of security agents and/or detention. He has also brought together eminent Nigerian leaders, military and civilian, for the sole purpose of deliberating on how to salvage Nigeria from the political and economic quagmire into which it has been plunged by many years of mismanagement and misrule.

In an opening address delivered at his Ota farm on 25 May 1993 at a meeting he had with Nigerian leaders, including Generals Mohammadu Buhari, Tunde Idiagbon, Yakubu Gowon and T. Y. Danjuma, Chief Michael Ajasin, Dr. Olusola Saraki and Commodore Ebitu Ukiwe—who was Babangida's first Chief of General Staff—General Olusegun Obasanjo characteristically and pertinently stated:

"We are here because we are concerned. We are concerned about the present and the future of our nation. ... We should neither be antigovernment nor pro-government, rather we should be pro-Nigeria and through our activities, government should find their task of nation-building eased and less problematic if pursued on the basis of fairness, equity, justice, transparency and honesty. We need to give confidence and energise or re-energise patriotism. If we believe in something, let us stand for it and by it. Those who cannot stand for something will stand for anything."

On the dangers of Nigeria's leaders being indifferent to the political instability convulsing the country, the General warned as follows:

" Those who could and should keep our hopes alive either lost or were made to loose their conscience and developed tight lips and withered hands. All that is necessary for enthronement of evil is for good people to remain silent and inactive."

The meeting gave birth to the Association For Democracy and Good Governance in Nigeria (ADGN) which threw its membership open to all Nigerians. The communique issued at the end of meeting is instructive. It read in part:

"The enthronement of genuine democracy is the first preoccupation of the assembly. Democracy is a process rather than a project, and one election does not establish democracy.

.... the assembly will strive to see that whichever part or group of persons are in government, the two elements of democracy and good governance are encouraged."

Commenting on the formation of ADGN, TELL magazine of 7 June 1993 had this to say:

"Nonetheless, the emergence of the ADGN is a great boost to the efforts of those who have tried to set up political pressure groups to promote very vigorously democratic ideals for the country. And the Third Republic and the Nation are certainly going to be better for it."

When General Babangida criminally indulged in devilish antics towards the prolongation of the military rule in Nigeria with its attendant ominous consequences for the Nigerian nation, Obasanjo condemned such an obsession with power in unmistakable language. In a speech sent to General Babangida and published by The Guardian newspaper of 16 November 1992, General Obasanjo said:

"Any prolongation of military rule in form of diarchy or any other arrangement will not only bring the Armed Forces into utter disrepute, it will amount to a declaration of war against the sovereign rights of the people of Nigeria to choose their own leaders and conduct their affairs in accordance with the constitution. Enough is enough. Asking NEC or governors to advise AFRC on such issues as timing and period of transition with a view to passing the buck is a joke and no mind is amused or deceived by it. The responsibility is squarely yours."

It admits of no argument that it is only a former Head of State who is genuinely and patriotically concerned about the corporate existence, stability and prosperity of a country of which he has once been the head that would show the type of concern that General Obasanjo has shown and is still showing for Nigeria. It is an open secret that some past leaders of some African countries are only concerned with luxuriating in their wealth, upon leaving office not caring about what happens to their countries.

The liberation struggles in Southern Africa

It would be recalled that the Apartheid system in South Africa, which was dismantled recently, evinced condemnation from various quarters in and outside Africa. It is also true that numerous efforts were directed towards the eradication of the monstrous and inhuman apartheid policy in South Africa. Even though Africa and the world in general recorded a resounding triumph over the apartheid system, the contributions of different individuals and different heads of state towards the eradication of the system would remain indelible on the sands of time. It is a thing of joy and pride to recall that General Obasanjo's administration did make monumental contributions in this regard. In his opening address entitled **"No Compromise With Apartheid"** to the World Conference for Action Against Apartheid—organised by the United Nations in collaboration with the Organisation of African Unity and hosted by Nigeria between 22 and 26 August 1977—General Obasanjo as Head of State said:

"I am calling on the world, regardless of material and other short-term advantage to join forces with us against apartheid and all which that evil philosophy represent. I must, however, state that in addition to response to our call which will be valuable, we are resolved and ready to fulfill our destiny."

"If apartheid is not dismantled", he warned, *"it may yet be cause of the greatest human conflict and tragedy in the world."*

The General minced no words on the uncompromising stance of Nigeria on the issue of apartheid when he continued:

"For our part, we are convinced that there can be no compromise on the apartheid problems of South Africa. We find it difficult to fraternise with enterprises and organisations that are party to the system that holds our brothers and sisters in Southern Africa in bondage and regard us on account of our colour as subhuman. We cannot continue to cooperate with those who benefit from us while at the same time reap large profits from the sweat and blood of our brothers and sisters held in slavery. It is our sovereign duty to review our relationship with them and take appropriate actions."

Also speaking at the 17th Summit Conference of the Organisation of African Unity (OAU) held in Libreville, Gabon, General Obasanjo reiterated the solidarity of the Nigerian government and people with the South African black people, when he declared:

"... the Nigerian Government and people are solidly and concretely behind the oppressed people of South Africa and are giving what we can to support not only their cause, but our cause also, and because we believe that they are not fighting only their cause, but our cause also, and because we believe that in their freedom lie our own dignity and security."

It would be recalled that General Obasanjo marched his words with actions. Some of the contributions made by the Obasanjo administration towards the eradication of the system included the granting of scholarships to many South African students to continue their studies at Nigerian institutions, the launching of the South African Relief Fund (SARF) and the making of monetary donations to the liberation struggles. Worthy of mention was the nationalisation of British Petroleum in Nigeria by General Obasanjo because of its activities in Southern Africa which General Obasanjo considered detrimental to the goal of eradicating apartheid.

General Obasanjo's support for the just struggles of Africans also extended to Angola, Zimbabwe, Sudan, Namibia and Mozambique. It was therefor no wonder that the OAU at its 16th Ordinary Session held in Monrovia, Liberia, from 17 to 20 July, 1979 passed an unanimous motion of commendation for him:

"Vote of congratulation and appreciation extended to General Olusegun Obasanjo, Head of State and Commander-In-Chief of the Armed Forces of the Federal Republic of Nigeria:

The Assembly of Heads of State and Government of the Organisation of African Unity meeting in its Sixteenth Ordinary Session in Monrovia, Liberia, from 17th to 20th July, 1979,

Considering the exceptional qualities of statesmanship of General Olusegun Obasanjo, Head of State and Commander-In-Chief of the Armed Forces of the Federal Republic of Nigeria,

Consenting the distinguished services he rendered to Africa,

Noting with high appreciation his immense contribution to the cause of liberation of the African continent and towards the peace in Africa as well as in the world,

Having heard, with emotion, the speech delivered at the opening ceremony of the Sixteenth OAU Assembly in which he announced his imminent handing over of powers,

Consenting that throughout the years of his office as Head of State of the Federal Republic of Nigeria, President Obasanjo never ceased deploying sustained and permanent efforts so that Africans could solve their own problems themselves so that Africa asserts itself in all its entity and authenticity in the world,

Considering finally the farsighted vision, a special quality of President Obasanjo, whose dedication, sense of responsibility and strong commitment are well known and appreciated by all,

1) Addresses its warm thanks to President Olusegun Obasanjo, worthy and brilliant son of Africa,
2) Commends President Obasanjo for all his achievements as Head of State of Nigeria, not for his own country alone but the entire African continent,
3) Assures him of the unanimous appreciation of his colleagues and the participants at the Sixteenth OAU Assembly."

It is noteworthy to state that General Obasanjo has also been working in collaboration with other African Heads of State to hold deliberations on the multifarious politico-economic problems facing Africa, and the means of solving same under the auspices of the Africa Leadership Forum of which he is the Founder and Chairman.

It is therefore not an overstatement to describe a former Head of State, some of whose activities—while in and out of office—have been characterised above as an exemplar. My advice is that other African Heads of State should take a cue from General Obasanjo rather than go into oblivion upon leaving office. Africa stands to benefit tremendously from their wealth of experience.

I join others in congratulating General Obasanjo on the occasion of his 60th birthday and wish him many more years of useful services to Africa in particular and to the world in general.

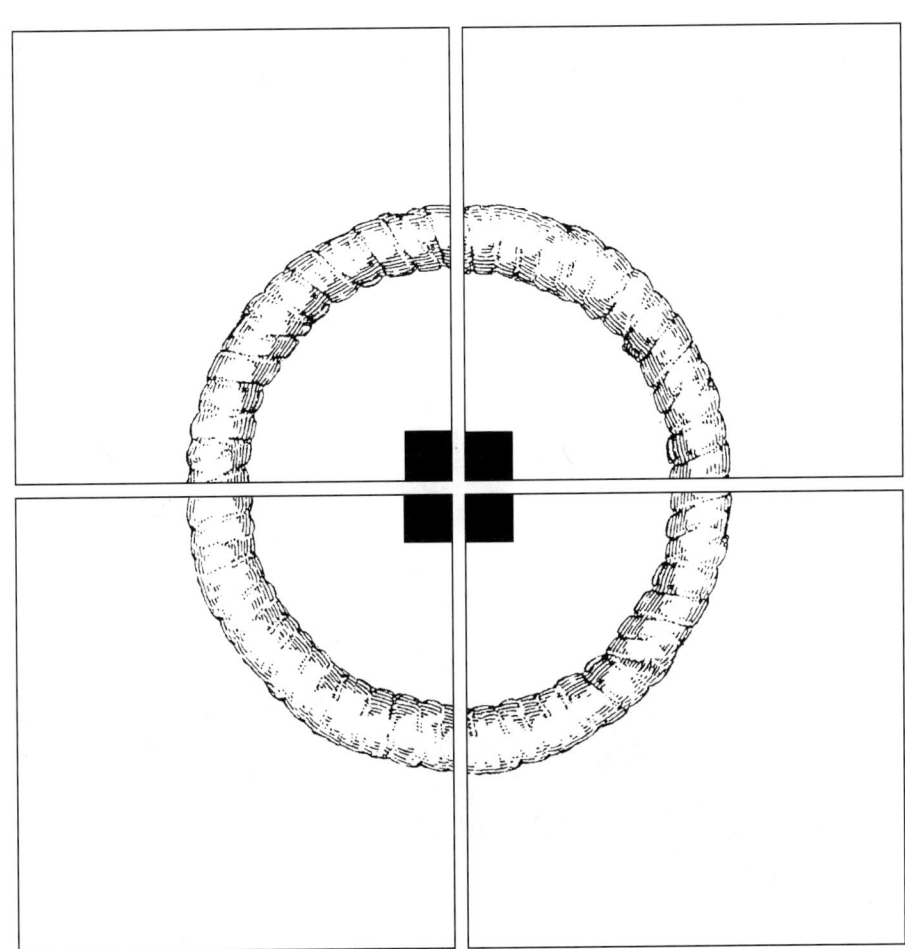

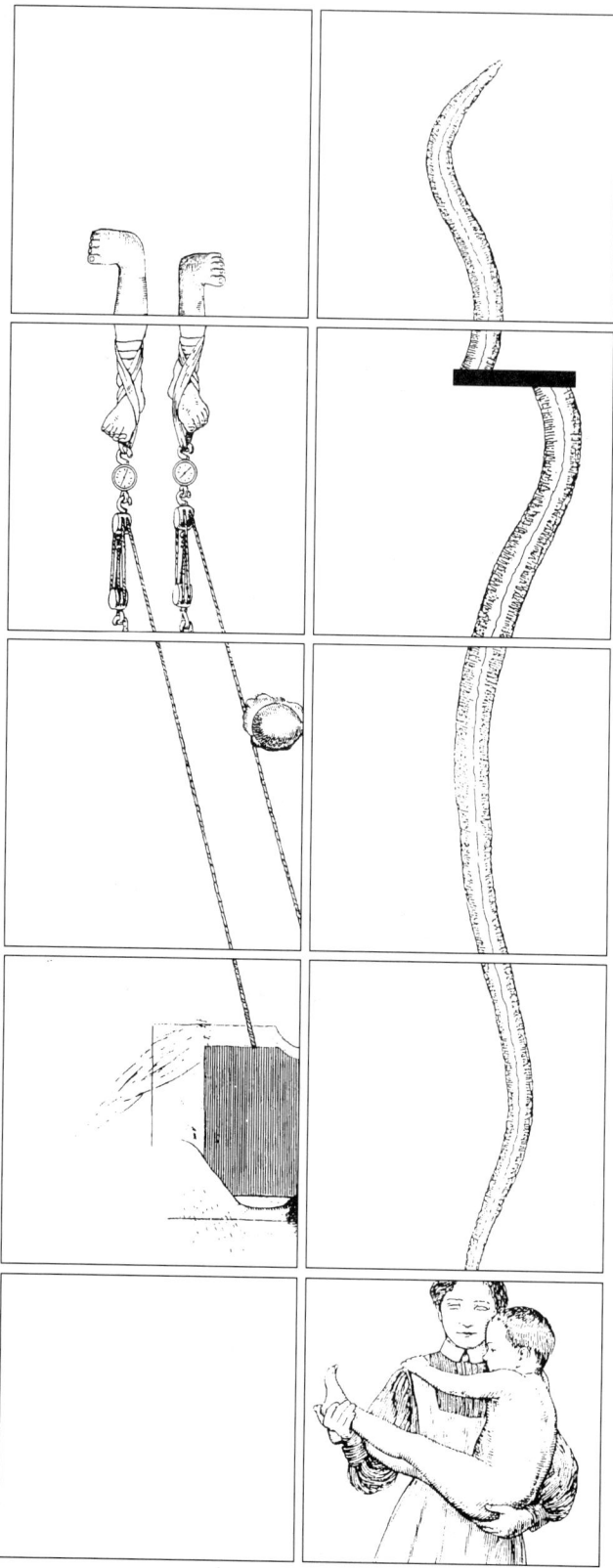

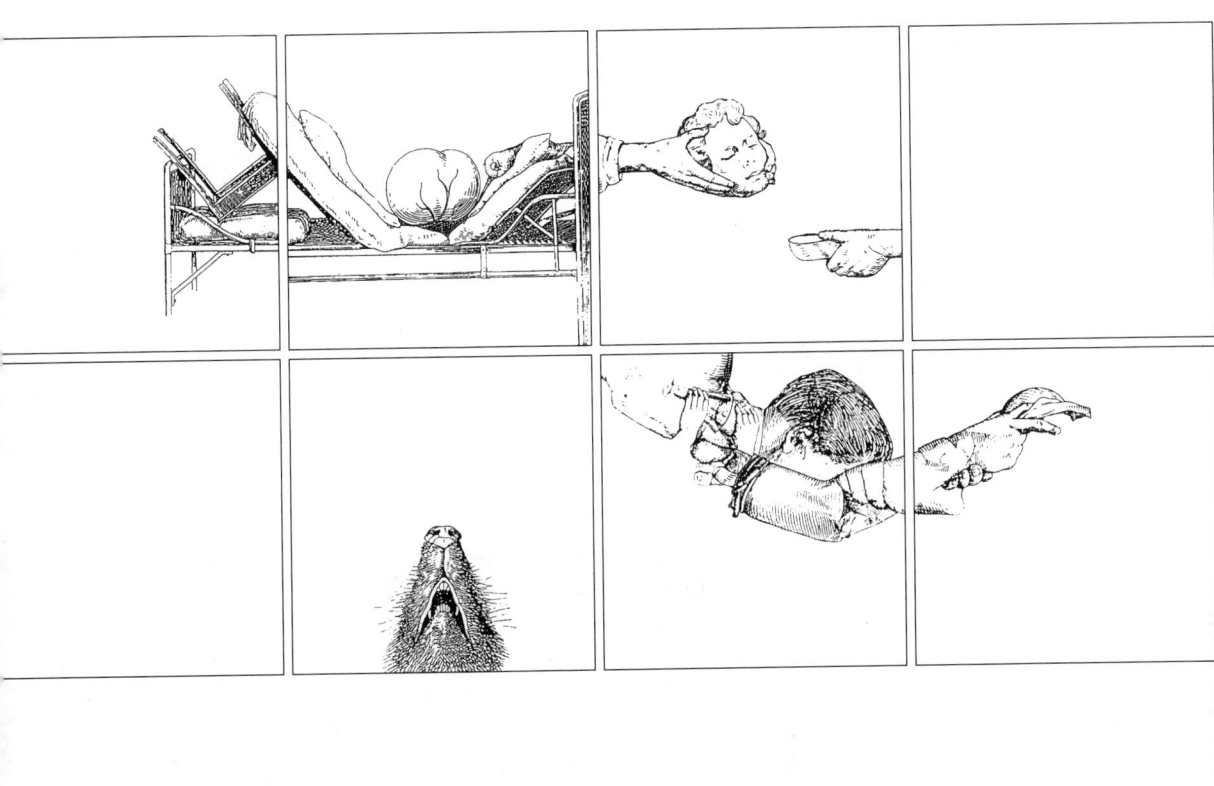

PINA + VIA LEWANDOWSKY
North – South, East – West, 1995

Onukaba Adinoyi Ojo

THE CAUTIOUS REFORMER

My companion was one of the old generation of reporters at the Murtala Muhammed Airport, Lagos, and his approach to news gathering and the amount of risk that should be invested in it, had been shaped and fixed by years of routine, unimaginative practice. We had gone to the international terminal to assist a departing relation through the notoriously "firm" barriers erected by security wolves. A man in an overflowing *agbada* ambled through the normally thick night crowd in the departure hall. Heads turned and eyes widened in recognition. We stood on our toes, craning our necks to see who it was. The hall clock nearest to us had died at 5.50 P.M.., three hours and ten minutes ago. On March 20, 1984.

"Ah, it's General Olusegun Obasanjo," my friend said. And hissed. The former Head of State was returning from Frankfurt, in the then West Germany, in one of his fairly regular diplomatic shuttles around the globe since voluntarily relinquishing power to an elected civilian administration in October 1979. "Let us go and chat him up," I managed to say with naive excitement. My friend promptly rebuked me for harbouring such dangerous thoughts. "Don't you dare. That man hates journalists. He will embarrass you today."

My enthusiasm was dampened. And I watched helplessly as the General walked past us. Then, something in me said I should defy my friend's warning, and dare the consequences. "*Wo* (look), don't waste your time. Don't play with that man. Just let him go with his *wahala* (trouble)", my friend said in a tone deep with cynicism and loathing. "I shall try." I did not wait again for his response. I dashed after the subject. Barely one year old in journalism, I moved with supreme confidence, youthful exuberance, and the aggressiveness of my generation of journalists. In *The Guardian* tradition, it'd still be news even if the former Head of State rebuffed my interview attempt. It was my first physical encounter with him and I wanted it on record that I once pestered him.

I introduced myself and my newspaper. He sized me up, then smiled and drew me closer to him, one arm stretched across my shoulders, almost cuddling me like his child. With my leather shoes, reasonably well-embroidered guinea brocade *dashiki* and *sokoto*, and a shiny black briefcase, I looked more like a young businessman than a typical Nigerian reporter. As I later found out, this seemingly dapper appearance contributed to the unusual cordiality of our encounter. For between the soldier and Nigerian journalists, there is no love lost.

"Yes, what can I do for you?"

"Let's chat on some national issues," I began, what I now recognise was not a particularly brilliant conversation. He gave me a velvet punch.

"That should tell you that I don't talk to the press."

His arm, hard and heavy, was still spread out on my shoulders. His eyes, tiny and twinkling, absorbed everything on our route. His face, dark and coarse, managed a smile.

"Perhaps I could get an appointment to come to the farm for a chat."

"No, I don't chat. Have you ever seen a farmer chatting?"

"Yes, sometimes to diffuse tension."

"What tension? That must be a very lazy farmer."

"No sir. It is a necessary interlude to the boring monotony of work."

By now, we were outside the departure hall, approaching his car and aides frenetically getting things ready for the 20-minute journey to Ota. He removed his arm from my shoulders, dismissed me, and turned to his aides. As soon as he left at 9.15 P.M.., I sat down and recreated our encounter. It was published under the headline "Obasanjo Parries Interview Attempt" in *The Guardian* of 23 March 1984.

Dele Giwa, who had earlier on similarly pestered the General for an interview, got it, and became one of his close friends, met me in *The Guardian* newsroom one day and said something about the General being impressed with both my appearance during that chance encounter and the entertaining story that came out of it. Giwa then advised me to keep in touch with the Ota-based chicken farmer "for he seems to like you very much".

I did not keep in touch until July 1984 when Nigeria found herself in a serious diplomatic row with Britain over the botched kidnap attempt in London of the former Minister of Transport, Umaru Dikko, who had been accused at home of corruptly enriching himself as a minister in the civilian regime of Shehu Shagari. A Nigeria Airways plane had been indicted in the highly embarrassing episode and seized at Stanstead Airport by the British authorities. Nigeria had responded by detaining a British Caledonian Airways plane on a regular London-bound flight from Lagos. The diplomatic face-off between Lagos and London was the hottest story at the time and reporters virtually camped at the airport to witness the behind-the-scene diplomatic contacts and deals that came after the public outbursts and denunciation.

The then External Affairs Minister, Ibrahim Gambari, flew in with General Obasanjo, apparently arriving from separate engagements abroad. Gambari pleaded for time to consult with his boss, the then Head of State, Major-General Muhammadu Buhari, before speaking to the press. We then turned to General Obasanjo who, predictably, had no comments. With two veritable news sources dry, colleagues froze in frustration. I ran after the former Head of State and introduced my self.

"Ah, are you? How are you?"

He held my hand and led me into the cozy presidential lounge and granted me an exclusive interview on the Dikko affair. At yet another chance meeting at the airport two days to Nigeria's 24th independence anniversary celebration, I got a food-for-thought from the General for a nation counting 24 years of freedom from British colonialism. Less than a month later, we met again and talked. In no time, he became familiar with my name and face. Because I was often around when he was going out or coming in, he began to credit me with an omnipresence and efficiency that I owed solely to chance. He thought I was such a damn good reporter that I had all his travel schedules in my head.

To my colleagues, I had naturally become "Obasanjo's boy". Even if tinged with certain amount of sarcasm and envy, the nickname had some truth. Familiarity imposes some measure of responsibility. For example, I wrote only on those things he cleared for publication. Whenever he said "and this not for your paper", I kept faithfully to the agreed boundaries, most of the time. Gradually, I began to gain his confidence. Then, something happened on 13 October 1984, which I thought had ruined our budding relationship.

In Yakoyo, near Ile-Ife, I was covering a thanksgiving service and reception for the former chief of defence staff, Lt. General Alani Akinrinade, who had just returned from a medical treatment in West Germany after a near-tragic encounter with armed bandits in January. Mrs. Stella Obasanjo stood in for her husband at the occasion and I succeeded in persuading her to grant me an interview for *The Guardian* of 17 October 1984. Certain aspects of the interview obviously did not go down well with the General's estranged first wife, Oluremi. She protested publicly and the lid blew off a sour affair, spilling into the streets. Scandal-loving news media picked up the story, trying to undo one another for the sleaziest coverage possible. It was only the threat of legal action from the General that would in the end force a section of the Nigerian media to exercise some restraint in its handling of the General's troubled private life.

I held myself responsible for everything and avoided him as much as I could. My editor, Lade Bonuola, and his deputy, Femi Kusa, counselled me constantly on the need to continue to have the General as a powerful source, they said his friendship was good for the paper and for my career as a reporter, that he was somebody I would find useful in future, and that I should save the friendship by writing him a letter explaining my role in what came to be known in the media as "The General's Wives Palaver." None of these persuaded me to venture near the man for a very long time.

I finally summoned up courage early in 1986—more than a year after the rumpus—and went to his farm in Ota. He was incredibly warm. I met him discussing with former Ogun State Deputy Governor Sesan Soluade. He promptly introduced me, adding, humorously, that I was "the young man who will not leave my wives alone". When we were alone, I wanted to explain what happened but he cut in, saying I should forget it for I was only doing my job. It was simply incredible. Relieved of the guilt I thought was mine, I reminded him over lunch of his promise to take me along to one of the world forums in which he had become very active since retiring in 1979. He reeled out a long list of them, before deciding that the fourth session of the InterAction Council of former Heads of States and Government in Hakone and Tokyo, Japan, in April 1986, would be the best for me to cover.

We left Lagos on 5 April 1986 for Brussels, Belgium, where he was billed to chair a working session at a leadership conference organized by the Washington-based Center for International and Strategic Studies. Here and in Japan I was to see his increasing relevance in world affairs, and meet his colleagues in the global efforts to save the world from environmental pollution and destruction, hunger and starvation, the debt squeeze, human rights violations, the threat to democratic values worldwide, East-West tensions, and a host of other problems. He introduced me to his colleagues, talked them into giving me interviews, and even suggested issues I could raise with them.

In Brussels, Tokyo and, two years later, in Moscow, I met the real man. Mentally alert (the letters he wrote in my presence and the contributions he made to debates at the conferences were so surprisingly deep and illuminating), earthy and humorous (he advised me to remember to readjust my taste to the harsh realities of a journalist's life in Nigeria when he saw me ensconced in chauffeured limousines and sampling choice cuisines and wines), and pathologically stingy (he woke me up at 1 A.M.. in a five-star Tokyo hotel presidential suite to collect the coins left from an errand I had done for him; and he bugged me almost to the point of irritation not to forget to tell my newspaper to refund the over Naira 3,000 he spent on my ticket).

Well, it's been some 10 years since that initial encounter. I have gone from being a reporter-friend to an adopted son, a confidant, and a trusted adviser. Personally, it's been a privilege knowing him. I have learnt a lot from him. Through him, I have heard rare access to eminent people and interesting places in different parts of the world. He has shielded me from the full wrath of oversensitive Nigerian security agents over stories I wrote that they had found very offensive. He arranged an institutional support for me to obtain a masters degree in Journalism and a doctorate in Performance Studies at New York University.

Quick upstairs, brutally frank, crude and practical, Obasanjo is a study in ambivalence and ambiguity. He has run his life on certain definite principles: diligence, temperance, fairness, justice, and parsimony. He is at times thoughtful and methodical, and at times, stubbornly unconcerned with the finer points of legality and propriety of behaviour, a man who sometimes raised expediency to a virtue. He is earthy and humble, but acutely sensitive about slights. He worked very hard for everything that has come his way. But it is also true that he owes a lot to providence, though he likes to de-emphasize it.

When he assumed power on 14 February 1976, he was still relatively unknown to the millions of Nigerians whose collective destiny he had been entrusted with. His leadership of the Third Marine Commando during the civil war, his command of the Army Engineering Corps, and the few months he had spent as Minister of Works and Housing had been exemplary. But most Nigerians were not so sure of his ability to lead the nation out of what was largely a self-inflicted social and economic malaise. The situation, for Obasanjo, was further compounded by an uncomely presence that many people often mistake for dullness and boorishness. Some distrusted him outright. But his friends and colleagues within his immediate constituency—the Nigerian Army—knew that his gracelessness was deceptive; they knew that he was the "ideas man" behind the tough-talking, fire-spitting General Murtala Muhammed. Though lacking the fiery temperament of his predecessor, his competence was never in doubt among these people. He also suffered greatly at the hands of public expectation. Because he was taking over from an immensely popular leader who had also been canonized by death, Obasanjo's actions, style and even his gait would frequently be compared to those of his predecessor by a populace that would refuse to see them as two different personalities.

Disciplined by a childhood of deprivation, he would bring into governance a responsible financial management and a frugality that his colleagues considered crippling. In a nation where public service is synonymous with greed, theft and corruption, his ethical crusade and his call for moderation in every aspect of our national life would be mocked by a cynical populace.

Obasanjo is a cautious reformer. The brutal termination of his predecessor's aggressive strides seemed to have imbued in Obasanjo a crippling sense of moderation and caution. He is a man who believes in the system, and leadership to him means tinkering with the existing structures to evolve a more dynamic one in which hard work is encouraged and rewarded, and indolence, waste, and indiscipline are discouraged with enforceable sanctions. He believes that it is the responsibility of the government, any government, to use the collective resources of the state to the benefit of every citizen; to help the disadvantaged to their feet; and to create an atmosphere in which each person could find fulfillments in life. His era, according to one political scientist, would be essentially a monitoring exercise for the fundamental policies had been initiated in the six action-packed months he shared with Muhammed. "... highly talented, shy, fearless, swift in action and deep," was how Obafemi Awolowo, western Nigeria's apotheosized leader, described the new man.

Because of the way things have turned out for him, he is often too quick to recommend his life to others while overlooking the unfair advantage that the military gave to people like him. He says he is intolerant of "thoughtlessness and uninformed criticisms," but in general, Obasanjo has often responded aggressively to attacks on his actions. Asked several times if with the benefit of hindsight he would have acted differently on some of the issues and policies taken by his administration between 1976 and 1979, Obasanjo said confidently that he had no regrets. But this feeling of infallibility, this belief that I-can-do-no-wrong is a major character defect in Obasanjo. Surely, time—the acid test of all policies and actions—has shown that some of the policy decisions of the Obasanjo administration could have been better thought out. For example, the first World Bank loan was unnecessary. With that loan, an access to easy funds was suddenly thrown open to be abused and perverted by the succeeding administration. Today, Nigeria is suffocating under the crushing weight of a foreign debt estimated at US $35 billion.

Obasanjo has a sound memory—for good or for bad—and he can be mean and ruthless when he thinks he is being taken for a fool. No matter how hard he tries to tout the altruistic motives in his actions, Obasanjo still leaves the impression that he is a man struggling seriously to be ennobled by history and to be appreciated and complimented by his fellow men. Some of those who have lived and worked with him have accused him of using and dumping them when they were no longer vital to his overall scheme. While this is not entirely untrue, it does not diminish at all the towering figure the General represents and his historical accomplishments. His 60th birthday is an occasion for me to renew the feelings of my respect and gratitude. I have recently completed a biography of General Obasanjo, entitled *In the Eyes of Time*, which I hope will soon be published and which will shed more light on his multifaceted personality than was possible in this short contribution.

Dear General Obasanjo:

I would like to convey my most hearty congratulations to you on your 60th birthday. Not only in Japan but throughout Asia, one's 60th birthday is considered to be a highly auspicious year in one's life. This is because the traditional Chinese zodiac calendar is organized on a 60-year cycle. So on one's 60th birthday, one returns to the zodiac sign under which he was born, and in a sense starts life anew. In Japanese, this birthday is called "kanreki." We look forward with great expectation to the valuable contributions you will make to Africa and to the world in this your "second life."

As you know, the Sasakawa Foundation administers a wide variety of international assistance and exchange activities. In the course of carrying out many of them, we have availed ourselves of your wisdom and expertise. The most significant among these and the one in which your contribution has been most impressive is the agricultural project in the sub-Sahara conducted by the Sasakawa African Association, on whose board you are serving as a member.

The Sasakawa Africa Association is now carrying out with marked success the "Sasakawa Global 2000" program in seven African countries. As you are well aware, this program is being conducted with financial support by the Sasakawa Foundation and under the leadership of Dr. Norman E. Borlaug, who won the Nobel Peace Prize for his "Green Revolution," in collaboration with former U.S. President Jimmy Carter. The insightful views and excellent leadership you have offered as a representative of Africa's intelligentsia on the Association's board have contributed greatly to the success of this project.

Again, we wish you sustained health and abundant happiness, and look forward to many more long years of fruitful association.

Yours faithfully,

Yohei Sasakawa
President
Sasakawa Foundation

Olatunji Dare

THESIS ON GENERAL OLUSEGUN OBASANJO

Of all the eminent public figures that I have known here and elsewhere, General Obasanjo is probably the easiest to underestimate. He is not your dashing, swashbuckling General. And yet, he is a master of strategic thinking and planning, and given to decisive action. He was the Commanding General who brought the Nigerian civil war to an end on the battlefield. He is not a stirring platform orator and rarely comes across as a charismatic figure. And yet, he has emerged in the last decade as an authentic statesman, respected at home and abroad, and much sought-after on the lecture circuit. It is a measure of his international stature that he was pressed into the race for the post of Secretary-General of the United Nations by world statesmen with whom he had interacted during his years as Head of State of Nigeria and thereafter. He did not win the race but his showing was respectable.

In Africa, instances of the soldier as intellectual are even rarer than instances of the soldier as statesman. In fact, the soldier is often seen as the antithesis of the intellectual. The one is regarded as given only to action. What else do they teach in military school anyway? The other, typically a holder of a string of university degrees, is regarded as concerned mainly with thought and ideas. Thus, when a leading Nigerian journalist and commentator reported some 16 years ago that Obasanjo wrote his own speeches, many Nigerians of the intellectual class thought that the claim was sheer propaganda, an effort by a journalist to ingratiate himself with the Head of State. When he added, as evidence of Obasanjo's intellectual disposition, that he had found the General absorbed in Bertrand Russell's *Authority and the Individual* on the plane during an official trip to Eastern Europe, the evidence was dismissed as anecdotal at best.

General Obasanjo straddles the military and the intellectual traditions. If, following Ali Mazrui, we define an intellectual as someone who has acquired a larger stock of ideas as well as the capacity for manipulating them, Obasanjo would have to be regarded as an intellectual.

He is author of five (or six?) books, and editor or coeditor of three (or four?) edited volumes. The quarterly Farm House Dialogues and the yearly international conferences that are held under the auspices of General Obasanjo's Africa Leadership Forum are veritable intellectual encounters dealing with a wide range of development and other issues. At these encounters, Obasanjo is an exemplar of the host as participant. The casual observer might think that Obasanjo's attentions are elsewhere, and that he is really not following the proceedings. Such an observer is invariably proved wrong when Obasanjo makes his trademark sharp, incisive interventions that usually compel a reexamination of the issue, or when he cuts through the miasma of contention to identify the core issue, or when he brings down matters needlessly gone arcane and obscure to a practical level. And when, at the end of proceedings, he produces a concise yet comprehensive report of discussions on complex issues of national, regional or global significance, no one is left in doubt that no participant had been more involved than the General.

Since leaving office voluntarily in 1974 and handing over power to an elected government, General Obasanjo has shown an astonishing capacity for growth.

It is a measure of the patronising nature of British colonial rule that whenever the authorities encountered a native who was smart and knowledgeable and could not be hoodwinked easily, they credited him with possessing "native intelligence". At bottom, this meant a raw, untrained capacity for grasping the essence of some things. The educated Nigerian elite have inherited this prejudice from the colonialists. If a man who does not have a string of university degrees shows a great capacity for grasping complex issues, they ascribe that facility to "native intelligence". And so, in Nigeria, Obasanjo is widely credited with possessing "native intelligence". But that which is called "native intelligence" is really nothing but wisdom.

Tunji Abayomi

IN HONOUR OF A MAN OF MANY MEANINGS

> "But Africa's road to political stability and solidarity is rough and tortuous. We have always had a tendency to find ready-made scapegoats for our problems, to blame other people for our shortcomings but after 25 years of independence, we can no longer afford to do that, we should now adopt a realistic, self-critical and indulgent appraisal of our problems to determine how we got where we are now and what we can do to get out it. We owe this much to the future generation of Africa if not ourselves."
>
> Olusegun Obasanjo
> Silver Jubilee Lecture of the
> Economic Commission for Africa
> Addis Ababa, Ethiopia, 1987

According to *The Standard*, a leading Kenyan newspaper, at Kisumu in Kenya where General Olusegun Obasanjo visited recently to mark the first anniversary of the death of the late Jaramogi Odinga, the General caused a stir at the Jubilee market in Kisumu district of Kenya where he was spotted drinking local porridge at a kiosk, while playing a local game "a jua" with the residents. This is General Obasanjo—the true son of Africa.

In a normal day at his farm in Ota, Ogun State, which is home to his searching spirit and body, he moves up and down with a common touch between the noble and the commoner treating all largely the same with adequate regard. I have seen Olusegun Obasanjo share in his messenger's bread, laugh with his cook, and drink with his gardeners—in the most ordinary manner.

A few months ago, I went to the Ota farm to see General Obasanjo. Shortly after I got there, he invited me into his car. He sat at the driver's seat and we took off. In a short trip around Ota, we discussed many issues of great significance, such as the value of education, reducing human anguish, nursing appropriate leadership cadres in Africa, wealth and poverty, war and peace. As we moved around, we stopped from time to time at the "monuments" he was putting in place to realise his many hopes for Africa. From the anticipated structure to establish the headquarters for the Africa Leadership Forum, which from the outset he did not want carry his name to avoid self-glorification, to his pet project "The Bells", a secondary school for boys and girls through which he hoped to instill character and knowledge in future leaders of Africa. At each point, I observed that he took time to review each project with his allies, workers or agents with whom he appears to be a comfortable and convivial allay.

It was during this hour of exchange between us that I asked General Obasanjo what he considered the most important characteristics of the many world leaders he has met. He reflected for a while and replied: "humility". I turned around and looked at him meditatively and was again struck by the willingness with which he drove me around. I remembered for a moment that next to me at the driver's seat was probably Africa's most important figure. The ordinariness of the uncommon commoner called Olusegun Obasanjo was simply infectious.

But among all General Obasanjo's preoccupations, the value he places on children has always been marvellous in my eyes. At any time, in any season, there is what could best be described as an eruption of love between him and his many children. Yet he is not a father without sin—for one, his inexorable demand for excellence often appears to be threatening—but his children always find it easy to forgive his sins without effort. Simply put, he anoints his children with the love and care of a father and in turn his children regard him even in disagreement like a mountain.

General Olusegun Obasanjo is immense by any standard. At a conference after he had delivered the keynote address, I once—in a thrust of natural expressivity—described him as "Professor General Olusegun Obasanjo". High intelligence, fecundity, insight—often unappreciated at first instance—is an intellectual symphony to a true cooker of the General's views.

In 1991, I invited him to speak at the Africa Conference on Human Rights and Democracy in Africa, an area where his reputation was most attacked at the time and perhaps at all times. It was an opportunity for deep reflection on the theory, practice and philosophy of human rights in traditional African society. There, he asserted before the world his disagreement with the generally acceptable thought that human rights in the West are at variance with human rights in non-Western societies or cultures.

To him, while a blanket application of the Western concept of human rights calls for care, a thorough study of traditional African societies shows a comparative and competitive enforcement procedure of human rights despite the predominant influence of the good society as an ideal from which the law regulating individual happiness is to be drawn. Human rights to him encompass with its penumbra human responsibility, responsibility by the leadership especially in Africa, the content of his preoccupation, and of course of the led too.

General Olusegun Obasanjo has always been guided, it seems, by two factors crucial for beneficial change. These are idea and hard work. His rather large intellect which manifestly began to unfold as he assumed the leadership of his country Nigeria, makes him often a missionary of a kind: from a farm project to set an example for Africa's food actualisation to the Africa Leadership Forum, developing a think-tank for appropriate governance, to education and many more projects. What strikes one most are not even the brave and bright ideas as such, but how they are projected.

Hard work appears to be more than clothing to him. A man who saw grinding poverty all around him as he grew up should know just how to conquer it. Obasanjo understood early that the medicine to conquer poverty is hard work and that hard work will bring self-reliance. The early avoidance strategy he chose was hard work. This has paid off. Today, few know that the General's victory over poverty began with a small loan through the assistance of a late friend and the careful utilisation of the loan to multiply and create seasons of harvest in the last 30 years.

Those who are sincere and able to dig deeper than the surface will regard his leadership in Nigeria the best time in the history of the country in terms of responsible management and accountability. His time as Head of State of Nigeria is often regarded as a time of immense change. What was conceived and realised during his tenure, no one could have foreseen that the evil days of the subsequent years would develop in Nigeria. Reminiscing on his tenure as Head of State of Nigeria, he speaks of change: "nothing is more difficult to arrange, more uncertain of success and more dangerous to carry through than initiating change". To him, for change to endure takes time to conceive (ideas) and effort "to push it through and sustain it" (hard work).

In the often cacophonous political uproar in national discourses, it is generally forgotten that if the nation had the courage to continue the implementation of the beneficial changes he initiated during his tenure as Head of State, Nigeria would have established a good government which would have benefited the greatest number of our people in terms of stability, harmony, freedom, security, order and general welfare.

General Olusegun Obasanjo is by and large the most nationalistic Nigerian I have met anywhere. You cannot but be convinced of the correctness of his insight on the values of true unity for the people of Nigeria. Leadership "involves tolerance and application of the place and points of others" he told me many miles above the sea level as he reviewed national political problems in a trip we took together last year. In a multi-cultural society leadership does not allow for immutability of views or rigidity of position. A man going to war needs to study the field before designing the strategy. Today, his vision of a united Nigeria is not commonly accepted by all people mainly because of ethnocentrism, but is this not also why national unity remains nothing but a matter of speculation in Nigeria?

Obasanjo the democrat. Those who are close to him must admit that the metabolic conquest by surrender of military command to civil consensus, typical of a democratic communion, is one of the major changes in the life of the General since he left government. Within the community of human rights activists, to which I belong, the commitment of the General to democracy is in itself a continuing debate. Strong arguments are proffered either way. But there is no counterpoint to his profile as a believer in the ultimate supremacy of democratic rule over dictatorship. This explains why in spite of pressure to the contrary by significant sectors, he handed over power to an elected government. He once told me how a few months before the October 1979 handover both sincere and insincere representatives were mounting pressure on him to resist the handover, especially given the uncertainties in the political state of the nation. He reflected on the suggestions made by those he considered sincere enough to build for others to run. He has subsequently expressed his views on democracy as the greatest form of government. Democracy may not be the ideal in a world full of changes but it represents more than any other form of government man's "imminent tendency towards freedom and thereby remains the best and the most humane form of power". Democracy to him compels a level of tolerance, "a game of inclusion rather than exclusion".

Periodic election through secret ballot, popular participation and the right of choice are among the crucial attributes of democracy. In spite of the long standing conflict in the past with the national press, which was initially engendered by military disposition, General Olusegun Obasanjo believes in a free press including the right of private ownership. But the point of discord really relates to completing the equation. While others over-emphasise freedom, he lays equal emphasis on responsibility and freedom. Freedom, he once asserted "connotes obligations and duties which must neither be ignored nor abused."

To speak of freedom compels me to go back to the human rights profile once again. When General Olusegun Obasanjo was a candidate for the post of Secretary-General of the United Nations in 1991, my colleagues fiercely attacked his human rights record. I am still of the view that the lack of support from my colleagues arose from a level of misappreciation of the General's position. While he views with suspicion the overassertive individual libertarian, he clearly shares the view that a responsible government must uphold the rights of the people. But these rights go beyond political rights, which he considers overprotected at the expense of the socio-political needs. He speaks of the "need to zero in on the humanness of human rights" by which he alludes to peaceful coexistence, security, shelter, food, clothing and even "the right to contribute one's quota to national development."

He considers human rights meaningless without strong effort to conquer poverty which he considers to be man's deepest search for victory. Human rights within human poverty and deprivation is to him nothing more than mere shadow casting. He asserted in his 1991 lecture at the African Conference on Human Rights and Democracy, organised by Human Rights Africa:

We must realise that the constant clamour for political freedom and the enforcement of political and civil rights in Africa is merely an appendage of a more serious oppression that is foisted by an existing socio-economic order. Freedom to live and die in abject poverty, disease, ignorance and squalor could not be one of the cherished freedoms by Africans. Redressing of human rights abuses must start with the lifting of our people above poverty line. Poverty limits, constraints, debilitates and kills faster than breaches of civil and political rights which are of course rampant all over Africa. Acts and policies that pauperise the citizen must be treated as acts against the fundamental rights of the people."

In conclusion, all that has been said of Africa's leading personality and child is to emphasise that, in truth, Olusegun Obasanjo deserves a very happy birthday. But as a commentary on his 60th Birthday, I know he would have had more to celebrate in a more democratic Africa.

Happy Birthday, General!

Joan Holmes

A GREAT SON OF AFRICA

I welcome this rare and auspicious occasion to write a tribute about a wonderful man, a great son of Africa and one its outstanding leaders. General Olusegun Obasanjo has been a passionate voice and advocate for many important international issues such as world disarmament and democratic governance.

We all know that in 1976, historical circumstances made him head of Nigeria's military government. While he was leading Nigeria's destiny, his major economic policy was to ensure Nigeria's self-reliance. He did so by steering his country away from its dependence on oil exports and towards sustainable agricultural production. His agricultural policy called "Operation Feed the Nation" has contributed enormously to increasing the number of farmers on the land and to raising the people's awareness of the importance of agriculture in Nigeria's development agenda.

In 1979 General Obasanjo became a pioneer as the first African military leader to voluntarily and in an orderly manner hand over power to an elected civilian government. In doing so he became one of the few military leaders in the continent to adhere to the principle of multi-party democracy and respect for the people's choice.

Since his retirement from politics he has given a personal example of how a former Head of State can continue to contribute to Africa's development. General Obasanjo did this by becoming an active farmer and as a passionate advocate for a better future for Africa's people.

He has demonstrated his great qualities of leadership and his commitment to building a new, committed generation of leaders by creating the Africa Leadership Forum in 1988.

Recognizing the crucial role that leadership can play in Africa's development, General Obasanjo has worked continuously through the Forum to enable promising figures in Africa to interact with experienced leaders from both inside and outside Africa.

As I said at the award ceremony for The Hunger Project's Africa Prize for Leadership for the Sustainable End of Hunger, held in his honor in New York City on 25 September 1990, "one of the striking characteristics of the General's leadership is his profound recognition that in charting the future of Africa, women, their education and their empowerment must be given the highest priority".

As a political strategist, General Obasanjo has forcefully presented the African cause to the world by speaking candidly and emphasizing that the primary responsibility of Africa's development rests with Africa alone. In his speech to a 1989 InterAction Forum, he clearly stressed that "We need leadership which links ideas and policy with action".

Who could be a better advocate for Africa than General Obasanjo when he frankly states "If there will be any realization of any hope for Africa, Africans must keep their continent at the center of their concern and raise the awareness and the conscience of the world for support in solving African problems".

It is this passion for Africa's well-being that has led him to become involved in a number of peace mediation efforts in Sudan, Angola and other parts of Southern Africa. In this regard we all recall vividly the key role he played in 1986 as Co-Chairman of the Commonwealth Group of Eminent Persons, which worked very hard to convince the Pretoria government of the need to eliminate apartheid from South Africa.

Beyond the problems of Africa, the General has also been preoccupied with international issues and particularly the cause of disarmament. As a member of the Independent Commission on Disarmament and Security he contributed immensely to the reduction of East-West tensions and the establishment of peace and cooperation in the world.

What has most impressed me personally is the General's commitment to supporting small-scale farmers in Africa and particularly in Nigeria. I saw this commitment in action when I visited his farm in 1991. Translating his commitment into real action, he established in 1981 a large farm in Abeokuta where he employs more than 600 workers in agricultural production, poultry farming and other aspects of rural development. In this manner, I am sure, he wanted to demonstrate to his fellow Africans everywhere that farming is an honorable occupation that can be undertaken by anyone—even a former Head of State—without any negative stigma.

It is very heartening to see that on top of this productive initiative, the General goes out of his way to support other, small-scale farmers in his area by providing training, advice and technical support.

It is so empowering, above all, to read the invitation to his fellow Nigerians on the sign at the entrance of his farm which says: "You too, can be a farmer, have an exciting occupation and join in feeding yourself and the Nation."

On behalf of all the staff of The Hunger Project, who respect General Obasanjo so much for his personal qualities and his commitment to the end of hunger, I believe that the best tribute that can be paid to him is for all of us, Africans in particular, to accept as he does the urgent need to mobilize the whole world to become committed to conquering world hunger and malnutrition.

Abul Maal A Muhith

NO TIME TO WASTE, NO TIME TO REST

We do not know for sure that Olu will be in a position to celebrate the days following his 60th birthday as a free man. He is at least out of the jail where he was locked up, but confined to home imprisonment. But can it be reasonably predicted that the big prisonhouse that Nigeria is today will change in a year's time? It is ironical and at the same time a great tragedy that General Olusegun Obasanjo, who as head of state of Nigeria tried to put an end to its prisonhouse culture a decade and a half ago, should be a victim of that culture now.

It is about a decade back that I first got acquainted with the genial General. Bradford Morse, a Congressman from Massachusetts turned a top international development administrator, invited me to work with a group of semiretired world leaders on the problems of the least developed countries. The InterAction Council had appointed a working group to study the issue and come up with practical recommendations on how to prevent the slide of these countries into the abyss of underdevelopment. Former Prime Minister Ola Ullsten of Sweden was chairing the group and I came up from my quiet meditation in Princeton to act as the anchor of the group (a very onerous responsibility indeed!).

Olu was introduced to me as the biggest poultry farmer of Africa. I was aware of his unusual efforts in empowering people by handing over the reins of government as the head of a military regime in Nigeria in 1979. I learnt then that besides being a professional soldier, he was also a professional engineer and builder.

It was in a gathering of the InterAction Council in Barcelona in 1985 that I came to appreciate the depth of Olu's concern for three issues. And on this occasion in celebrating his life I take the opportunity to dwell briefly on these issues. First, the need for a resolution of the debt problem of the developing countries, especially of African and least developed countries. Second, the need for a change in the military culture of the third world and reduction in the spiralling military expenditure of these countries. Third, the importance of dedicated leadership in moving forward with economic and social progress, particularly in the African continent.

This is not intended to downplay his other various interests which are equally important. He has many other interests like poultry farming or improving cassava products. Surely peacekeeping is another of his abiding interests, with which he was introduced as a young man in the United Nations Congo operations and a decade later in the Biafra settlement in 1970.

Looking at the problems of the least developed countries in 1984-85, it was found that the structural problems of these countries warranted a change of ethos, a renaissance of the spirit of enquiry and enterprise. The key to success lay in good governance, a stable macro-economic framework, freedom of enterprise and spread of education. But the debt burden had to be lightened for allowing a level playing field. For the least developed countries it meant more than the write-off of official bilateral debt, it required restructuring of debt from official multilateral sources as well as a more efficient and longer term settlement of commercial debt than that provided by the Paris Club at the time. In the fall of 1989 when Obasanjo launched his Africa Leadership Forum, he was still eloquent on the debt owed by the poor countries to the multilateral development institutions. The World Bank today, despite the IDA window, is a small player in net transfer of resources to the developing countries. In the Africa region which accounted for the major portion of the Bank's net transfer, for example, with an IDA disbursement of US$ 2770 million in 1993 the net transfer was a mere US$ 874 million. Starting with the Trust Fund in 1977 and moving ahead with the CCFF, SAF, ESAF and STF facilities the IMF has been trying to change its image of a Shylock; but after all it is not a development financing institution, it is truly an economic policy policeman.

In 1985 the InterAction Council, I thought, was considering a working group to look at the military expenditure of the developing countries, which was running at about 23 percent of global military expenditure of about a trillion US dollars at the time. But those were still the days of cold war mind-set and so the issue had to be looked at in the context of global military expenditure. General Obasanjo led the working group to explore the subject. It was then that I noticed Olu's concern at the waste of resources in military expenditure in the developing countries. In 1989 at Ota in the presence of General Babaginda, then the military ruler of Nigeria, there was an opportunity to dwell on the subject. Olu made the point with considerable deftness that growth of able leadership in Africa would not make much headway without empowerment of people through mass literacy and democracy. In 1990 in Costa Rica, one of the few really pacifist countries in the world, Olu welcomed the idea of demilitarisation of the third world parallel to disarmament in the erstwhile eastern and western blocks. There the Nobel Laureate President Oscar Arias proposed in his open letter to build a new Panama without an army, a feat accomplished by Costa Rica in 1948 at the conclusion of its revolution under the able and farsighted leadership of General Jose Figueres, the father of the present President of Costa Rica.

I understand that it was a statement, made in Copenhagen at the end of the Social Summit, recommending diversion of military expenditure to social development that landed the General in jail on his return to his country. Developing countries have talked loudly about disarmament and denuclearisation but have always shied away from controlling their own military expenditure. Not till 1991 has there been a decline in their military expenditure; even then it was a little less than double the net resource inflow—US$ 242 million against US$ 131 million. In 1950 the developing countries accounted for 7 per cent of global military expenditures but it went up steadily to 25 percent by the early 1980s and is still about there. They account for 67 per cent of the world's total men in uniform and 76 per cent of global imports of armaments (1991). At the end of the Cold War there is no reason to delay action on demilitarisation of the third world, where resources are needed for more urgent and beneficial investment. The military culture in the less mature polities of the third world is epitomised by secrecy, corruption, wastefulness, lawlessness and repression, which are the worst enemies of good governance and freedom of enterprise.

It is natural for Obasanjo to be concerned with the problems of his region. But his region is not just West Africa but all of that vast continent. One of the difficult problems in Africa has been nation-building, forging broader ties above narrow tribal and ethnic allegiances. A large number of military regimes sprang up there mainly on the ground of consolidation of nations. Olu has identified the problem correctly and building of leaders enjoys his top priority. I had the privilege of being present at the launching of the Africa Leadership Forum in Ota in the fall of 1988. Whatever other problems may have occupied his interest now and then, my impression is that he is most deeply committed to this programme. It is leadership that can make a difference in the renaissance of learning and inquisitiveness that is so badly needed in most of Africa. It is leadership again that can develop participatory politics in Africa, a test case of which is in evidence in the new South Africa. In Uganda, leadership is the prime mover of propitious economic upturn. In my view social and economic development needs a propitious economic framework and accompanying spurt in investment, but the success of the effort depends nearly fifty per cent on commitment of the nation, which is basically inspired by good leadership. The good thing about Olu's leadership development programme is that it is anchored to democracy and that is the guarantee for its sustainability.

All the three issues I chose to dwell on are with us still. Thus, Olusegun Obasanjo has no time to waste nor any to rest.

Tunji Lardner

OUR GENERAL

My first encounter (such as it was) with General Olusegun Obasanjo was sometime in 1977, when as Head of State and Commander-in-Chief of the Nigerian Armed Forces, he visited the campus of the University of Lagos, where I was then an undergraduate. He was playing host to Dr. Agostinho Neto, the late Head of State of Angola, and both were scheduled to deliver some lecture or the other.

We, the fractious student body, cared less about the lecture, we were more interested in "Aremu," as we called the General, using his middle name, and as the object of our ire, we had reserved a particularly boisterous welcome for him. At issue was a protest against the quality or price of our heavily subsidized meals, or some such thing; but as students fancying ourselves as militant radicals, our *angst* was in actuality that vaguely defined "anti-authority" post-adolescent petulance that students revel in.

Perhaps so, but for us, it was serious business. As his motorcade wound its way through the long driveway into the campus, essentially naming a gauntlet of raucous student, it stopped at the entrance of our "great hall", the venue of the lecture. General Obasanjo ambled out of his limousine, clasping the hand of his guest, a smile fixed on his face, waving it would seem in appreciation of his welcome.

Something was wrong here; here we were hauling epithets at the man and sorely trying to embarrass him before his guest, and he was on the face of it, calm and looked as if he was actually enjoying it. Although, he within earshot urged us to behave ourselves, his delivery was made through that improbable smile fixed on his face. Years later, I understood why the General was so smug about the whole episode, his guest Dr. Neto spoke Portuguese and little if any English, and our animated welcome could quite easily have been misconstrued to read as a jubilant welcome from students to their leader.

Determined to wipe the smile of his face, and propelled by the unthinking peevishness of youth, I suddenly broke through his security cordon, and gave the General, my Head of State, and the Commander-in-Chief of the Nigerian Armed Forces, a forceful push on the shoulder.

I was immediately engulfed by soldiers and security men. General Obasanjo, quickly reading the situation, gave nonverbal orders that I should be released, vigorously shaking his head in the negative, he signaled that I should be left alone. My fellow agitators immediately surrounded me and spirited me away from the scene to the rooftop of one of the female hostels, where I spent the next couple of hours waiting for the dying echoes of the sirens of his motorcade to subside. Needless to say, I missed the lecture.

Subsequent encounters with the General were happily less dramatic. I met him again in 1980 at his farm in Ota, just months after he had been midwife to Nigeria's Second Republic and handed over power to a civilian government, the first African military ruler to voluntarily do so. I had, purely out of curiosity accompanied a friend who had to deliver a letter to him. The General, after being told of our presence, emerged wearing Khaki shorts and shirt and on his head a rumpled *fila*, looking every inch the farmer that he was. Here I was before a latter-day Cincinnatus, like that other Roman general, this one also retired to the farm having successfully ended his tour of duty, dealing with the weighty responsibilities of the State. A first in Africa and equally remarkable anywhere else.

In spite of my muted fears about possible recriminations over our first encounter, he was jovial and engaging as he ushered us into his office. He evidently had no recall of our encounter, for him as he told me years later, it was just another inconsequential episode with students spoilt by the oil boom's state-subsidized educational system.

In the intervening years, our paths were to again converge in New York City, where I, irresistibly drawn to the stated idealism of the Africa Leadership Forum (ALF) became a willing conscript for the cause. By so doing, I became a member of an irregular battalion of young and not-so-young Africans and Africanists rallying behind "our General" as he marshaled national and international forces for the good cause of Africa.

Whatever complex reasons that other members of the "Obasanjo battalion" might have had for enlisting, my own reasons were simple enough.

Out of his own generation of leaders, especially within the Nigerian context, he remains one of the very few that has actually tried and in fact "given something back". Contrast this with the malevolence and evil of say a "Babangida" or the effete blandness of a "Gowon", and General Obasanjo's unceasing effort to leave the world a better place than he found it is better appreciated. I once told him that ordinarily, I wouldn't touch him with a barge-pole, but that he in my estimation has somewhat redeemed his generation before the inquisitorial *angst* of mine and possibly younger generations of Nigerians.

I have since come to know and appreciate the General, as they say, up close and personal, having traveled with him as his personal assistant, essentially his majordomo, worked for the ALF, and spent many hours arguing with him about Africa, Nigeria, and the plight of the "blackman". I came to appreciate his demanding and grueling schedule, his phenomenal stamina, and of course his authoritative and even domineering style of management. I clearly recall being roused from deep sleep at 3 a.m. in the morning for a briefing about a conference later on that morning, and then being ordered to make arrangements for a VCR to be brought to his suite, so that he could watch a video about the ecological and political consequences of further damming the River Nile. Never mind that he went to bed just four hours earlier after a strength-sapping trans-Atlantic flight, and I, finally going to bed an hour later. I also remember at the historic ALF's Kampala conference seeing him meeting with all sorts of groups at 4 a.m., and then promptly heading a formal session at 8 a.m., with no outward sign of fatigue or loss of acuity.

Of course we all know that his carefully maintained dour, even phlegmatic exterior, conceals a mind sharper than a tack and a resolve better imagined than experienced, but then, this is the stuff of leadership.

I again recall one memorable trip to China in 1991, after another heroic debate, the General wired back to his New York office a fax that said amongst other things that "Tunji is both rude and cocky". He added that he never wanted to have anything to do with me again. Luckily, in spite of my rudeness and cockiness, after due penance the General, like in our first encounter, again displayed the magnanimity and plain common sense that further endears him to a great many people. This is not to imply that the General is an angel; far from it, many have felt the weight of his ire—it is not a pretty sight, his legendary parsimoniousness and his stubbornness at sticking to his point ... his point!

But the flip-side of that is a caring and devoted father, who genuinely cares about his children, his family, his people, his country, his continent, his world.

The General cares. History will adjudge him so. That is why he will always remain for some of us, "our General".

FRANÇOIS VAN HOEK

AVENUE JACQUES PASTUR, 131
1180 BRUXELLES

Brussels, 19 March 1995

Dear Hans,

Upon my return to Brussels these days, I found your letter of 28 January containing your invitation to contribute to the book to be published on the occasion of the General's 60th birthday. Although it probably is too late for a contribution to the book, I would be most obliged, if you could transmit my most sincere congratulations and very best wishes to the General. Over a certain number of years I have constantly admired his vision and sense of realism on international affairs and particularly on Africa and have enjoyed immensely his active participation in several activities that I had the pleasure to organize during my stay at the European Centre for Development Policy Management in Maastricht. Although I belong already to the "club of the seventies", I still hope for an opportunity to resume and expand the very stimulating discussions and cooperation with the General as well as with yourself.

With best personal regards,

François

TWINS SEVEN – SEVEN Custodian Of Democracy, 1995

Chief Jonathan Adio Obafemi Olopade

THE MAN OBASANJO—A DISCRETE NEGOTIATOR AND MEDIATOR

It will be extremely difficult for one so close to him before becoming Head of State and after leaving the office on 1 October 1979 not to try and give a detailed account of his life as an insider. I must confess that I can state categorically that I am one of his many friends who has had the rare and privileged opportunity of travelling within and outside Nigeria with him on national and international matters since 1979. As a matter of fact, one Nigerian newspaper styled me once as "his Chief of Protocol".

During our many travels, I have watched him with great admiration and amazement: his bargaining skills; tactics; patience; strategies; comportment; and his preparedness to listen to the other side. Obasanjo's commitments are those of a visionary and a missionary. He goes all out to do those things which he believes would create a world of peace for humanity. As a Honorary Rotarian, he is an ardent believer in the 1993/1994 Rotary theme "Believe in what you do and do what you believe in". It is very important to state the role he has played in Angola whilst he was Head of State and after leaving office. He has visited Angola; Cuba; the United States of America; South Africa; Russia; Zambia and Britain on several occasions in search of peace for Angola.

His several visits since 1992 to South Africa to discuss the future of that great country with its various factions like President de Klerk; President Nelson Mandela; Chief Buthelezi; Lucas Mangope and a host of prominent South Africans of all races and colour, have yielded results today.

He seldom takes up an assignment that he cannot see through—he is a tireless dedicated and relentless worker. When one considers the number of travels he makes in any one month, one asks the question as to how he can manage and at the same time have sufficient time for his family, his personal business, and private life.

Obasanjo is a true family man. This aspect of his life is not made public, but those of us close to him see it glaringly. He loves and adores children. There was a moving experience I had with him when we visited the children of freedom fighters from Central and Southern Africa who were being cared for by Fidel Castro's Government in Cuba. He wept for joy when he saw the first-class care given to these children by Fidel's Government. I was also moved and could not control my feeling for these children who could not say much about their parents or background.

During our travels to China, Cuba, Angola, South Africa, Namibia, Zambia, Ethiopia, the United States, the United Kingdom, Singapore, France and the Caribbean, Obasanjo would routinely telephone at ungodly hours to discuss issues that he feels very strongly about. He may sit up till the early hours of the morning putting his thoughts on paper. He also takes great delight in calling some of his friends late at night when he is out of the country and within the country to discuss matters affecting Nigeria. He is a very concerned Nigerian and Africanist. In 1973, Obasanjo unwittingly disclosed his Africanist's inclination in the presence of the Head of the Africa Department at the Federal Ministry of External Affairs, Lagos. It was therefore not surprising when during his administration cautious efforts were made to assist in liberating those African countries that were still under the imperialist yoke.

Obasanjo has made great sacrifices for Nigeria and Africa. I recall that as Second-in-Command, he was bereaved but only a few persons knew about his bereavement, namely General Murtala Muhammed, the deceased person's mother, a medical Colonel, the registrar of deaths and births, a close friend and I. Obasanjo visited the grave site after leaving office in 1979.

He is a detribalised Nigerian who has, in his own little way, made several efforts to bring Nigeria from all corners of the country together. He has friends and associates throughout the country, but he is known amongst his friends as one who would not hesitate to condemn a friend if that friend does anything wrong, and will also reinstate a relationship if the friend changes for good. Yet, he has never been in business with his very good and confidant friends. He does not ever close a door completely and he also would publicly admit and apologise if he had misjudged or condemned someone wrongfully. At times, he is blunt in his words to the point of obstinacy. If you ever need an assistance from him, please make sure that you have your facts and requirements ready. Don't just go to him and say that "you want anything", he will tell you to go back and make up your mind as to what you actually want.

I sincerely hope that, some day, some historians would sit down with him and ask pertinent questions as to why and how he has managed to live his life style as he did.

I pray that he and his family will live to enjoy the fruits of his labours. Unfortunately, Nigerians do not have the word "Thank You" in their vocabulary, but I would say *"a big thank you to General (Chief) Olusegun Obasanjo* for making some of us *proud Nigerians* by his exemplary actions on matters affecting Nigeria, Africa and the world at large".

Ayodele Aderinwale

THE ESSENCE OF OBASANJO

Ordinarily, writing about one's boss is difficult enough a task. The added problem is writing about someone as complex as General Obasanjo. My intent in this short piece is to try to depict the man through a number of anecdotes.

I still recall most vividly my first encounter with the General in November 1988. I arrived at the General's farm in Ota at about lunch time in the company of Femi Badejo and Cyril Obi. Having expected someone with all the paraphernalia and trappings of power, we got to the farm gate to find normal security personnel, no soldiers. I shrugged my shoulders and went on believing that the soldiers would come on later. When we were ushered into the reception area of his office quite a number of people were already waiting. By all standards, this outer office was bare and functional, one might even say austere and spartan. Stephen Okine, his secretary, was tucked away in one corner banging away at an archaic manual typewriter in between bits and chews of kolanut. There was no air-conditioning, the floor was covered with some tiles that seemed to imitate a rug, a tiny refrigerator was tucked in one corner and the only item of noticeable "luxury" was a pile of the London Guardian newspaper on a shelf which immediately caught my attention. Upon close scrutiny I discovered that the most recent of the lot was three weeks old.

After about thirty minutes the General himself emerged from his office in all his peasant majesty, clad in faded jeans with a green overall and a white beach hat—quite a shock for me. He was still deep in conversation with his visitor when he suddenly stopped by the door, took one sweeping look at the motley crowd in the outer office and began what I was to later see as usual practice: he asked each person what he or she wanted, gave instructions and dispatched each person. As he turned towards me I squirmed in my pants, tried to courtesy while at the same time not wanting to be obviously scared out of my wits. As he asked what I wanted I answered in a croaking voice that I was with Femi Badejo. He nodded his head. In a short while he had managed to reduce the crowd to a manageable number, I think of about seven or eight, all of whom he invited to lunch with him. Off we trudged to the restaurant of the farmgate complex, like a band of sheep flocking after a shepherd. Lunch was altogether a simple affair of a straight forward choice between rice and eba.

After lunch I was called to be introduced to the General by Femi Badejo. I do not know what they had discussed before I was summoned. Squinting his eyes he looked at me and said "your teacher said you are good, yet I am not sure you will last two weeks; but you can surprise me, just like Stephen. I didn't give him a chance and he did it. Start in two week's time and we shall see."

One early morning he called me and asked me for my honest and candid opinion on an issue. I looked at him straight in the eye and without thinking shot my mouth. Funnily enough he squinted his eyes, gave that usual mischievous grin of his and went into his room. Suddenly the import of all that I had said dawned on me and I said to myself: I probably will be lucky if I get out of this place in one piece—but nothing happened. I will never forget that day.

When I first joined him, I saw the breakneck speed with which almost every little task and assignment had to be done. I couldn't understand—was he afraid he would die tomorrow? But we kept on at it and he did not die. There is usually frenetic pace about him. Every time he moves on like a colossus, he expects you to move at the same pace. He is, in one word, a hard task master. But one of the General's guiding principles is that it pays to be humble and I have never forgotten that.

Travelling with the General can be both fun and exhausting. He carries with him his usual frenetic pace and tireless schedule. I recall a trip to Zimbabwe in 1990. We were supposed to visit a number of farm settlements in Zimbabwe crisscrossing the country side and thereafter cap it with a meeting with the Vice-President before leaving for Lusaka and, thereafter, Maputo. As we were getting ready for the trip to Lusaka, we were informed that because of an ongoing SADCC meeting we would not be able to meet key officials. The trip was postponed and I was besides myself with joy realizing that at least I would be able to relax and have an opportunity to explore Harare and savour the beauty of the city which I had only seen from the golden cage of the Harare Sheraton Hotel. I was still feeling great when the General called and asked that I explore with the travel agent how we could leave Harare this very night. I couldn't believe my ears. Anyway I smiled believing there was no way we could catch a connecting flight back to Lagos. The travel agent was eager to find a solution yet I couldn't tell him that I did not want him to satisfy us. He eventually threw up his hands in resignation and concluded there was no way he could accommodate us. I hurriedly scampered back to tell the General—with some hidden glee—that we could not leave tonight and that the earliest possibility for a plane back home was the evening of the next day. Even that would mean to spend at least one night in Nairobi. He asked if there was any flight out of Harare that night that could take us to anywhere in Europe, preferably

London and that if that were possible we could then of course connect and travel home on a British Airways flight out of London. Tough luck for me: there was a ZIMAIR flight to London that very night and we left for London. I was so tired that I slept all through the flight. As we arrived in London, I wanted to spend the hours in between flights to window shop at the airport. Such thoughts were quickly dismissed as we arrived and the General said that we had to complete our reports now before returning to Nigeria. He was eager to send his reports and observations to President Mugabe immediately and so he dragged me to the first class lounge under the pretense that I was his personal doctor. There I was in London and spending six hours at Gatwick airport drafting my report while he drafted a letter to President Mugabe.

The second experience was during a trip to Singapore in November 1993. Arriving in Singapore via London after a fourteen hour nonstop flight, I was suffering from serious jet lag. I assumed everyone else, including the General, was going through the same period of disorientation. As I was about to settle down in my room, I got a call from him saying I should come over as we had work to do. That was the pattern that continued until the last day of the conference. And so, I was looking forward to a day's rest before catching the flight back to London. Yet, he insisted on our departing Singapore that very night. Of course, this time I smiled because I had anticipated it. Knowing him he would not spend an extra day in Singapore even if it meant that he must fly to Sydney to connect to another flight to Nigeria. What lesson to draw from this? Don't ask me, when next you see General Olusegun Obasanjo ask him.

There are times he goes at great length to please people. In March 1994, Bill Zartman invited him at a meeting in South Africa to address a conference in Baltimore. General Obasanjo's schedule was already too tight for any normal person. He told me of Zartman's invitation and my instinctive reaction was to advise "impossible". He had an engagement in Nigeria and about two or three days thereafter he was supposed to go to Lome to deliver a keynote address at another event. But for him it was an opportunity to further sensitize a non-African audience with regard to the proposed Conference on Security, Stability, Cooperation and Development in Africa (CSSDCA). This was an opportunity not to be missed. The next minute we were in the escalator on our way to the travel agent. As it were, he returned home leaving me in Johannesburg (thank heavens!). His departure was hectic, but his return trip proved to be even more crazy.

Over time, I realised that he does not encourage backbiting. I remember several instances when farm employees were going behind each other to tell him tales, founded and unfounded. His characteristic reaction has always been either to ask one, while he was sending for the other. If this was not possible, he told a person at the next possible encounter exactly what was said about him—no embellishment, no deductions and no add-ons. While this appeared to be putting somebody on the spot, I soon drew the import of his action: as a responsible leader or manager you must learn to discourage backbiters and tale bearers. To do otherwise is to allow yourself to be distracted and confused from your main goal and target.

Prudence and maintenance must be your watchword. One of the things that initially used to amaze me is the Obasanjo penchant for used items. In fact the joke around the farm was that if it were possible to hire a fairly used human being, Obasanjo would go right ahead and buy it. From generating plants to cars to every conceivable item General Obasanjo would invariably buy fairly used items.

One basic trait of General Obasanjo has always been the tenacity with which he pursues whatever he is convinced is right. You must learn to have the courage of your personal convictions. Although one may appear to be intransigent in some people's eyes, once one wavers one is open to all types of advice and misadvice. However, before making up one's mind one must consult as widely as possible. Most times, General Obasanjo couldn't care what you think of him or whatever names you may choose to call him. This has in fact remain his greatest handicap in terms of his involvement and role in the Nigerian political process. Take for instance the whole debacle over the 12 June crisis and the material loss that has suffered in the process. I know for sure that he was as much a facilitator of the Abiola victory and was already making preparations for the Abiola presidency. As I was the one who drafted a letter requesting Professor Adebayo Adedeji to prepare the economic blueprint for an Abiola government. This blueprint was to be broken down into the first 100 days, the first six months and so on. General Obasanjo was also instrumental in facilitating the Igbo votes for Chief Abiola and he was making inroads to Bauchi state through the efforts of Ambassador B.A.T. Balewa.

Being frugal to a fault is one drawback of the General. He is definitely not a believer in material rewards rather going for something more deeper and more enduring. When he is bargaining with Hans d'Orville, I do not know who is a more shrewd and hard bargainer. There are three things he does not joke with: his children, his money and his women. In each case even with his children there is no iota of indulgence. I recall the last time one of them came from the United States. When he was sending the next cheque for the upkeep he deducted the cost of the air ticket from the annual allowance. The allowance itself a niggardly amount and I could only shake my head in utter disbelief. Such is the fervour with which he guards every penny of his that he would never carry a credit card.

Another interesting dimension is that he enjoys bluntness and robust exchanges. He even seems to court them—as is the tradition of the Farm House Dialogues of the Africa Leadership Forum. I remember a Dialogue on Youth and Development, when the General turned during lunch to Abubakar Momoh, an avowed Marxist, asking Momoh what he would tell his friends. Momoh looked at him straight in the face and said "Well, I will tell them that the General is improving, we are reforming him". The General stared at him in mock horror and feigned an attack. In reaction, Momoh moved to increase the distance between them. Settling back into his chair, the General said "After eating my food you are still abusing me". To which Momoh retorted, "This is not your food, sir, this is a product of the workers' sweat". Everyone laughed uproariously. Such is the stuff the General is made of. He actually interacts with you at your level and has never despised the company of either the young or the old, the rich or the poor.

Thus it is easy to understand why he finds it easy to hound all of us into marriage. In most cases you would have been either a victim or beneficiary of his unsolicited and generous match-making once you let him know you are getting married and the date can somehow be accommodated within his impossible schedule. Even if your marriage is to take place on the North Pole, he will insist to be there and he would fulfil all the traditional wedding requirements. That is why one picture I admire most is the one showing the General going full length prostration during my traditional wedding ceremony.

Happy Birthday, General!

Terencia Leon-Joseph

THE ABILITY TO RESPECT OTHERS

I first met General Obasanjo in 1985, but it wasn't until December 1986, while we were working on the first official draft of what would later become the project document for the Africa Leadership Forum, that I began to work with him more closely.

Since then, I have seen and come to admire his commitment to the principles and beliefs that he stands for, his optimism and for his support and concern for youth. While putting together all the contributions received for this book in honour of his 60th birthday, I realized more than ever what an honour it has been to be associated with him.

General Obasanjo is one of those outstanding and rare persons that always appreciate the true worth of people, whether they are, like himself, heads of states or simple workers. In these many years, I have observed him approach humble people with genuine interest in what they have to say and he applies the knowledge acquired from these conversations to his quest for peace and a better world. Although his interests are primarily in Africa, it extends to all parts of the world. His inquisitive mind is at work at all times.

But the quality that I find most outstanding is his ability to respect other points of view, even if they do not agree with his own. He, of course, delights in a healthy discussion and will try to persuade you of his own position, but at the end he will respect you the more for standing in defence of your own values.

Thank you, General, for the kindness you have always shown to me, for your words of support, and for your continual encouragement and appreciation, whether at a particular stressful moment or at the end of a long day. Whatever effort I have put into the production of this book is only a very small way of saying thank you for the many times you have stood by my side.

God bless you!

Mehri Madarshahi

LETTER TO GENERAL OBASANJO

My dear General,

Although it was less than a decade ago when I met you for the first time at a meeting of the InterAction Council in Tokyo, it seems to me that I have known and respected you all my life. It was not difficult—at first sight, during several encounters in Zimbabwe, Mexico, Brussels, Germany, Russia, Ota or any of the other numerous meetings you were attending in New York—to like and respect you as "statesman", "Big Chief", "fair conciliator", "Chairman" or as an honoured and celebrated member of the African community.

What was particularly impressive for me was not only your presence and charisma but your humble demeanour and modesty. Contrary to many others, you never tried to impress anyone by showing whom you know and how closely you are associated with "haves" or those wielding power and influence. I remember that often you wore a pair of white shoes which you dropped as soon as you seemed to be comfortable. I never forget the story which I heard from one of your collaborators in Government. Once upon a time he had decided to give you a pair of *Pierre Cardin* shoes, in a nice brown colour, matching your many beautiful African gowns. However, he soon found out that you in turn had passed on the shoes to your assistant—and you still continued wearing the same simple white shoes of yours. You surely demonstrated that it was not the luxury of riches which made you what you were, but your personality, your wisdom and your wit.

I still remember the day in 1988 when we had a intensive discussion of a paper I had prepared on the persisting conflict in the Persian Gulf and what should be done to end that human tragedy. We met over lunch and I had prepared a simple meal to be served at the table. While in and out of the kitchen, I noticed that you had already finished your salad and the main course—without me having a chance to join you even for the first course. Well, I had the choice, either to lose precious time and continue eating or to continue discussing the subject which was so close to my heart. The choice was very clear, I went hungry, but fulfilled by your words of wisdom.

Talking about your modesty reminds me of another occasion where you, my husband, my five-year old son and I went to a Chinese restaurant—which you liked a lot—for dinner. Our discussion on Africa and the future of the continent, its leadership crisis, its economic problems and the fact that there is an acute need to put it back on the map of the world community was so engaging that I totally forgot about my little son and his need to sleep. At the time of our departure we found him sound asleep and totally immobile. My husband was about to wake him up, when you signalled that you wanted to carry Anoush on your shoulder. To my greatest surprise, you did carry him all the way home. My dear General, this memorable event has been captured in a beautiful photo which is still hanging in my son's room and we all cherish it.

As you know, working in the United Nations for almost twenty years, has exposed me to many meetings and proceedings on various multilateral issues dealing with economic, political and social matters of importance to the world community. Seeing you in the chair and observing your unique style and command of the issues on the agenda, however, was a completely different and exhilarating experience for me. I remember particularly well a meeting in Harare, Zimbabwe, in 1988 on conflict resolution in the Sudan. You presided over a meeting which was attended by all protagonists of the Sudanese conflict, including the wife of the then Prime Minister of Sudan on one side and former Foreign Minister Mansur Khalid on the other. On the battlefield, the two rivals would have been satisfied only by shedding blood, yet, as usual you managed to bring them face to face and encouraged them to discuss their case in public and in front of a panel of high-level international personalities. You left no room for bargain or dispute. You set the rules of the game and they had to respect them: three to five minutes were given to each party to present their case and to express their grievances. If the process was interrupted or the rules were violated, you admonished them like unruly children. At points, being an international bureaucrat, I was frightened whether the meagre prospects for orderly negotiations would dissipate given your towering command of this verbal battlefield, or whether one of the two parties would object to the procedure. As the discussion got protracted, you were gradually getting impatient with the repeated bickering and—with your shoes off—you relaxed and pretended to fall asleep in your chair! I was deadly sure that this would mark the end of another goodwill initiative to find a peaceful solution to the Sudan crisis.

How wrong I was! Soon, I found that all your antics were part of a grand tactic and strategy vis-a-vis naughty children—those who have not yet grown up enough to respect the rights of their neighbours and regard each other as fellow human beings with all the freedom of thought, without infringing on each other's rights. You had to show impatience and disregard for their unreasonable posturing and probably this was the only language they understood. The shouting match between the two parties subsided shortly thereafter and while they were waiting for your ruling, you devised a magic solution: a luncheon with all of them, at one table. You knew full well the effectiveness of sharing earthly goods and of engaging divergent minds to relent in a different setting, a peaceful coexistence of sorts. This tactic was certainly not new in history and might have been used especially at the time of French Emperor Louis XIV and his Prime Minister Richelieu, who were famous for securing the most impossible deals over meals.

Sure enough, that very afternoon in Harare, you had extracted a tentative agreement between the warring parties—even though it lasted only for a short while.

Your masterly negotiating skills served you equally well in your involvement in South Africa and your indefatigable efforts to arrange for a peaceful end to apartheid. Here again, you commanded unquestionable respect from all sides.

Recent events in your country have caused you much grief and pain, as it did to me. We, the people, feel deprived of your chiefly wisdom. Africa is feverish and longs for selfless leaders who could save it from its rapid downfalls in economic, political and social deprivations. As you have often said, however, colonialism can no longer be blamed for the malaise of Africa—it is the Africans and their leaders that have to accept their responsibilities. You told me once that a leader should adopt a set of responsibilities and that a leader should serve the people, who entrusted him or her with power. A leader should act without self-glory or cheap excuses. This principle is too often forgotten. I, nevertheless remain hopeful and always remember what you once told my little son: never hate anyone, try to change them—nobody is beyond redemption!

I do not know when and how you will read this letter. All I know is that we are patiently waiting for you. The time has come for the greatest Son of Africa to return into the arms of the world community.

Magemeso Namungalu[1]

THE UNIQUE GENERAL

Mother Africa besmeared dirty red
With fresh blood
Absurd clotting blood
Rotten dirty blood
From the barrel of the gun
Of Africa's callous politicians
Wanting to grab power
By the force of arms
Perpetuating themselves in power
By the force of arms
Unconcerned about Africa's security
The much needed stability
Development and cooperation
But only concerned about
Acquisition and retention of power

There in Uganda however
Notorious for intermittent bloodbath
Where Idi Amin sat on a throne
To plunder and murder
Where in the Central Districts of Luwero

Mubende and Mpigi
Hundreds of thousands
Of pathetic skulls and skeletons
Of victims of thirst of power
Were displayed on hundreds
Of stalls at junctions
Market places
And trading centres
Where another hundreds of thousands
Of lonely skulls and skeletons
Are yet to be displayed
In the Northern Districts of
Gulu and Kitgum
Apac and Lira
And the Eastern Districts
of Kumi and Soroti
Or the Western District of Kasese
Where bloodbath is at play since 1986

There in Kampala
In the International Conference Centre
Where the democratic General
Former Nigerian Leader Olusegun Obasanjo
And other African men and women
Sat to design the seal
Of Africa's bloodbath
Foreign visitors learnt
Through visual aids
That in Uganda
Only one man
Was not a security risk
Only one man
Was entitled to security
Only one man
Was not subject to search
Because the foreign visitors saw
A thousand security men in plain clothes
Were at the Conference Halls
To make Ugandan delegates
Uganda's Ministers and foreign delegates
Open their handbags
In order to make sure
The only man entitled to security

Was surely secure
And hundreds of other security men
In military or police uniform
Sealed off the Conference Centre
Or loitered in Kampala City
To ensure security
As if to report to the visitors
The guns roaring
In Uganda's Northern and Eastern

There in turbulent Uganda
At the Conference in Kampala
Known as Africa Leadership Forum
Unique General Obasanjo
Stood bold
And commanded the healing
Of the wounds of Africa
By embracing plural democracy
To bring an end to bloodbath
From the barrel of the gun
Of those wanting power
Those perpetuating themselves in power
Those who terrorise
In order to rule
Those who murder
In order to sit on the throne
Those who have no ability
To seek mandate to lead

As democratic General Obasanjo
Still made his point at
Africa Leadership Forum in Kampala
Ethiopia's Mengistu Haile Mariam
Who for fourteen years dreamt
He was the Socialist Lion of Juda
Through resounding echoes of guns
And human bloodbath
Saw his offence against democracy
And realised his life was in danger
So he took to his heals
Faster that a frightened dog
Up to Zimbabwe
Where he now lives very scared

When Mengistu collapsed
Some African leaders
Began to say publicly
That Mengistu was bad
But for the fourteen years
When they sat with him
At the OAU Summits
None of them ever told him
It was bad to kill
It was bad to detain
Or institute Kangaroo Courts
As a means to remain in power
Because according to them
That was interfering
In the internal affairs of other countries
So they condemned South Africa
Talked about Namibia
Or blamed Reagan for supporting Savimbi

Unlike Mengistu anyway
Obasanjo lives in Nigeria loved
Because as a leader of Nigeria
With state power secure in his hands
He realised he was a professional soldier
And there were Nigerians
Better suited to polities
So like Paulo Muwanga of Uganda
He organised democratic elections
And peacefully handed over power
To the victors in the democratic elections
In order to see Nigeria secure and stable
In order to see Nigeria happy and prosperous
In order that human blood
In Nigeria remains precious

By relinquishing power
When he was still loved
Obasanjo retained the respect
He had acquired
By relinquishing power
Obasanjo broke the mirth
That African leaders only knew
The way to power

Not the way out of power
And Obasanjo is not alone
Leopold Sedar Senghor of Senegal
And Tanzanian Julius Nyerere
Joined him on that errand
Who because of their compromise in politics
Are free in their motherlands
Loved and not haunted

Talking about the democratic General
At the Africa Leadership Forum
Julius Kambalage Nyerere
Said Obasanjo was a unique General
The General who had power
And peacefully gave it to civilians
(According to military discipline anyway
When there is no law and order in a State
A General takes power
And promises the Chief Justice
That after he has restored law and order
Power would be handed back to politicians)
But according to Africa's History
Such Generals are rare
Generals who know
That the gun cannot rule
That the gun cannot breed stability
That only loved ones can give love
That only peaceful ones can give peace
That the feared ones only emit fear
That violence breeds violence

Lamenting Africa's past 30 years
Nyerere regretted his mistakes
As President of Tanzania
He regretted the mistakes
Of other African leaders confessing
We tried to build socialism in Africa
Without real socialists
And then poured out his heart
That Africa would never be secure
That Africa would not be stable
That Africa would never develop
Without real democracy

Concretising Obasanjo's mission
For pluralism in politics

If this General Obasanjo
Who won hearts of many
Both men and women in Kampala
Through his democracy can command
Guns to go silent
In the Northern and Eastern Uganda
In Angola and Mozambique
In Rwanda and Sudan
In Racist South Africa
Or verbal military jets
Rocketing between Uganda and Kenya
Rocketing between Uganda and Rwanda
Then the General could as well stand
In civil war torn Sri Lanka
To command South Korea
And the Democratic Republic of Korea
To stop useless quarrels

If is a Cherub Obasanjo can fly
And from the air command
Immediate silence for
The millions of bullets shot
At those opposing some African leaders
The millions of bullets shot
At those talking about pluralism
The millions of bullets shot
At those pleading for justice of children
Command immediate silence for
The millions of bullets shot
By those wanting to come to power
By the force of arms
Then Mother Africa will embrace
Economic development
Because the money for buying firearms
Will be spent on
Exercise books for school children
Medicine for the sick
Tractors for the farmers
Or the civil servants
Who guide economic development

What a heaven then will Africa be
If Obasanjo's poetry of peace
Penetrated the hearts
Of some of those African leaders
Who sit on thrones of clotted blood
With fortifications of human skeleton
And use human skulls
As shield against those opposing them
Determined to stay on their thrones
Without fear or favour
Unworried of how many they kill
So long as they stay on their thrones
Because they cannot resign
And confess their wrongs
Like Mwalimu Nyerere did

One thing is clear however
Obasanjo has set the ball rolling
So even without his breath
He will command
Africans to acquire
Governments of the people
By the people and for the people
Or as one of his admirers put it
Obasanjo can move mountains
His poetry of pluralism
Will lull brutes out of brutality
Will instal power-seekers
Into the right steps
Will flood peace into Africa
And if given chance
He will sing a lullaby
To the Irish people
Blowing up cars
Because they want understanding
From the English people
If he had the power to command
From the United Nations in New York

---

[1] The writer, then Editor-in-Chief of the Uganda News Agency, wrote this poem in May 1991 on the margins of the Kampala Forum on a Conference on Security, Stability, Development and Cooperation in Africa organised by the Africa Leadership Forum.

II. Africa's Leadership Challenge

Ali A. Mazrui

POLITICAL LEADERSHIP IN AFRICA: SEVEN STYLES AND FOUR TRADITIONS

The history of leadership in Africa has stood on seven pillars. Were they seven styles of command or seven categories of commanders? At the time of independence there was a lot of discussion about *charismatic* leadership. This discourse was greatly influenced by the man who led the first Black African country to independence—Kwame Nkrumah of Ghana. He himself was a charismatic leader with considerable personal magnetism. I first met him in New York in 1960 and fell under his spell.

I also happen to think that Idi Amin Dada of Uganda had a lot of charisma, which enabled him to survive in power for eight years until a foreign army (Tanzanian) forced him out. Idi Amin was a brutal ruler who nevertheless captivated a substantial following, both at home and abroad.

A *mobilization* leader is another category. Nkrumah tried to use his charisma for mobilization, but in reality Nkrumah was not a particularly successful mobilization leader in Ghana. On the other hand, Julius K. Nyerere in Tanzania was both charismatic and mobilisational. He succeeded in arousing the masses to many of his causes. Gamal Abdel Nasser in Egypt was also both charismatic and mobilisational from the Suez crisis in 1956 until his death in 1970.

A *reconciliation* leader seeks areas of compromise and consensus from among disparate points of views. Nigeria is a difficult country to govern. So far mobilization has not worked for long. Reconciliation as a style of leadership is often essential. Ironically both General Yakubu Gowon (who led the Federal side during the civil war) and General Olusegun Obasanjo (who succeeded him a year after Gowon's overthrow) were reconciliation leaders. They attempted to find areas of compromise in widely divergent Nigerian points of view.

The intermediate head of state between them was Murtala Muhammad, the nearest approximation to a charismatic and mobilisational leader that Nigeria has had. He was assassinated within months of capturing power from Gowon. Nor is it certain that a mobilisational style is what Nigeria's ethnic and sectarian realities can really sustain. But this option should at least be carefully considered.

A *patriarchal* system is one in which a father figure emerges, using the symbolism of the elder and the patriarch. Jomo Kenyatta was already about sixty years old when he emerged from a colonial prison in Kenya to assume the reins of power. He carried the title of Mzee, meaning both "the Elders and the Old Man". He ruled Kenya from 1963 until he died in 1978. Felix Houphouet-Boigny of Côte d'Ivoire was also a patriarchal leader who presided over the destiny of independent Côte d'Ivoire from 1960 until his death in 1993.

Nelson Mandela is both a reconciliation leader and a patriarchal figure. His long martyrdom in prison (1964-1990) and his advancing years have given him the credentials of the patriarch. His moral style in his old age is a search for legitimate compromises. The latter is a style of reconciliation. Is Nelson Mandela also a charismatic figure? Or, is he only a hero in history? That is a more open question.

Has Africa really produced *technocratic political leadership*? The answer is yes—but not at the level of the presidency. Some vice-presidents have been technocrats or potential technocrats. Kenya has had a series of quasi-technocratic vice-presidents, some of whom got "debased" in office. They include Vice-Presidents Mwai Kibaki (distinguished economist), Josephat Karanja (former University Vice-Chancellor) and George Saitoti (former professor). They say "power corrupts, and semi-absolute power corrupts semi-absolutely". Does that apply to at least some of the technocratic Vice-Presidents in Africa's experience?

Personalistic political style in Africa is sometimes indistinguishable from *monarchical political style* in our sense. Both entail the personification of power. But the monarchical tendency goes further and sacralizes authority while simultaneously seeking to create an aristocratic impact. Hastings Kamuzu Banda of Malawi was definitely a personalistic political leader, demanding unquestioning political allegiance. But was he also a pseudo-monarch, seeking to give his authority a semblance of sacredness?

More literally Jean-Bedel Bokassa of the Central African Republic tried to create a new monarchical dynasty, with himself as the first Emperor. He even renamed his country "the Central Afican Empire". He held an astonishingly lavish coronation that was supposed to be paradoxically Napoleonic.

In addition to these seven types and styles of leadership in the contemporary context, there were a number of underlying *pre-colonial cultural traditions* which affected those types and styles. The most obvious was the *elder tradition* in pre-colonial African culture, which has probably conditioned the patriarchal style after independence. The reverence of Jomo Kenyatta as *Mzee* (the Elder) in Kenya was substantially the outcome of the pre-colonial elder tradition still alive and well.

Also obvious as a continuing tradition from precolonial times was the *monarchical tendency*. Even African societies which were not themselves monarchical were influenced by the royal paradigm. Kwame Nkrumah attempted to create a monarchical tradition in independent Ghana by declaring himself life-president, by sacralizing his authority with the title of Osagyefo (Redeemer), by surrounding himself with a class of ostentatious consumers passing themselves off as Ghana's new political aristocracy, and by increasingly regarding political opposition to the president as the equivalent of treason (a monarchical version of intolerance).

Less obvious as a precolonial conditional factor was the *sage tradition*. This involved respect for wisdom and expertise. In the modern period the sage tradition was rapidly modernized to include the new products of western-style high schools, and later western-style colleges and universities.

The sage tradition from the post-colonial period has sometimes resulted in promoting ostentatious display of Western learning.

Tapping on modernized versions of the sage tradition a number of founding fathers of independent Africa tried to become *philosopher-kings*. They attempted to philosophize about man and society and about Africa's place in the global scheme of things. Kwame Nkrumah wrote books and became the most prolific head of state anywhere in the world. Leopold Sedar Senghor of Senegal was a more original political philosopher and poet.

Some leaders attempted to establish whole *new ideologies*. Julius K. Nyerere of Tanzania inaugurated *ujamaa*, intended to be indigenously authentic African socialism. Kenneth D. Kaunda of Zambia initiated what was called "humanism". Gamal Abdel Nasser of Egypt had previously written *The Philosophy of the Revolution* and subsequently attempted the implementation of "Arab socialism".

The modernized version of the Western tradition also popularized the use of honorary doctorates as regular titles of Heads of State. Thus the President of Uganda became "*Dr.* Milton Obote", the President of Zambia became "*Dr.* Kenneth Kaunda"— just as the president of Ghana before them had become "*Dr.* Kwame Nkrumah". These had been conferred as honorary doctorates, but they became regular titles used in referring to these heads of state. The sage tradition was attempting to realize itself in a modern veneer. African presidents were trying to become philosopher-kings.

Finally, there was the *precolonial warrior tradition*, emphasizing skills of combat, self-defence and manhood. Did this survive into the colonial period and onwards into independence? The Mau Mau fighters in colonial Kenya in the 1950s were greatly influenced by traditional warrior virtues, especially those of the Kikuyu. Even liberation fighters in Rhodesia/Zimbabwe two decades later, who were using much more modern weapons, were mainly recruited from the countryside and were deeply influenced by traditional concepts of the warrior.

But were African soldiers in regular African state armies part of the continuities of the warrior tradition? Were the Olusegun Obasanjos fundamentally still old warriors? It largely depends upon how much of the old African cultural values are still part of their attitudes to combat, self-defence and manhood. Sometimes those old warrior values go awry in a modern military ruler. The warrior tradition went wrong when personified in Idi Amin Dada of Uganda. Idi Amin was a warrior-soldier who was miscast as head of state in the modern world. He fluctuated between brute, buffoon and genuinely heroic figure. He courageously took on some of the most powerful countries in the world—and yet pitilessly victimized some of the most powerless individuals in his own country from 1971 to 1979. In Idi Amin the warrior tradition had gone temporarily mad.

Seven types of political leadership and four precolonial traditions of political culture have helped to shape post-colonial Africa in the twentieth century. The question which now arises is whether the 21st century will either reveal totally new styles of leadership or create new combinations of the old styles and traditions and produce better results than Africa has accomplished so far.

Reginald Herbold Green

AFRICAN LEADERSHIP FOR AFRICAN AGENDAS

> *To plan is to choose*
> *Choose to go forward.*
> Mwalimu Julius K. Nyerere

> *Rabbit, rabbit what are you doing?*
> *I am going out to kill the elephant.*
> *Rabbit, rabbit can you really do that?*
> *Well, I'll try... and try again.*
> African proverb

Crisis Management, Strategy; Reacting, Leading

To view Africa today in terms of the hopes and expectations of the 1960s is to weep. This is not because no progress has been achieved—education is more widely available, infant mortality is substantially lower. Nor is it because there are no signs of hope—since 1990 about half of Sub-Saharan African countries have achieved food and overall output production growth comparable to population. Even on the political front breakthroughs exist as well as disintegration: nationally, Namibia 1990, South Africa, Malawi, Mozambique 1994 and regionally, SADC 1980 onward not least in response to the 1992-94 drought/food security crisis. Afro-pessimism in the North is highly selective and often appears to be a sublimation of Northern (or global) problems (e.g. rising poverty, social crumbling, growing cynicism about violence, personal insecurity, inner city poor area wastelands, HIV) by "exporting" the blame for them to Africa.

However, the problems confronting the majority of Africans and of African states are terrifyingly real, severe and immediate. So too are the gaps between what was anticipated a third of a century ago and what has been achieved and between the record of forward movement (even if uneven, with setbacks, often painfully slow) between 1957 and 1979 and the period marked by disintegration and decline which has followed.

The most appalling long-term consequence is not the physical and social setbacks nor even the global marginalisation and loss of respect which have been only too prevalent for a decade and a half. It is Africans', African states' and Africa's loss of self-belief and of ability to set, to negotiate and to act in terms of their own agendas. External constraints and the conditions of other actors always limited African freedom of manoeuvre, but the general nature of dialogue and of agenda setting through 1980 was quite different from what it is today.

Crisis Managers or Managed by Crises?

In part, the loss of sense of direction and of vision flows directly from a decade and a half of generalised crises. The international economic and political, the literal weather and the internal social, political and distributional context of the 1980s and 1990s have been a far harsher, more complex and more demanding climate than those of the 1960s and 1970s.

African households and African leaders are all too frequently in the position of the man halfway across a swamp, standing on crumbling clay, with quicksand up to his nose and crocodiles converging. It is rather hard at such a point to remember that the big idea was to drain the swamp and harder yet to see any way to project present thought or action beyond (very) short-term survival.

Crisis management is necessary—for those who die today (whether individuals, communities, systems of governance or societies) there is no future in which to win back present losses. But it is never enough for two reasons:

a. Survival is a condition precedent to, and largely justified as well as secured by, future recovery. How crises are handled now determines whether survival builds into recovery;

b. short term capacity augmentation through fragmentation—e.g. the proliferation of direct foreign donor and foreign NGO programmes—may, or may not, facilitate survival. But it surely fragments and decapacitates government and the domestic social sector both operationally and intellectually at a grievous cost in respect to national recovery and renewed development.

Whose Agendas For Action?

Linked to and interacting with the shortening and narrowing of perspectives caused by crisis management has been a surrender of agenda setting with Africans—not just African governments—increasingly **responding and reacting to outside agendas for**

Africa not drafting African agendas and defending, dialoguing amending them in light of outside concerns and contributions.

A symbol and a major example of this shift is the World Bank's 1991 "Berg Report" quite literally entitled: *What Agendas for Action?* In retrospect three basic criticisms arise:

a. The report was too narrow, too ideological and too a contextual;

b. it—at least as read and used—conflated a tool kit for halting decline and reducing certain imbalances with a medium term prioritised development strategy based on stabilisation won through use of the tool kit and a long term neo-liberal moral catechism;

c. and, because of its global and—less uniformly or unquestioningly—African acceptance, "structural adjustment" as a Bank-Fund agenda not structural transformation from crisis to sustainable African development came to dominate intellectual dialogue and nearly monopolise practical governmental discourse (even—or perhaps most of all—when it focused on African objections to parts of the external agenda). That—however intended—was, and is, intellectually decapacitating and neo-colonialising in the extreme.

To be fair, the World Bank—especially Vice President Jaycox—have become gravely concerned with these trends. The first—up to a point—has been corrected. The reintroduction of the struggle against absolute poverty and the insertion of that for environmental sustainability and the reprioritisation of human (health, education, water, nutrition) and physical (transport, communications, power) infrastructure as well as learning by experience to give contexts greater weight have structurally adjusted structural adjustment. So has the appearance—with a decade's lag from the time the problem's parameters became clear—of the Bank's full-blooded endorsement of and proposals for write-down of unserviceable external debt (implicitly on their formula 75 per cent or more for some African states).

But the expansion of the scope and the domestication of the form of Structural Adjustment has had two problems:

a. first, whether the additions and modifications receive the same weight in the crunch from the dreaded, cut brandishing PER (public expenditure review) teams is open to grave doubt;

b. the more Structural Adjustment (SA) expands its scope the greater the conflation or confusion between technical tool kit and substantive strategy—despite the efforts of the 1989 *Long Term Perspective Study* to present both in a way showing interrelationships but also distinctions.

Further, ironically, the more Structural Adjustment has been broadened, domesticated and humanised, the greater the temptation for Africans to take the easy path of responding to it, seeking further modifications to it and letting the Bank play the role of flagship for African recovery with a flotilla of African states and commentators bobbing along in its wake.

ECA's experience highlights this risk. Its early attempt at an African Priority Programme for Economic Recovery and Development was co-opted into a UN

Programme (UNPAERD—or, as grim observers and burial analysts dubbed it, UNprepared) which was treated either as an endorsement of Bank led SA or as a tedious irrelevance. Later in *African Alternatives*, ECA sought to make a broader, longer term strategic case—albeit one hampered by confusing 1985-90 Bank Structural Adjustment in SSA with 1960s IMF Stabilisation in Latin America. However, 90 per cent of the actual proposals are well within the Bank's SA parameters and the more original reflections on governance and life style read almost as if presented to donors to seek new conditionalities rather than to African states, leaders and people to initiate and sustain African changes.

At least since 1993, Vice President Jaycox has spoken for an increasing and increasingly alarmed Bank constituency which asserts Africans must design, draft own SA and—even more—strategic development programmes and the Bank resile from agenda setter, architect and Platonic Guardian to critic, advisor and—when convinced—cooperating partner. He welcomed the report of the December 1994 Nairobi "Africa's Priority Agenda" conference chaired by Mwalimu Nyerere and organised by Philip Ndegwa, precisely because it focused on African priority goals, their interaction and how to resume agenda building and implementation—with SA and the World Bank in fact not mentioned in that report (as opposed to in background discussion of contexts).

The Africa Leadership Forum and General Obasanjo

1995 sees an opportunity for progress toward restoring African agenda setting. This is not because all crises have been resolved—far from it. It is the result of more experiences of viable African initiatives; of the failure of external agenda responding to deliver what it was thought (in Africa and more broadly) to promise; and of the realisation that African leadership and involvement (nationally and sub-regionally) was crucial to successful crisis resolution on a sustainable basis (contrast for example the results of the Gambia and Lesotho coups of 1994 and the 1992-94 peace process experience in Angola and Mozambique).

General Obasanjo has done much to prepare the ground for capitalising on that opportunity. He has always set—and stuck with—medium term priorities. As President he had the priorities of completing a peaceful, honest process of return to democratic and civilian rule and of handing over a more competent and honest governance structure and legal base and a less weak economy than his government inherited. Whatever the merits or otherwise of some economic decisions taken during his term, he delivered on those priorities. He then retired from national politics resolutely refusing to allow himself to become a catalyst for critics or even an omnipresent elder statesman as kibitzer. Like Cincinnatus, the Roman Tribune of the People, he literally retired to his farm.

But he did more. In the African Leadership Forum (ALF) he created a vehicle for keeping alive informed African dialogue on themes, priorities, issues and strategic components. In that dialogue ALF has brought together political decision takers, officials, intellectuals, journalists and experienced outsiders sympathetic to African goals and accepting that on the bottom line the future of Africans depends on what Africans do because they believe in it, not on what outsiders tell them to do.

Similarly, he has served effectively in cross-country roles—notably but not only the Commonwealth Eminent Persons group to South Africa. Like Mwalimu Nyerere he has demonstrated that Africans can design strategy and mediate/guide change in Africa and influence that of the South to incorporate African priorities. It is on such foundations of continued thought and real contributions that **Africans' redefinition and reconquest of their own agendas** (and deployment of tool kits like Structural Adjustment) in the next decade can be, and need to be, built. That is the challenge not only to him and to ALF but to the many other African leaders (of social sector institutions, of thought and of civil society as much as of political office) acting after listened to and hearing their constituents feel a need for a **rebirth of the goals, hopes and aspirations of the 1960s ruthlessly prioritised and directly related to the contextual requirements, limitations and potentials of 1995-2005**.

If that can be achieved—and it will not be easy—the earliest bemused comment of an outsider whose African agenda and interpretation went wrong, Pliny The Elder's "Out of Africa there is always something new"!, will indeed be a message of hope.

Francis M. Deng

LEADERSHIP BEYOND POWER: THE OBASANJO MODEL

The title of this paper emanates from a piece I wrote nearly ten years ago proposing to General Olusegun Obasanjo the establishment of a council of African senior statesmen to serve as informal mediators in the resolution of internal and regional conflicts in Africa. General Obasanjo liked the idea, but was initially reluctant to push it forward, lest it be misconstrued as a self-serving search for a role. However, he shared it privately with former President Julius Nyerere of Tanzania and the then President Kenneth Kaunda of Zambia. Although both leaders approved of the idea, they too felt reticent to press forward with it, presumably for the same reasons. Nevertheless, the idea gradually gathered momentum, received increasing support and was eventually incorporated in the Kampala Document on the proposed Conference on Security, Stability, Development and Cooperation in Africa (CSSDCA). A similar idea was also incorporated in the OAU Secretary-General's initiative on conflict prevention, management and resolution within the Organization. I give this background not to reintroduce the idea, although I still stand by it, but to express my appreciation for the opportunity to apply the title to a paper saluting General Obasanjo as a true leader beyond formal state power.

General Obasanjo has become known worldwide not only as an African statesman, but also as an international personality. His major accomplishments in his own native country, Nigeria, in the continent of Africa, and in the international community are competently covered elsewhere. Here, I thought I would do him and myself justice by building on my personal experiences with him, focusing on two interrelated attributes: his overriding commitment to the cause of peace, security, stability and prosperity worldwide, especially in Africa, and his emphasis on substance and results rather than on protocol and status symbolism.

My first encounter with General Obasanjo was when I was Minister of State for Foreign Affairs of my country, the Sudan, and he the Head of State of Nigeria. I first witnessed his commitment to the cause of peace in Africa through his efforts to mediate in the conflict between Sudan and Ethiopia. In order to appreciate the delicate and sensitive diplomatic issues involved in the mediation process, some background is necessary.

Relations between the two countries had deteriorated considerably over Sudan's support for the Eritrean liberation movement, aggravated by the Cold War ideological differences. The animosity had become personalized in the relations between Mengistu Haile Mariam of Ethiopia, who was Marxist and pro-Soviet Union, and Gaafar Mohamed Nimeiri of Sudan, who had gone full circle from a pro-Soviet socialist to a pro-West, born again Muslim fundamentalist.

The OAU mediation committee on the Ethiopia-Sudan conflict under the chairmanship of Nigeria convened a series of meetings, the most crucial of which was hosted by Sierra Leone in Freetown in 1977. Ethiopia's Foreign Minister Felleke Gedle Giorgis headed the Ethiopian delegation and I the Sudanese. That meeting made significant progress in trying to reconcile the competing claims of all the parties concerned in the conflict—Ethiopia, Sudan and the Eritrean liberation movements. We argued that the issue of Eritrea could not be considered an exclusively internal matter for Ethiopia, not only because it had its roots in international decision-making mechanisms, but even more specifically because Sudan was affected by the influx of refugees and the spill-over insecurity in the region. We therefore offered a formula endorsed by the mediation committee that aimed at reconciling the territorial integrity of Ethiopia and the legitimacy of the Eritrean cause. Toward that end, the committee urged the two countries, Ethiopia and Sudan, to cooperate in the search for a solution within those parameters. Such specific measures as the secession of media attacks, resumption of flights by the national airlines, and convening joint ministerial committees were agreed upon, both to create a conducive climate and to improve bilateral relations toward the solution of the more serious problems.

This understanding was both applauded and criticized by various domestic constituencies. Since one of the pressing objectives of Ethiopia was improvement of bilateral relations, that aspect of the understanding was evidently welcomed in Ethiopia. But there was apparently an overwhelming disapproval of the agreement on the ground that the Ethiopian delegation had conceded too much on the Eritrean question which impinged on Ethiopia's sovereignty. Years later, while General Obasanjo and I were meeting with the Heads of Mission of the Horn Countries in Khartoum, the Ethiopian Chargé d'affaires of the Mengistu regime recalled that I had given their delegation a hard time.

In Sudan, the opinion was more sharply divided between those who thought the agreement had significantly advanced the Eritrean cause and those who wondered what interest the Eritreans could find in it. I was asked by President Nimeiri to brief the African and Arab diplomatic corps and the Eritrean leadership in Khartoum. Nimeiri and I subsequently met with the Eritrean leaders to explain and discuss our

FREE OBSANJO!

THOMAS FLORSCHÜTZ
Without Title (Free Obasanjo), 1995

TWINS SEVEN – SEVEN
Without Obasanjo's Freedom, No Peace, Democracy, 1995

CLEMENS WEISS
Free Olusegun Obasanjo, 1995

WE MUST SAVE AFRICA -
NOUS DEVONS SAUVER L'AFRIQUE

Elimo P. Njau

For me, Obasanjo represents a symbol of contemporary African presence in world affairs, at a crucial time when Africa is being discredited and disowned by the materially rich Western world. Obasanjo, Nyerere and Mandela have taken over where Nkrumah left as humble but bright and humane candles shining in a dark and corrupt world full of vested interests, a world that has lost faith in God. Destroying Obasanjo is equal to destroying Africa, the new hopeful Africa that Obasanjo created tirelessly through his travels, seminars, workshops, publications and the Africa Leadership Forum with which I was happy to be involved in Addis Ababa, Kampala and Nairobi. May the Almighty God let his light shine on the dark shadow of General Abacha and inspire him to save Africa rather than destroy, uplift humans rather than oppress, be generous with his power in the name of democracy. You can see the shadow of General Abacha behind, below Obasanjo. If he harms Obasanjo, the curse of Africa will be upon him and he will be haunted like 'Hamlet' to his grave. If he saves Obasanjo, he will have saved a harmless African 'Lion' and Abacha will be as strong and as loved as the "Lion" he will have saved. 'We must save Africa" by all means at our disposal.

ELIMO NJAU
We Must Save Africa, 1995

agreement with Ethiopia. I recall the response of the Eritrean leaders quite vividly: they appreciated our efforts on their behalf, but made us know in no uncertain terms that the future of Eritrea would be determined by the Eritreans themselves and that they would not want anyone, even their best friends, to negotiate on their behalf. They were sincerely appreciative, polite, but unequivocal in their stance.

In a follow up meeting of the mediation committee which was held in Dar-es-Salaam, Tanzania, several months after the Freetown talks, Ethiopia sent a delegation led by Dawit Wolde Giorgis (to the best of my knowledge, not a relative of Felleke Giorgis), the head of the Relief and Rehabilitation Commission, who was reputedly close to Mengistu. This was evidence of the fact that the regime held Felleke, the foreign minister who had led the delegation in the Freetown talks, responsible for what they saw as their disadvantage in those talks. At the Dar-es-Salaam meeting, Ethiopia reversed its position by insisting that they could discuss only bilateral relations and would not allow any discussion of the Eritrean question. Privately, however, Dawit intimated to me that they would be prepared to discuss everything on a bilateral basis and that their seemingly hard line was due to the fact that President Mengistu was hurt because I had visited all the countries in the region except Ethiopia to deliver personal invitations to the heads of state to attend the forthcoming OAU summit in Khartoum. I told him that the reason we had not included Ethiopia on my itinerary was that we could not be sure I would be received by President Mengistu, given the state of our bilateral relations. If I could be assured of that, I could not see why President Nimeiri would not send a personal invitation to President Mengistu. Dawit promised to discuss the matter with President Mengistu and report back to me within a few days after his return.

Dawit was true to his word. I received a personal invitation from President Mengistu with a request that I be formally authorized to discuss bilateral relations with him. I went to see President Nimeiri to seek his approval. Nimeiri listened attentively to my presentation, but then responded unequivocally that I should decline the invitation. According to him, the Ethiopians were playing a game. He informed me that our First Vice President had conveyed to Ethiopia his desire to visit. His proposed visit had been welcomed in principle, but Ethiopia was supposed to come back with specific dates. They had not. Their inviting me instead was part of the game they were playing. Nor was he inclined to send Mengistu a personal invitation to attend the OAU Summit. "He is not my friend," Nimeiri reasoned, "why should I send him a personal invitation? He is welcome to attend the meeting as an OAU head of state, but I am not going to send him a personal invitation." In any case, he thought the argument about the invitation was only a pretext for other calculations. According to him, it was insulting to keep the Vice President waiting and send an alternative invitation to the Minister of State. I argued in favor of seizing the opportunity to improve bilateral relations which both sides wanted, but Nimeiri was adamant. "Do you really think you can persuade me to change my mind?," he asked rhetorically, and instructed me to send an excuse.

I had barely been back in my office when my secret phone rang; it was the President calling to tell me that he had changed his mind. I sighed with relief until I learned exactly what that meant. He had decided that instead of sending a polite excuse, I should just ignore the invitation the same way Ethiopia had ignored the proposed visit of the Vice President. I acknowledged the President's instructions, secretly wondering how I could possibly obey them. On reflection, however, I decided to send an excuse through our Ambassador.

Understandably, President Mengistu did not attend the Khartoum Summit of 1978. The Ethiopian delegation was led by Foreign Minister Felleke. As though to compensate for his Freetown fiasco from his government's perspective, he delivered a scathing attack on the Sudan for harboring and aiding the rebels and Nimeiri responded in kind. I thought the interaction was beneath Nimeiri's presidential stature, especially because he was disputing with a minister and not with his presidential colleague. I requested permission from President Nimeiri to make a statement. He willingly obliged. In my statement, I gave an account of what had transpired in Freetown and Dar-es-Salaam, stressing the balance the Sudanese delegation and indeed the committee made between three sets of considerations: the degree to which the internal conflicts in Ethiopia spilled over into the Sudan and made us become unavoidably involved, respect for the sovereignty and territorial integrity of Ethiopia and recognition of the legitimate demands of the Eritrean people. My message went across very well and messages from several Foreign Ministers, some of whom were members of the mediation committee, among them Joseph Garba of Nigeria, Cecil Dennis of Liberia, and Abdullai Conté of Sierra Leone, came to me, both congratulating me for my statement and supporting my account as an authentic reflection of what had transpired. By the time I made my statement, Minister Felleke was out of the assembly hall. Ambassador Berhane Dinka, the Director of the Africa Department at the Ethiopian Foreign Ministry, spoke for Ethiopia. He said he was pleased to hear what I had to say about Ethiopian unity, but noted that it differed from what the President had said. Was the minister reflecting a change in the policy of the Sudan or did he and the President disagree? I immediately asked for the floor on a point of order and argued that if my statement reflected our desire to help our Ethiopian brothers to preserve the unity of their country, should they in turn pay us back by wanting to tear our unity apart. My comment elicited a supportive applause from the Assembly.

President Julius Nyerere then took the floor to say that the issues involved were extremely sensitive, that my statement had elucidated those issues, and that the Assembly should take note of the efforts of the mediation committee and urge it to continue its work. He thought that any further debate would be counterproductive. His advice was heeded by the Assembly and the issue was resolved accordingly.

In the aftermath of all that, President Obasanjo paid a visit to Khartoum. Chad and Western Sahara figured prominently in the talks. But he informed President Nimeiri that he was expecting a visit from President Mengistu and wanted to seize that opportunity to sponsor talks between Ethiopia and the Sudan. He wondered whether Nimeiri could pay him a visit at the same time, but if he could not, he wanted me to go and meet with Mengistu. Nimeiri excused himself, but was less certain about the suggestion that I visit. Looking in my direction, he said he did not know whether my program would permit, leaving it for me to decide. Knowing his state of mind, I was deliberately ambiguous. Of course, I could not dismiss President Obasanjo's invitation, but I did not make a firm commitment either.

When the time came, our ambassador in Lagos sent frantic messages, inquiring on my plans. Nimeiri was visiting his native town of Dongolla, where he was difficult to reach by telephone. When I eventually reached him through a telephone with a very poor connection, he still sounded noncommittal about my visit, not objecting, but vague, still leaving the decision to me. I seriously considered going, but the difficulties of flight connections, combined with Nimeiri's obvious ambiguity, persuaded me to cancel the plans and send my apology.

The next time both President Nimeiri and I met General Obasanjo was at the OAU summit in Monrovia, Liberia, in 1989. The General lightheartedly, but poignantly, referred to my insubordination for not heeding Presidential instructions. I gave some defensive response which he received in good spirit.

The occasion of the Monrovia summit was however significant for another incident that confirmed to me General Obasanjo's commitment to substantive results above the formalities of protocol. Although I was Minister of State, I consulted with him directly on several issues relating to draft resolutions and at no time did he give me the feeling that there was any status barrier between us.

President Nimeiri's chairmanship of the Organization was coming to its end after a turbulent year that had been marked by a series of dramatic events, the most conspicuous of which were Chad, Western Sahara and the Tanzania-Uganda war that had ended in the ouster of the Idi Amin regime by the joint forces of Tanzania and exiled Ugandans. The OAU was severely divided between those who welcomed Amin's ouster and those who saw in Tanzania's invasion a dangerous precedent for the continent. Nimeiri and Obasanjo shared the latter view. And since Nimeiri was the chairman of the Organization during that crucial period, his views were especially pronounced and subject to public scrutiny. The Liberian press was particularly critical in a way that enraged Nimeiri. At one dramatic moment during the debate on the issues, he walked out of the assembly hall, sat with members of his delegation in one of the surrounding rooms and instructed his aides to request his plane to come from Khartoum so that he could leave the following morning. President Nimeiri, the outgoing chairman of the Organization, was boycotting the summit.

It was clear that the move would damage the image of the Sudan in the OAU and possibly harm the Organization. I approached Vice President Rasheed El Tahir Bakr, who was also the Minister of Foreign Affairs, and the President's Press Advisor, Mohammed Mahmoud, to persuade the President to stay, but they were convinced that Nimeiri could not be persuaded to change his mind. I approached President Tolbert of Liberia, who had assumed the chairmanship of the Organization, and urged him to plead with Nimeiri to change his mind. Tolbert went to talk to Nimeiri. But Nimeiri would not be persuaded. Tolbert apologized for the Liberian press, explaining the freedom of the press in Liberia and his total lack of control over it. That did not mean anything for a President who did not believe in the freedom of the press in his own country. For Nimeiri, Tolbert's arguments merely added pain to insult. He was totally unconstrained in his expression of anger, which now seemed to be directed against Tolbert himself for failing to control his media. I watched helplessly as my effort through President Tolbert failed dismally. Nevertheless, I felt strongly that we should do all we could to prevent Nimeiri from leaving. Both the Vice President and the President's press advisor remained totally submissive to the declared will of the President.

In desperation, I decided to approach General Obasanjo and explained the situation to him. "Don't worry, we will not let him go," he declared confidently. The manner in which he said it reassured me. But as the day passed, I began to be concerned, especially as President Obasanjo had left the meeting and I could not find out where he was and when he planned to see Nimeiri. By the evening, I was panicking. I approached Nigeria's Foreign Minister and asked him to convey a message to his President to remind him of his undertaking. Word came back to me later with the reassurance that he was still planning to call on President Nimeiri. It was now late in the evening, and it seemed impossible to expect Nimeiri to change his mind at that late hour. As the night session was still underway, I again approached the Foreign Minister to find out from his President whether he still planned to meet with President Nimeiri that night. Once again, I was reassured that he would see him shortly.

Several members of the delegation, myself included, were still with Nimeiri when we heard the commotion of Obasanjo's entourage approaching. We withdrew to give them privacy, but as I had a vested interest in their conversation, I directed my ears toward their conversation. After an intense exchange in which Nimeiri continued to voice his indignation with fervor and Obasanjo asserted that he could not leave in that spirit, I could sense Nimeiri's resolve weakening. At one point Nimeiri argued that he had already given instructions for the plane to leave Khartoum early in the morning and that he was expected back that day. I recall Obasanjo saying, "Mr. President, are you telling me that somebody else is in charge!?" That was a stroke of genius, since Nimeiri would not entertain the thought that he was accountable to somebody else. The critical issue had been resolved. Nimeiri not only stayed for the rest of the session, but made a very constructive contribution on vital issues and to the overall success of the summit.

My next pertinent experience with General Obasanjo occurred after we had both left our respective positions in Government. He had heroically coached his country back to parliamentary democracy; I had resigned from the foreign service of my country when I saw the regime drift into an Islamic fundamentalist agenda that I could no longer represent in good conscience, especially after the resumption of hostilities in the Southern part of the country between the government and the Southern-based Sudan People's Liberation Movement (SPLM) and its military wing, the Sudan People's Liberation Army (SPLA). I had, however, resolved to remain engaged in the affairs of the Sudan and of Africa, an objective which I would pursue in a variety of positions over the years: as a visiting scholar at the Woodrow Wilson International Center for Scholars, a Distinguished Fellow of the Rockefeller Brothers Fund, a Guest Scholar and then a Senior Research Associate at the Woodrow Wilson Center, a Distinguished Fellow of the United States Institute of Peace and a Senior Fellow at the Brookings Institution.

General Obasanjo and I later converged on his work in the newly formed InterAction Council of Former Heads of State and Government. He had been asked to chair a high-level group assigned the task of looking into the problem of armament and development in the third world, and I was asked to prepare a concept paper for the meeting. Over the years, my collaboration with General Obasanjo would broaden and extend into other areas pertinent to Africa, including the conceptualisation and formation of his Africa Leadership Forum and its extensive agenda which among many other things, included the initiative on the proposed Conference on Security, Stability, Development and Cooperation in Africa (CSSDCA), the so-called Helsinki process for Africa. But perhaps the most significant instance of personal cooperation between General Obasanjo and myself has been the search for peace and unity in the Sudan.

General Obasanjo had already informed me of his willingness to help in any way I thought him useful. And so, while I was in the process of organizing a workshop on the conflict in the Sudan at the Woodrow Wilson International Center for Scholars where I was back as a Senior Research Associate, I thought of inviting him together with the then Mayor Andrew Young of Atlanta as senior statesmen whose leadership and wisdom would enrich and help guide the meeting. This was in 1987 shortly after the return of parliamentary democracy to the Sudan. The meeting was attended by all the major political forces, except for the Communist Party and the National Islamic Front. The latter however sent its National Charter, a proposed constitutional framework for the country, as a conference document.

I tracked General Obasanjo down in Hawaii by telephone to extend to him the invitation for the workshop. He reminded me of his commitment to the cause of Africa and his pledge to do whatever he could to promote peace and unity in the Sudan and readily agreed to attend the workshop. When the time for the meeting came, we read in the papers that General Obasanjo's wife met with a tragic death. With such a tragic loss occurring at precisely the time of the meeting, I concluded that he would of course not be able to attend. To my astonishment, I received a call from General Obasanjo to confirm that he would nevertheless attend, but would have to leave early to attend the funeral. I was speechless with emotion. What greater commitment to the demands of leadership could anyone have demonstrated! His presence at the workshop, availing the meeting with comparative reference to the Nigerian situation, his own experiences in managing the problems of ethnic and religious diversities in that country, and his vision on how the Sudanese should approach their problems were an enormous boost for the meeting.

Several months after the workshop, I received a call from General Obasanjo inquiring about the results of the meeting. I informed him that the Wilson Center was about to publish a book incorporating the papers and summary of the discussions under the title *The Search for Peace and Unity in the Sudan*. General Obasanjo expressed the view that we should not just produce the book and leave it to gather dust on the shelves. We soon agreed to use the book as a basis for initiating a peace process that kept us engaged for several years, shuttling between the warring parties and among the regional and other international leaders concerned with the cause of peace in the

Sudan. It was through the chain effect of this initiative that the former United States President Jimmy Carter, the InterAction Council of Former Heads of State and Government, Assistant Secretary of State for Africa, Herman Cohen, the US State Department, the Norwegians (first through Bergen University and then through the Ministry of Foreign Affairs) and General Ibrahim Babangida (first informally through General Obasanjo and then later in his capacity as Chairman of the OAU) and many others became involved in one way or another. Although the initiative itself did not end the conflict, it certainly contributed to widening the circle of involvement in the search for peace and raising the level of awareness about the war in the Sudan in its multiple dimensions.

It was during those visits to the neighbouring leaders that I witnessed another evidence of Obasanjo's humane attitude to leadership. The head of the country involved was briefing us rather impassionately about the sins of the regimes that had preceded his ascension to power and how he had initialed investigations aimed at severely punishing all those who had been involved in gross violations of human rights and other crimes. General Obasanjo preached magnanimity and cited the experience of Nigeria following the Biafran war. His host argued that the Nigerian case was quite different. It seemed obvious that he was determined to exact stringent penalties on his predecessors. Obasanjo was also adamant in defending his point of view. "Mr. President, vengeance breeds vengeance. When it becomes your time to go those who will follow you will also be tempted to find faults with your government. If you must, then I would support your limiting punishment to the man at the top and no more." By the time we left, the issue was not resolved, but the attitude of our host seemed affected by Obasanjo's plea for magnanimity. As we drove away, Obasanjo turned to me and said, "Do you think we saved a few lives?"

In a somewhat similar quest for magnanimity, I recall Obasanjo telling me about his visit to South Africa as Co-Chairman of the Commonwealth Eminent Persons. They met with South African leaders from all political factions, including Nelson Mandela in prison. A white South African told me later how much Obasanjo had won the confidence of South Africans of all races because of his ability to see the problems from their respective points of view. He was said to have been particularly popular with the Whites, even though his mission was to end white domination. After explaining the polarization of the nation and the dangers of a bloodbath not only between Blacks and Whites but also among the Blacks themselves, Obasanjo spoke very optimistically about the impact Mandela had made on them. "Nelson Mandela is the only hope for South Africa," he said emphatically. "They must release him if they hope for peace in South Africa." I never could have imagined the potential role Nelson Mandela would play in bringing Blacks and Whites together in a democratic, nonracial South Africa. Obasanjo foresaw what now seems like a miracle and he certainly tied it to Nelson Mandela personally.

General Obasanjo told me many times that he was less popular among his own Yoruba people than he was among the other Nigerians. The reason is that as President, he reached out to the others more than he did to his own people. In that respect, he reminded me of a principle which was impressed upon me early in life in my own family as a principal value of leadership in our traditional culture. A leader must always cater more for the interests of those farthest removed from him than of those closest to him. That way, he brings the more distant group person closer to him and thereby unite his people.

Africa's place in the world or more accurately its marginalisation has been a major concern for General Obasanjo over the years. But he has placed most of the blame for Africa's marginalisation more on African leaders themselves than on the international community. Sometime ago, I attended a weekend meeting convened by the United Nations Secretary General with a small number of scholars, policy makers, and senior UN officials in which the mounting emergencies around the world and the response of the international community were discussed in light of Robert Kaplan's article *The Coming Anarchy*. Unfortunately, although the meeting had been planned as a conversation with the Secretary-General, Boutros Boutros-Ghali, he was unable to attend at the last minute for emergency reasons. While there was no consensus on Kaplan's view of the world, there was unanimity on the seriousness of the situation and the need for developing an effective system of international response. Controversy, however, focused on the scale and scope of the required response. The general trend was to argue that the capacity of the international community to respond was grossly limited in comparison to the magnitude of the crisis. It was therefore necessary to be selective in the efforts to save situations. While it was important to rescue certain countries, others might have to be allowed to collapse and die a natural death. One scholar went as far as saying, "I hate to say this, but the Rwandas do not matter much." His argument was that while the collapse of such major countries as Nigeria, Egypt, or Pakistan would destabilize international order, the collapse of small countries like Rwanda was of relatively insignificant consequence. I was naturally outraged by that perspective although I felt sure that Boutros-Ghali himself would not have shared that view. I argued that while I could understand even as powerful a country as the United States argue that its capacity for international rescue operations is limited, the same could not be said of the United Nations to which all nations and humanity must look.

Following that meeting, I learned that General Obasanjo was somewhere in the vicinity of North America. After several calls to different cities, we eventually connected. When I reported to him about the meeting I had just attended, he shared my reaction, but expressed no surprise. He had heard similar views expressed elsewhere and felt that in any case, the primary responsibility for the situation fell on African leaders. He suggested that we should meet to discuss the situation in more detail and to determine what if anything could be done, perhaps through the Africa Leadership Forum. He invited me to meet him in New York, but also offered to come to Washington if I preferred that option, yet another instance of substance having priority over protocol. I said that instead of going to meet him alone, I would prefer to organize a small brainstorming session at the Brookings Institution, where I headed the Africa Project of the Foreign Policy Studies Program. The meeting included government representatives, policy analysts, and other experts on African Affairs. The discussion centered around several themes: the extent of disintegration or deterioration of conditions in Africa; the international response to the African tragedy; and Africa's own responsibility for the problems and the solutions. The meeting resulted in a proposal to convene a high-level consultation by African statesmen, scholars, diplomats, and activists, in collaboration with foreign friends of Africa, to review the current international and regional climate and to develop appropriate principles, mechanisms, and strategies for Africa and international response to the African challenge. The Africa Leadership Forum was tasked with spearheading the initiative.

Shortly afterwards, a workshop on conflict resolution in Africa was held in Washington in which several people spoke in favour of the CSSDCA initiative which General Obasanjo had spearheaded but which had been forestalled by the OAU. The issue was how to revitalize the process through external support and stimulus. I informed the meeting that the founder of the idea, General Obasanjo, was scheduled to come to the United States in a few days' time. We could arrange a meeting with him and interested American partners during his visit. Since I was myself about to leave for Africa and both the General and our American counterparts wanted us both to attend the meeting, the question was whether he could leave immediately to be in Washington a few days before his scheduled meetings in the United States. He did.

It is not my intention here to exhaust the occasions when I called on General Obasanjo to make his good offices available to the cause of Africa. Whether it is to make keynote addresses at conferences, attend and chair meetings on African issues, participate in policy briefings, or undertake peace missions, I have found General Obasanjo ever ready whenever and wherever he is called upon to apply his good offices and statesmanship to the service of Africa and indeed of humanity. And knowing how much in demand he is around the world, it is not surprising that he is nearly always en route, having learned the art and skill of travelling lightly.

To say that the examples I have provided here give an adequate portrait of General Obasanjo and his *leadership beyond power* is to limit the intensity, the scope and the overall profile of his leadership. There is hardly an international initiative these days in which his name does not figure in one way or another. That he was a serious contender for the position of the United Nations Secretary-General underscores his global vision and outreach. It is in this broad perspective that my modest contribution to the celebration of his leadership should be perceived. My account is merely a pinhole glimpse of a man I have come to know well and admire immensely, on all accounts a truly remarkable national, regional, and global leader.

Olusegun Obasanjo has demonstrated to Africa and indeed to the world that true greatness lies not only in ruling wisely, but perhaps even more importantly, in a humble, but towering service to society and humanity after leaving the formal institutions of government. I hope and trust that his example will provide a model for other leaders to follow. Recognizing and rewarding such accomplishments nationally, regionally and globally is an important reinforcement of the values of statesmanship behind true leadership. That indeed could provide a constructive incentive for democratic transitions in and out of power.

Oyeleye Oyediran

THE MILITARY AND POLITICAL TRANSITION IN AFRICA: THE OBASANJO MODEL

In recent times scholars and students of political structures and processes in West Africa have come to argue that perhaps the single most important challenge confronting the democratization process in the subregion may be the identification of an effective and lasting formula capable of checking and putting in permanent abeyance the seizure of political power and authority by the military. Such is the widespread nature of the problem along the West Coast of Africa, that it has probably become the most engaging concern of scholars, practitioners as well as the casual observer of the political structures and processes in Africa with specific reference to West Africa.

1 October 1979 remains an important landmark and therefore evergreen on the democratic history and calendar of Nigeria as a nation and I dare say the African continent. For that was the day a military ruler handed over the baton of Nigeria's presidency to a democratically elected civilian president. The symbolism of that occasion would for sometime to come remain indelible in the minds of many Nigerians and many Africans.

Perhaps with the exception of Toumani Toure in Mali who led a military government for eighteen short months during which he executed a political programme culminating in the transfer of political power to a democratic elected government, the West Coast has remained deprived of similar experience. Again the military have in country after country repeatedly taken the path of dishonour and disgrace by clinging to power at all costs and under a gamut and variety of reasons, guises and manifestations.

It may be argued today that the military as an institution does not organise coups rather than a select group of individuals within the military does. Nonetheless the individuals within the military tend to structure the public perception of the military.

Some of the often bandied argument is that military men appear to be men who find it difficult to keep their honour. The implication of this are many and have severe consequences for the institution itself. In a similar vein it is perhaps also important to note that within the desert of failed promises t here have been individual military officers who have been party to pronouncements and who made pledges and who in spite of possible diversions, managed to keep their word. In this instance I refer to the likes of Toumani Toure, and Olusegun Obasanjo before him. However my focus in this short piece is on General Olusegun Obasanjo, my schoolmate and friend of many years standing. Although I was not part of his team in government I was nonetheless involved in the political programme of his regime. I was part of the Constitution Drafting Committee in 1976.

Although with benefit of hindsight we are wont to find fault with political transition programme, the important point to note here is that whatever may be said of Obasanjo he kept faith with Nigerians, with his military colleagues, with the world and with the rest of Africa—when it was largely fashionable to break such promises. More importantly, for the military as an institution he showed that honour and integrity can be found among the members of the black race that are in uniform just like their colleagues elsewhere. The point for me is not to seek to proffer answers or explanations as to why he kept faith, the point to note is that having done this, Nigerians have come to once again to trust and believe their military rulers who assume the reigns of power at their own behest and for whatever reasons they may choose to decipher.

I was at the sixth annual international conference of the Africa Leadership Forum when President Kenneth Kaunda openly recounted his plea to General Obasanjo not to hand over power and to remain at the helm of affairs of Nigeria. I have on other occasions heard General Obasanjo recount the several similar pleas by other African heads of State and presidents to renege on the promise to hand over the reins of government. If he had chosen to act otherwise there would have been an antecedent. There was the excuse of the dispute surrounding the election, there were other opportunities. The fact that he maintained his position and handed over power as scheduled given the numerous opportunities available to act otherwise is an indication of a mind-set typical and characteristic of Obasanjo.

To attempt to rationalise why he kept faith will not be within the scope of this short piece to adduce reasons for the shortness of the succeeding civilian government of Alhaji Shehu Shagari would as well be beyond the scope of this paper. Suffice to note that his represents a model that is worthy of examination and emulation by other present day military usurpers of political power.

Happy birthday, General Obasanjo! "*Nulli secundus.*"

Ibrahim Agboola Gambari

THE SPECTRE OF MARGINALIZATION OF AFRICA IN THE EMERGING NEW WORLD ORDER: A PERSONAL REFLECTION

General Olusegun Obasanjo has become more than a national asset of Nigeria. He symbolises the aspiration of a troubled continent while operating as a true citizen of the world. The General is a very special person in a special period of world history and international relations. Throughout his career, General Obasanjo has been dedicated to the proposition that dangers are in fact challenges in different forms. Therefore, this warning that Africa faces a new danger of marginalization in world affairs in this post-Cold War era, is an appeal to him to rededicate himself, mobilize all necessary resources and do battle in order to help reverse this trend.

When the novelist Charles Dickens, in *The Tale of Two Cities*, said so eloquently that "these are the best of times; these are the worst of times", he spoke for his time as well as ours. The prospects of a new world order capable of strengthening world peace and international cooperation contrast sharply with the realities of increasing intrastate wars, poverty and social disintegration in all countries of the world. This is the sad duality of human condition that we are faced with.

The international political and socioeconomic environment in the post-Cold War era poses great challenges for Africa. Following the diminution of our continent's political, economical and strategic value which existed in the heydays of the Cold War, there is a real prospect that Africa may simply become irrelevant in world politics and international economic relations. This situation may be worsened by the fact that the only superpower left in the world is becoming increasingly inward-looking especially following the assumption of control of both Houses of the United States Congress by the Republican Party. The choice for Africa is therefore between that of heading towards continuing marginalization or taking advantage of some of the positive elements in the changing international order to reverse the marginalization process and register our collective interests in the global arena.

For African countries to be credible actors in world affairs, realistic and definitive strategies need to be fashioned which can take them into the 21st century. Such strategies should aim first and foremost at eliminating poverty and building the economic and political clout to enable African states to participate meaningfully in international affairs. This should, of necessity, encompass the full exercise of sovereign powers resting on the foundations of peace, economic growth, sustainable development, democracy and social justice.

There are a number of ways in which recent developments in world politics could be exploited to Africa's benefits as the continent strives to achieve desired relevance. The concept of Non-alignment could, for instance, be redefined and its focus changed. Africa could help steer the Non-Aligned Movement (NAM) towards tackling pressing global problems such as the environment, the problems connected with the production, consumption and trafficking in narcotic drugs and psychotropic substances, population explosion, refugee problems, international trade and finances, etc.. Furthermore, those African countries which have developed relevant experience and greater capability in the area of international peacekeeping operations, especially at the United Nations, could play a credible role of becoming more actively involved in such operations whose demands appear to have increased the world over. We could also develop our capability to respond quickly and effectively to conflicts in Africa and promote their resolution peacefully.

In the economic sphere, the international scene is now largely dominated by economic giants some of which came about as a result of regional economic integration. African countries should therefore strive to make existing subregional economic communities work more effectively. The subregional economic communities could then serve as credible pillars upon which a full-fledged African Economic Community would be built.

Africa could also attempt to reverse the imminent threat of marginalization through the United Nations. With the end of the Cold War the virtual completion of the decolonisation process and the termination of apartheid, the United Nations continues to be the global organization within which African states seek to pursue their respective national agenda, contribute to international peace and security and enlist support from other regions of the world for the promotion of their peoples' welfare and the defence of their sovereignty, independence and territorial integrity. However, there is an urgent need to restructure and revitalise the United Nations to enable Africa and other developing countries play a greater role within-the Organization. Nigeria has consistently argued Africa's case for the democratisation of the United Nations, especially its principal organ, the Security Council, in order that more legitimacy would be conferred on the decisions of the world body. It is through such changes that the United Nations will reflect not only the new reality in world affairs, but will also register equitable geographical representation at the highest level of the Organization. Africa would then be in a position to assume its rightful place in the United Nations beyond the 50th anniversary of the world Organization.

Africa must not consent to its own marginalization. Having been a beneficiary of Africa's united concerted efforts to rid the continent of the humiliation of colonialism and the degradation of apartheid, the new South Africa has a special responsibility to help reverse the marginalization of Africa by joining hands with sister countries in the enormous tasks of converting the continent's abundant human and natural resources into real assets for economic growth, political stability and social development. Further democratization and decentralisation of political structure, together with good leadership, creative and sound economic and fiscal policies are needed urgently in order to move our continent forward into the 21st century. For the rich industrialised countries of the West, it is imperative for their leaders and peoples to realise that the prospect of lasting international peace and security and global socioeconomic development in which a better life will prevail and the interest of the weak and strong harmonised, will be illusory unless all people of the world believe that they have a real stake in a new world order.

In this connection, the observations of another great novelist, Chinua Achebe, are instructive. In his celebrated lecture *African Literature as Celebration*, Achebe argues that the world of the African people interlocks more and more with the world of others and quotes a pertinent expression that: "We have not had the same past, you and ourselves but we shall have strictly the same future. The era of separate destinies has run its course." Africans appreciate and recognize the presence of the white peoples of the world. In return, the peoples of Africa insist that their own presences hopes and aspirations be appreciated and recognised by the others. Of course, we Africans cannot command the respect of others unless we accord respect to ourselves and take full responsibilities for our own destinies. We can then demand from the international community the acceptance of our human dignity and urge our partners in the rich, industrialized world to cooperate with us in the efforts to strengthen our capacity to contribute meaningfully in the definition, design and defence of a truly new world order.

In paying a well deserved tribute to General Obasanjo as he turns sixty, this is a reminder that for a man of his experience and talent there is much more to do for Africa and humanity in this new post-Cold War era.

Gabriel O. Olusanya

AFRICA: WHAT FUTURE?

Many will find it very strange that a topic such as the above laden with pessimism is part of the series of essays in honour of General Olusegun Obasanjo. This is because General Obasanjo is a man whose commitment to the development of Africa is a passion, and who has been working tirelessly both as a Head of State of Nigeria and ever since he left office to see that Africa has a future which is characterised by development and dignity. The setting up of the African Leadership Forum is one of many steps towards this end. Besides, his optimism for Africa remains strong and unyielding, the current situation notwithstanding. But the choice of this topic has nothing to do directly with General Obasanjo himself. It is directed to millions of others throughout the world who are beginning to despair about Africa. And this is necessary because General Obasanjo's unceasing efforts in promoting the development of Africa must find a fertile environment to succeed, and despair certainly is counterproductive to the creation and maintenance of such an environment. And yet this kind of environment is needed because no nation or people has ever achieved development by its own efforts alone. While it is true that the major effort must be by the people or the nation concerned, nevertheless, a helping hand, adequate and timely, is equally needed.

There can be no gainsaying that there is a growing pessimism about the future of Africa. Indeed, Africa has become so totally marginalised that hardly does it come into reckoning whenever world events are being discussed. In fact, the choice of this topic was conditioned by the talk I delivered recently to *The First Tuesday*—a Group of American Democrats resident in Paris. In the invitation letter to me, I was asked to discuss whether *Africa has a future; whether it is dying or dead*. This illustrates perfectly well the current pessimism about Africa.

This is not altogether surprising because anyone looking at current events in many parts of Africa may, if he does not look closely, be forced to conclude that the continent has no future. Witness events in Somalia, Sudan and Liberia as well as the observable maladministration, misrule and corruption in different parts of Africa. There is also the fact that military rule still dots the African landscape. Thus, many people, try as they may, cannot see the light at the end of the tunnel. And yet, there is light at the end of the tunnel if one cares to look closely. For side by side with the problems mentioned above are positive developments. The peaceful transition from apartheid to a nonracial democracy in South Africa, the transition from autocracy to democratic rule in Malawi, the end of the conflict in Mozambique and the establishment of a democratic government, the fact that Botswana has remained democratic and stable since independence and has over the years registered an annual growth of 9 per cent annually—one of the highest in the world, the quiet, peaceful developments in Benin, Burkina Faso and Ghana, the peaceful transition from the old order to the new in Cote d'Ivoire and the fact that Senegal has remained stable and democratic since independence—all these are positive developments and certainly constitute the light at the end of the tunnel. If even we discount these positive developments, we cannot come to the conclusion that Africa has no future or any future worth talking about.

I believe the basic problem with many who feel pessimistic about the future of Africa is the failure to look at Africa's problem from a historical perspective, and the tendency on the part of some to make an unfair comparison with South-East Asia.

Africa has been a victim of history. She has undergone an experience unequalled in any other continent. We should remember that Africa was subjected to slavery and slave trade from the 15th Century to the 19th Century. This development destroyed all that had been achieved by then, made any further development very difficult, because the slave trade involved the carrying away to the New World millions of able-bodied men and women who, in any society, constitute the main force behind development. Furthermore, it created a crisis of confidence in Africans. Thus for five centuries, Africa remained in a state of "arrested development".

The end of the slave trade was followed by colonial rule, which was authoritarian and exploitative in nature. Besides, it was both cohesive and divisive in its effect; cohesive in that it integrated into one nation-state various multi-ethnic groups but divisive, in that it did little or nothing to weld together on an enduring basis the heterogeneous groups of people that had been brought under one control. As a matter of fact, in many cases, it exploited the differences amongst the various groups to perpetuate itself. I refer here to the colonial policy of "divide and rule" whose chief legacy has been that African leaders have so far been unable to weld together the diverse groups within their states into one single nation. Thus, every Black African state presents the appearance of "many nations warring in the bosom of a single state". The consequence, of course, was tension and violence giving rise to intra-ethnic conflicts.

Besides, colonialism bequeathed to Africa the intractable problem of border disputes and territorial claims. This is because the partition of Africa was done with great levity and ignorance. The result is that colonial and now national boundaries cut across ethnic groups giving rise to irredentist claims. And these are the frustrating events which make people to despair about Africa. Certainly, time is needed to overcome such great handicap.

The end of colonial rule did not, unfortunately, provide a respite, for African states were born into the ideological conflict between the West and the East. And although the Cold War had in itself contributed towards destroying colonialism, it did not help very much the situation in Africa. This is because the Cold War exploited the intra- and inter-state conflicts and in doing so, helped to internationalize them. The internationalization of the conflicts logically led to unprecedented importation of weapons into Africa and consequently led to a higher degree of militarization of the region with dire consequences for social and economic development. Moreover, the arms were used to destroy resources; both human and material. The constant cycle of violence with its insecurity ensured that African states either became more impoverished or remained in a state of arrested development. It was this situation that put many of the African countries in heavy indebtedness.

In the first instance, African states are not arms producers except for South Africa and Egypt and in the case of the latter only to a limited extent. This means that the arms used in fighting interstate wars were purchased from other countries, mainly from the superpowers and the great powers. Worse still, these arms were paid for in foreign currency, which these countries could ill-afford and which made it difficult for them to put money into the development of their societies. This led to diminishing investment in social services, in health, education and training, particularly vital for development in countries with limited amount of trained manpower and low-level of technology and management expertise. It is well to remember this when we look at Africa as incapable of responding to efforts at development.

From the discussion above, it is obvious therefore that what Africa achieved at independence was not true independence. It was what has been characterised by some scholars as "Flag Independence". This was because, as has been demonstrated, Africa became a pawn in the ideological conflict and many of the proxy wars were fought on her soil. She was, therefore, unable to chart her own course and take her destiny into her own hands. Her interests were totally subordinated to the interest of the superpowers who shifted support from one side to the other as suited their own interests, and who helped not only to intensify and prolong the conflicts but also to retain in power most of the dictators in Africa; because they served their own interest. Thus the Siad Barres, the Mobutus, the Bokassas, the Haile Miriam Mengistus of Africa were sustained in power contrary to the wishes and desires of their own people. This is often forgotten nowadays when we accuse Africans of being incapable of evolving democratic states. In addition, Western intellectuals and nongovernmental bodies contributed their own quota in preventing the emergence of a democratic order in Africa. As Chester Crocker aptly observed:

"Diplomats of East and West, International Civil Servants and nongovernmental groups all played their role in legitimizing Africa's new rulers. The needs of the time called for cultivating "good relations" with the emerging Life-Presidents and Uniformed

Oligarchs who came to rule too many African countries. Prevailing relativist and liberationist fashions in Western academia caused African studies to take on the aura of a solidarity rally. Rationales for "one-party democracy" proliferated. We Westerners acted as if it would be unfair, impolite or downright dangerous to expect African systems of governance to meet universal norms."

Thus as long as the Cold War was on, what mattered to the East and West was not democracy or African interest but their own selfish interest. Thus from colonial rule to the end of the Cold War, African states had little or no opportunity to experience or experiment with democracy. It is therefore downright unfair to accuse Africans of inability to establish democratic rule in so short a time as the end of the Cold War.

We must appreciate that democracy is a "plant of slow and tender growth". It is not a matter of constitution and rules. It is an attitude; a way of life. It has to be cultivated and nurtured with great care to take root. This fact is evident elsewhere for apart from Britain and France, there was really no sustained democratic rule in other states of Europe until after World War II, and in the case of Spain and Portugal only recently. If many European states with their long history of development became democratic only within the last fifty years, how can we expect Africa with the kind of past that is discussed above to achieve same, given the newness of their independence, which, strictly speaking, began with the collapse of the Berlin Wall in 1989.

And as regards development, the comparison that is sometimes made with South-East Asia is unfair. South-East Asia did not undergo the kind of experience Africa went through between the 15th and 19th centuries. It is true that it experienced colonialism and was also born into the Cold War, but it benefited more positively from the Cold War than Africa. This is because Africa did not occupy as strategic a place as South-East Asia during that period. Thus the amount of resources and assistance poured into South Korea by the United States and into South-East Asia by the Japanese who at one time devoted over 98 per cent of their total official development assistance (ODA) to that region alone was not paralleled anywhere in Africa. It cannot be denied that access to such vast resources and assistance was very significant in the development of these states. It is in fact, what accounted for the difference between North and South Korea.

There is also a weakness in the argument, particularly when economic development is tied up with democracy. The newly industrialised countries of South-East Asia cannot, by any stretch of the imagination, be regarded as democratic except South Korea and even then only in recent times. Thus the argument that economic development can only be achieved under a democratic system of government cannot be made using these states as case studies. What was crucial was leadership; selfless and committed. Such leaders are few and far between in Africa.

This is not to deny that democracy, by ensuring participation on the part of the citizenry, helps to release the creative energies of the people for development and that in the case of Africa, it is an imperative necessity, because of the nature of the African nation-states and that is, its multi-ethnicity, a factor much less pronounced in South-East Asia. For it is only a democratic government in which every individual and group is given the right to participate in the political processes that can ensure stability, and it is within the context of stability that economic development can take place. But, it must, at the same time, be emphasized that democracy cannot really thrive without good leadership and in a condition of poverty, and most African states suffer from these. Herein lies the importance of Western democracies. If they are sincerely concerned that democracy should be established in Africa, then the need to help Africa get out of her economic, political and social quagmire is obvious.

As is obvious from our discussion so far, the current pessimism which tends to see no future for Africa and looks at Africans as if they are a breed apart from the rest of humanity is unjustified. Africa's current problem is a product of the heavy burden of the past—a past which has only been terminated recently. *Indeed, the fall of the Berlin Wall in 1989 marked the true beginning of Independence for Africa.*

Armed with the knowledge of the past, it is a miracle what Africa has achieved. This is not to rationalize the failings of Africans, because they are not altogether blameless as regards the events of the past. Whatever her past, Africans have a great deal to do and which they must do to get out of the current predicament. But she certainly needs assistance urgently on the part of the outside world. What is needed is understanding, patience and assistance. Africa is currently shedding off her post-colonial structures which had been held in check by the Cold War, and is in search of her identity. The false steps being taken now are the false steps a baby takes before he or she can walk properly. There should therefore be no room for pessimism and despair. The French have pointed the way forward by remaining engaged in Africa. It may not be altogether altruistic; but it is valuable and is worth commending to others.

Finally, recent history should dispel whatever despair exists. I remember very well that in the sixties and seventies, the West tended to write off India as a country with little or no future as is being done today as regards Africa. And yet, it is remarkable how many are today rushing to India to benefit from the surge of economic development. What we should do is to collectively assist in resolving a problem that has been collectively caused. We do not, as the Canadians believed in the thirties until the outbreak of the Second World War, "live in a fireproof house far removed from inflammable material". No part of the world can be immune to what happens in another part, much as we would like it to be so. Black Africa should not be neglected because it is not strategically located vis-à-vis the superpower or any great power or because she does not possess a nuisance value such as nuclear weapon potentialities or extremists or "boat people". To do so is to teach a very bad lesson. With the necessary understanding, patience and assistance, Black Africa can and will get out of her current predicament and her future will be as bright as that of any other continent.

Hans d'Orville

THE NEW CHALLENGES OF GLOBAL COMMUNICATIONS

In this contribution I am focusing on one global policy issue which over the past years has increasingly attracted General Obasanjo's attention and concern, namely global and instant communications. Not known to many persons, he undertook a number of consultations with international media executives, driven by two motivations: to avoid the marginalisation of Africa in yet another field; and to help to bring about diversity of ownership (and hence programming) of national media as one element of creating a vigorous civil society, based on democratic principles and pluralism.

In this age of globalisation and interdependence, the linkages between the problems of population, resource use and pollution have for many years been recognized, if not always tackled effectively. Global and instant communications represent a new, and maybe missing, link in this nexus. "The information society is of relevance to all humanity and therefore cannot ignore the position, the needs and role of the developing world."[1] Communications may be seen both as the conveyor belt for educating, sensitising and mobilising the global population with respect to the threats to the environment; the dangers inherent in a replication of Northern life-styles and consumption and production patterns; and the impact on political processes and governance—especially given the growing spread of television and radio in the developing world. They also may radically change traditional patterns of work. Representing as they do cutting-edge and rapidly evolving technologies, their ownership and control may hold ominous consequences for the future distribution of global wealth, power, influence and markets and the evolution of political culture and governance. It is no accident that the notion of the *information superhighway* has quickly entered the political vocabulary and is captivating politicians at the highest levels, even entering political campaigns.

Special care must be taken to avoid the emergence of new rich-poor disparities and the covert or overt imposition of cultural and political values, attitudes or processes. Globalisation need not and should not lead to one single global outlook and the emergence of a unified political system. In the following, I am developing pointers for discussion and action that must be taken up by governments, the private sector, the journalistic profession, media companies of various types and the civil society at large, the sooner the better.

With the advent of CNN, BBC/World Service Television and a host of other continent-spanning broadcasters television news coverage has entered a new era. On its heels has quickly followed a spate of corporate mergers resulting in a handful of global media conglomerates—combining television, cable, TV programming, on-line services, entertainment and movie production, telecommunications, computer hardware and software, electronic publishing, manufacturing and industrial interests seemingly unrelated to communications -, amassing in the process an awesome potential power beyond the control of national entities or international treaties. This process is still under way. While it is labelled as one feature of the ongoing globalisation processes in the world economy, it is contrasted by the dominance of a few American and European, to a lesser extent Japanese corporations. American firms made a record US$ 22 billion worth of multimedia mergers and acquisitions in the first half of 1995.[2] To this must be added numerous other joint ventures and alliances that leap across whole industries, most notably the recent merger agreement between Disney and ABC (worth: US$19 billion), the deal between the Westinghouse Electric Corporation and CBS (worth: US$ 5.4 billion) and the sale of VIACOM's cable interests to Tele-Communications Inc. for US$ 2 billion. Well before the calendar year 1995 is over, an amount equivalent to the entire flow of official development assistance (ODA) from industrialised to developing countries in 1994 has thus already been invested in the new industries in the United States alone.

Can the developing countries keep up and stake out a role for themselves in these new global markets? Is a disconcerting new North-South divide in the making? Will developing countries be mere importers and consumers of content produced in a few industrialised countries or can they also become producers and exporters? "More than half of humanity has never made a telephone call. There are more telephone lines in Manhattan than in all of Sub-Saharan Africa."[3] And similar disparities as at this highly aggregated level exist within the societies of the developing countries.

Is a new form of surreptitious political and cultural colonisation about to emerge? Has it even already occurred in a stealth manner unbeknownst to the world at large? What are the effects of a deepening maldistribution of access, resources and opportunities on individual societies?

As the *Economist* noted, "the losers will those who stood still and watched", no matter what the multimedia age will bring. As yet unknown synergies may exist and crop up between traditional markets and the future media-markets.

Foreign news has always been an important element in any national news system, but with the rise of satellite-based broadcasting, the smooth line dividing "domestic" from "international" coverage has been irrevocably blurred. The availability of global coverage is growing enormously quickly and is bound to grow further in the context of the evolving information superhighway and through the new global media giants. Star-TV, the Hong Kong-based service has a signal that reaches from Indonesia to Israel, an area encompassing more than 2.1 billion people. CNN is now seen in more than 140 countries, and every month brings announcements of new regional systems, satellites, channels, and programmes that consolidate, fill in and expand this vast new global network.

The revolution in global and instant communications has brought an immediacy of reporting—as events occur—hitherto unknown to the political process, before the eyes of a global audience and constituency (depending on the issue). Political leaders begin to rely on the same satellite-based coverage to communicate reactions and voice strategic positions, often bypassing traditional foreign ministry channels.

The new technologies and new forms of news coverage exercise powerful effects and create mass awareness (and opinion) about otherwise distant events that in turn are bound to influence the behavior and judgement of leaders worldwide.

These TV news developments are complemented by worldwide operating wire services providing information on screen virtually instantaneously, affecting decision-making in the political, economic and business spheres.

The explosion of technological capacity, the deepening of global interdependence and the emerging new global media corporations raise a host of fundamental questions:

What will the impact of transnational coverage be on the politics of individual nations and their leaders? How do nations and leaders adjust their behavior in an era when they can be minutely and instantaneously scrutinized, not only by other leaders, but by hundreds of millions of citizens in other countries? Can the new media be used to project positive role models in politics, business and civic life?

What will be the impact of global communications on democratic (or autocratic) systems and governance structures, their responsiveness, transparency and accountability? What is their potential to help bring about a more participatory and people-centred decision-making process? What will happen if and when viewers will be able to interact with and express their views on any issue through interactive multimedia? Will that affect the legislative process (electronic democracy)? Will—and should—it lead to the introduction of more elements of direct democracy into present political systems (plebiscite), neutralising to some extent the pervasive influence of lobbyists in the present process? What are the perils of such a course? How can undue interference and inappropriate programming be prevented? Do we need new ethical approaches and how can they be made to permeate globally? And lastly, do we need new journalistic ethics acknowledging the enormous power wielded by global media personalities, without democratic legitimacy and accountability?

The new technologies promise to be powerful engines of growth and economic development. *What will the economic impact be as the infrastructure of a new global communications industry develops, with the inevitable struggle not only over technical standards and control of bandwidths, satellite standards etc., but where the hardware and software industries of the 21st century are located. How will those industries be organized, which nations and individuals will control them, will there be the need to establish an international oversight and regulatory body? How will various stages of design, manufacture, and distribution be allocated, and where will the immense potential profits from them flow? Is there a need to strive for a better balance between public and private interests, between governments and the private sector, e.g. by launching industrial policies and a modicum of re-regularisation? How can the rapidly evolving hard- and software and programming output as well as the related know-how be made available to the developing countries to avoid uncoupling them from what arguably will be the technologies of the next century?*

What will be the impact of globalised financial markets, so critically dependent on the new global communications networks, on the role and functions of the traditional nation state, its sovereignty and ability to conduct national policies? Will the global markets provide sufficient savings to finance and support the exceedingly expensive technologies and needs of the ever-hungry conglomerates without crowding out other urgent needs?

How can the new technologies and media conglomerates be used in an invigorating way to further the necessary measures and action in the areas of population, migration, sustainable use of natural resources and curbing global pollution? How can media conglomerates be induced to create clean technologies, i.e. hardware that reduces the amount of energy required for its operations? The private and the public sectors, together with civil society and academia must work hand in glove, forging a global compact of a new type to devise practical and realistic solutions—commensurate to the enormity of the challenge—and to get things done. *Should the regular provision of certain types of (ecological, cultural, educational) information be made a political precondition for the multimedia future (in much the same vein as public broadcasting had been devised in the United States)?*

What will be the impact on the viability of other media, such as newspapers and other publications, including books?

What will be the effects of the new technologies be on national cultures, social structures, values and beliefs? The ongoing dispute over the export of Hollywood's vision of human life to Europe and elsewhere and the intensive discussion about the projection of European/Judeo-Christian values to Asian countries with their Confucian/Taoist foundations, underscore the problematic question of culture, civic, moral and religious values—quite apart from the political questions—as the products of local evolution versus the output of a multinational corporate imagination.

How can multi-cultural and multi-linguistic diversity be safeguarded? With the explosion of worldwide interest in on-line services, especially the Internet, English is ever more becoming the global lingua franca, relegating other languages. Yet, the vast majority of the world's population does not speak English. *Can the on-line servises become multilingual? Will digitalisation of letters and characters help to overcome this barrier?* Censorship and control may not be appropriate responses to these challenges. But "the best insurance against the swamping of people's cultures is the reinvigoration of their creative spirit and universal appeal" (Thabo Mbeki).

[1] Thabo Mbeki, Deputy President of the Republic of South Africa, at the G-7 Conference on the Information Society, Brussels, 24 February 1995
[2] see "Multimedia's no-man's land", in: The Economist of 22 July 1995, p. 57
[3] Thabo Mbeki, op. cit.

Dragoljub Najman

DEMOCRACY AND GOVERNANCE IN AFRICA

On 13 January 1990, i.e. two months after the fall of the Berlin wall, I wrote the following:

"The victory of the system of Government based on pluralist democracy (in short a system derived from the British Parliamentary democracy) has two immediate consequences:

a) First of all, the long debate on whether Parliamentary systems based on a multiparty system are adapted to the cultures, the traditions, in short the way of life in a wide variety of countries (such as Chad, Saudi Arabia or Afghanistan) is over. It now appears as if only those countries which will have a multi-party system more or less derived from the British Parliamentary conditions will in the future be considered as respectable.

b) But the respectability or non-respectability of certain countries is not the only thing which is at stake. Since the Elysée dinner of 18 November 1989, it has become evident that only those countries which will introduce a multi-party system would be eligible for economic assistance. Eastern Europe is trying to oblige. The Soviet Union is confronted with serious problems about the place and the role of the Communist Party, but those who will probably suffer most will be the countries of the South, more specifically Africa and the Arab world. More and more messages about the need to introduce pluralistic democracy as a condition **sine qua non** *for receiving any substantial economic assistance are aimed at them."*

There is a direct relationship between a system based on centralized planning, often called command economy, and a political system based on one-party rule. One could say that a centrally planned system in the economy practically requires a one-party system. This however has nothing to do with socialism. A score of examples can be quoted (of course, in Africa and in the Arab world), but also Argentina under Peron and Japan.

There is also a direct relationship between a system based on a free market economy and a pluralist democracy based on a multi-party system.

Both of those relationships should not be interpreted as automatic. There are exceptions to the rules but mostly those exceptions are eventually corrected if one factors in the time element.

The present difficulty in both the former socialist countries and Africa in the relationship between democracy and market economy stems from the complexity of both processes. The transition from a centrally planned economic system, in which the means of production are owned by the State, to a market economy system based on private ownership is an exceedingly complex one.

The transition from a one-party system or for that matter from military dictatorship into a democratic system based on a multi-party democracy is equally a complex one. We are, therefore, confronted here with one complexity being added to another—one creating a transition period without precedent in history.

In our search of solutions history is of little or no help. First of all because as Hegel noted in his introduction to the Philosophy of History:

What experience and history teach is this—that people and government never have learned anything from history, or acted on principles deduced from it.

And secondly, because—as mentioned above—this transition period is a totally new one requiring a genuine cultural revolution and above all deep mental changes among all citizens.

Confronted with very complex societies and undergoing a transition process in which the complexity becomes exponential, it is of little help to look into the past. Granted, an increasing number of people are deeply disappointed by the functioning of democracy in Western Europe and other democratic countries. They have the feeling of being alienated by the nature of the decision- making process in which essential decisions are taken at fora further and further away from the citizens. To them it is of little use to look for solutions in the so-called direct democracy in Athens (conveniently overlooking the fact that "direct democracy" was based on the work of slaves who did not have any democratic rights). In the same vein, Africans disappointed with the functioning of democracy will not find solutions by idealizing the system of democratic decision-making at a level of a village. Modern industrialized States in Europe cannot be run in the way Athens was governed. Modern African States cannot be run as African villages were and, in some cases, still are.

Both dissatisfied Europeans and unhappy Africans should reflect the words of Winston Churchill which date back to 1947:

Many forms of government have been tried, and will be tried in this world of

> *sin and woe. No one pretends that democracy is perfect or all-wise. Indeed, it has been said that democracy is the worst form of government except all those other forms that have been tried from time to time.*

The question which is at the center of the debate in Africa is the relationship between democracy and development. More precisely the question being asked is the following one: will a democratic system based on multi-party democracy bring development to African villages? Will it improve the lot of citizens? The answers should be here as candid as the questions are.

First of all it should be clearly stated that there is no development without economic growth (there might be economic growth without development). From the point of view of economic growth the past 50 years have shown that systems based on the free market economy and private ownership over the means of production have had a much faster economic growth than those based on centralized planning and State ownership over the means of production.

On the other hand, as stated above, all multi-party democracies, without exceptions, have developed on the basis of market economy and private ownership over the means of production.

It is true that there are countries which had a remarkable economic growth and in some cases even development based on a one-party system or even a military dictatorship (Chile for instance). However, in terms of history, the trend is absolutely clear. Those countries are shifting to a system of pluralistic democracy. This is the case for Chile, South Korea, Taiwan, Singapore etc.

Here, when analyzing the successes of some of the countries, it might be useful to ponder over the words of John Maynard Keynes written more than 60 years ago in the "End of Laissez-faire":

> *The important thing for government is not to do things which individuals are doing already, and to do them a little better or a little worse; but to do those things which at present are not done at all.*

There is an area in which the democratic system of government is certainly much better for the people in any and all countries. It is the area of protection of human rights. If one considers that the integrity of the human being, whether white, black or yellow, is absolutely essential; if we agree that in every part of the world human life has the same value (every other approach is clearly a racist one), then it is absolutely certain that only systems based on pluralist democracy are ensuring a proper protection of the individuals.

It is worth quoting here Reinhold Niebuhr who wrote in 1944:

> *Man's capacity for justice makes democracy possible; but man's inclination to injustice makes democracy necessary.*

In Africa the question is often asked: in what way, anyhow, are human rights in a remote African village endangered? It is ironic that this question should be asked by Africans who fought against colonialism, which was a system based on gross violation of individual human rights even in the remotest African village. It is ironic for Africans to ask such a question when since the independence of their countries, they fought against apartheid which was again a gross violation of human rights. Or was it easier to fight when the violators were foreign powers or were located in a remote country than it is to fight for the defence of human rights on the national ground?

If the protection of human rights appears, at the end of the day, to be the only advantage of a democratic system over dictatorship, it is worth the fight.

African countries are in most cases composed of people of a variety of ethnic origins. And it is quite legitimate to ask the question whether the cohesion of such countries can be preserved in a democratic system. The recent examples of Yugoslavia, the Czech and Slovak Republic, and above all the Soviet Union, clearly show that it is the lack of democracy which has destroyed the cohesion of those countries. On the other hand, democratic solutions providing for federal, confederal or cantonal systems have, in a much more successful way, tackled the problem of cohesion.

If one wanted to generalize, then one could say that the fall of dictatorial systems has often provoked the disaggregation of countries, while democratic countries have tended to follow the opposite path: the path of integration.

Africa has been the continent in which military coups were more the rule than the exception. The question has been most appropriately asked whether pluralist democracy represents a guarantee against coups d'etat.

It is necessary here to reflect on the true nature of pluralist democracy. Pluralist democracy does not mean only the existence of a multi-party system in which there is at more or less regular intervals a change in the leadership as a consequence of a democratic electoral process.

Pluralist democracy means the existence and development of counter powers: a powerful free press, strong trade unions, a wide variety of associations, political, cultural, youths, women, professionals etc. It is that counter power existing at each and every level that constitutes the backbone of democracy. There is no democratic system without counter powers, but counter powers are the strongest defenders against military or other coups. The passive resistance, the general strikes, the interruption of all communications organized by the counter powers will stop any coup d'Etat in any democratic society.

Africans are often complaining about pressures by the international community aiming at forcing them to introduce systems based on pluralist democracy.

For the sake of objectivity it is indispensable to stress that those pressures were first of all aimed at countries in Central and Eastern Europe and the Soviet Union in the form of the so-called political conditionality. In clear terms, any assistance including loans and credits was conditioned by the following:

i) establishment of the rule of law;
ii) introduction of a multi-party system;
iii) free elections with international observers;
iv) the defence of human rights;
v) the introduction of the market economy.

The same criteria are now being applied to Africa. Here also one should be totally clear: each and every African country has the right to choose the system of government it wants. Cynics might add the famous quotation (1811) from Joseph de Maistre:

"Every country has the government it deserves."

However, aid-giving governments have taken the right to award assistance through imposing the political conditionality mentioned above.

It is quite legitimate to ask the question why the Western democracies discover democracy, human rights and market economy only now as tools in their relations with Africa. The answer is simple. During the period of the Cold War and the existence of two antagonistic ideological and military blocks, the political priority was to make alliances with as many governments as possible, irrespective of their nature.

This is no longer the case. Therefore, political conditionality is there to stay and will probably be imposed in a more and more agressive way.

TRANSPARENCY INTERNATIONAL (TI)

Heylstraße 33, D-10825 Berlin, Germany
Tel: 49-30-787 5908, Fax: 49-30- 787 5707, E-Mail: ti@kabissa.com

Dr. Peter Eigen
Chairman, Board of Directors

Dr. Alberto Dahik
Chairman, Advisory Council

General Olusegun Obasanjo
Africa Leadership Forum
New York

by Fax

6 March 1995

My dear General,

On behalf of the whole team of Transparency International I would like to convey my heartiest congratulations on your 60th birthday. Our very best wishes for the success of your widely appreciated fight for African people, for humanity and democracy! May good health and personal happiness give you the strength to continue this noble work.

Transparency International is very proud having you with all your energy and experience on board. I do hope that our common fight against corruption will result in many concrete initiatives and finally contribute to a better and dignified life of the poorest, in Africa and everywhere.

With my very best wishes:

Yours

Herzlichen Glückwunsch! Peter

Peter Eigen

All the best

pp. Jeremy Pope (still in New Zealand)

Dresdner Bank AG, Berlin (BLZ 100 800 00) Nr. 09 332 145 00

Peter Eigen

THE "MORAL RELATIVITY" OF CORRUPTION

There is one particular "ideological difference" (that used to divide North and South) that needs much better appreciation—the myth in the North that traditional culture of appreciation and hospitality fosters corrupt practices.

I can speak only for Africa. But what holds true in my own continent may apply in other parts of the developing world. I shudder at how an integral part of my continent's culture can be taken as a basis for rationalising otherwise despicable behaviour. In the African concept of appreciation and hospitality, a gift is a token; it is not demanded; its value is in the spirit of the giving, not the material worth. The gift is made in the open for all to see, never in secret. Where a gift is excessive, it becomes an embarrassment, and is returned. If anything, corruption—as practiced by exporters from the North as well as by officials in the South—has perverted positive aspects of this age-old tradition.

Let us strip away excuses and explanations. In no society—North, South or East—is it acceptable to the people for their leaders to feather their own nest at public expense. Once this simple truth is widely accepted, more meaningful social and economic development will follow.

General Olusegun Obasanjo[1]

A Northern Myth

This is the Year of Fighting Corruption. Corruption is everywhere—it is a global phenomenon. The issue can, indeed must, unite those of every political persuasion who share a genuine concern for their societies. Of course, no political grouping has a monopoly on virtue. Just as we see around the world that none has a monopoly on vice. This is an issue which calls for a grand coalition of political, social and economic interests.

It is therefore important to address a deep seated prejudice, which has become part of the folklore of capitalism in established business and government circles in Europe and elsewhere in the North, which would if unchallenged undermine the basis for building such a grand coalition. It maintains that corruption is considered morally wrong only in the North, while it is considered acceptable, even desirable, in other parts of the world, in particular in developing countries. This theory of cultural relativity of corruption, is in the face of present economic stagnation and unemployment in many industrialized countries coupled with the politically appealing argument that jobs have to be created at all cost—even at the expense of your neighbour. There are many striking examples of politicians, high officials, business and opinion leaders in the North, who publicly pronounce this position. The by now famous statement in a BBC interview by Lord Young, Chairman of Cable Wireless and former UK Minister for Trade and Industry, illustrates well this widely held position:

"The moral problem to me is simply jobs. Now when you're talking about kickbacks, you're talking about something that's illegal in this country (UK), and of course, you wouldn't dream of doing. ... But there are parts of the world I've been to where we all know it happens. And if you want to be in business, you have to do (it). In many countries in the world the only way in which money trickles down is from the head of the country who owns everything. Now that's not immoral, or corrupt. It is very different from our practice. We must be very careful not to insist that our practices are followed everywhere in the world."[2]

For proponents of this theory, it follows that firms from industrialized countries should, if they want to do business in the South, put their ethnocentric scruples aside. "When in Rome, do as the Romans do": Bribe politicians and civil servants, pay kickbacks, distort decision-making and economic management, undermine open market forces—in short enter a competition of corruption.[3]

The passionate statement of General Obasanjo quoted at the outset captures brilliantly the thrust of a growing consensus about the universal condemnation of corruption, particularly grand corruption in international business transactions, with its devastating impact on democracy and social development all over the world. This statement is part of the untiring campaign for democracy and good governance of this extraordinary man of courage and integrity. His energy and wisdom have placed him at the vanguard of Transparency International (TI), the movement committed to building a global coalition against corruption.

The movement was initiated in the early 1990s by a group of concerned personalities from the developing and the developed world, who were convinced that most of the benefits of economic development are being negated because of corruption. The scant hopes for development of the South are dashed, the countries of transition in the East see their chances undermined by corruption even before the benefits of open economic and political systems can be experienced. The impact of corruption on economic development, democracy and the moral fibre of societies is devastating. Even strong and mature countries are thrown into crises.

The purpose of this article is transparent: I want to help "strip away excuses and explanations", as General Obasanjo suggests, and to chart out two key elements of a global campaign against corruption, that are presently hampered by the theory of moral acceptability of corruption in the South.[4] These two elements are, firstly, a multi-dimensional coalition building effort against corruption and, secondly, a realistic, gradualist approach to deal with corruption in relatively well defined markets, to create, what Transparency (TI) calls "Islands of Integrity".

Myth or Mystification?

To build a global coalition against corruption it has to be based on an evenhanded vision. Both sides are responsible, the giver and the taker. Action is needed in the North and the South and the East. Cooperation cannot flourish on the basis of allocating blame or moral superiority.

The proponents of the moral acceptability of corruption in the South, let's call them "culturalists", see wide spread corruption in foreign societies often as an inherent part of traditional cultures that are based on strong loyalties to family and clan. They see that such "clientilism" as essential for survival in the face of low civil service salaries and weak official social security systems. "Those who have to struggle continuously for survival and live at the same time in a tradition where loyalty to your relatives counts more than that to the state, do not understand complaints of corruptability".[5] Of course, there are important differences, some culturally determined, in the reality of corruption in different countries. They have to be taken into account in dealing with corruption in various situations.

But these differences exist also within the South, say between Botswana and Gabon, or within the North, say between Denmark and Italy[6], or between different sectors within one country, say construction and other sectors in Germany, or between different times in the same country. Corruption may have been seen as acceptable in Marcos' Philippines, but will hardly be judged to be a morally condoned by present observers. Inversely, the perhaps reluctant acceptance of corrupt conduct in a given society can take root very quickly; this has been shown by investigations in Germany, which show that systematic corruption in the construction sector in the Frankfurt area is perpetrated by professional marketing experts and managers without any sense of impropriety[7]. They are, after all, only doing at home what their government (in common with other European governments) actively encourage them to do abroad.

But to recognize the importance of local factors for dealing with corruption is a far cry from suggesting that it is ethically acceptable in the South. It is true that many young states are particularly vulnerable for corruption. Administrative capacities are often weak, political structures unstable, individual and social commitments to modern norms and institutions are still fragile. In spite of these complex factors, it is difficult to understand how so many can draw from this the conclusion that corruption is not morally contemned in these societies.

All the evidence is to the contrary. Practically every political campaign is driven by anticorruption rhetoric, suggesting at the very least a widespread disapproval of corruption among the electorates. In some countries corrupt officials are jailed or even executed in significant numbers. Most opinion surveys in the South show that the vast majority of the populations consider corruption as one of the most devastating problems for their lives. Individual campaigners risk their lives in fighting corruption.

And yet the myth of moral acceptance of corruption abroad survives. "We must not forget", writes Father Rupert Lay, S.J., "that corruption is prohibited only in our European cultural area. I was recently for four weeks in Indonesia. There this is not only a morally permitted, but even a desired form of conduct".[8] One explanation could be that such theories serve the psychological needs of businessmen and officials, who feel that they have to bribe abroad in order to get or keep contracts. Without such rationalization, what would they tell their families, their friends, and especially their shareholders about bribing foreign officials?

Hence, it is comfortable to believe the myth about moral acceptability of corruption abroad. Or is it sometimes self-deception? Or even blatant mercantilist propaganda? The distinction can be blurred. It still serves as justification for many exporters to carry corruption systematically into the South.

Of course many Northern firms and governments do not attempt to justify foreign bribery by its acceptability in the South. They know it is forbidden, both morally and legally, but they also see that it is widely practiced. They therefore decide that it is necessary to "howl with the wolves", if they want to do business abroad. Having done so they now do not want to make the first step to end bribing while the others, or some others, continue.

Particularly during the present period of relative unemployment in Europe it has become fashionable to justify foreign bribery in order to protect jobs. "The ends justify the means?" The problem was a distant one when only the developing countries and their peoples were the victims. But look at what it means now—a German firm can bribe a UK defense official to steel 300 jobs from his UK competitor in Lancashire?[9] British bribes in Austria? Italian bribes in Belgium? A free for all in an international corruption market as employment policy?[10]

Posing these questions means answering them: There can be absolutely no justification for bribing abroad, and particularly not in the South, which is especially vulnerable and can least afford mismanagement and waste. Accordingly, there are many important international companies, that never bribe, albeit sometimes at what seems to be a painful cost, at least in the short term. Also, it points to a positive example among Northern governments: the United States of America introduced in 1977 strong laws and policies to prohibit corruption by its nationals abroad.[11] No other OECD country has followed this example—so far.

Building Coalitions Against Corruption

There is today a growing consensus that corruption has to be reined in. This consensus includes concerned leaders from all continents, and it draws from all segments of society, from all sectors. It includes business, academia, NGOs and religious groups, media, political leaders and civil servants. The time is clearly ripe to forge effective coalitions for concrete actions against corruption. The following summarizes the response of Transparency International (TI) to this opportunity for coalition building.

TI itself is an international coalition against corruption. It spans continents, cultures and religions, social strata, and the professional orientations of its supporters. An essential element in TI's country programmes is the initiation of active citizens groups to accompany, as independent and supportive partners, the anticorruption strategies of their governments. These groups, normally incorporated as National Chapters in the form of NGOs under local law, are expected to translate the international concepts and strategies of TI into a concrete, country-focussed and sustainable reality.

By the end of 1994, after barely a year of operation, there were more than forty national chapters formed or in the process of formation. Although a number of them are in the developed world, the majority are being formed in the South and in the East. They replicate, at the national level, the coalitions being forged by TI on the international plane. The chapters are free to define their own mandates and work programmes. There are only two important caveats which all chapters have agreed to respect:

- TI does not investigate and expose individual cases of corruption. This would undermine its role of a coalition in search of professional and technical improvements of anticorruption systems.
- TI avoids party politics. It would damage the credibility of the movement if a national chapter fell under the control of a certain government or, inversely, focused on political opposition to government.

The objective of this policy and structure of national chapters is a two-pronged coalition approach: the responsibility of controlling corruption has to rest with both, the government as well as with the civil society. TI's role in building this interaction is mainly catalytic. Generally, country programmes follow the same sequence and methodology:

First, it is ascertained from both the government and leading figures within civil society that a TI visit would be regarded as constructive. Discussions are held initially with senior government figures (usually including the head of government in person) to explain the nature of the mission and of TI's mandate. The purpose is to lay a sound basis for constructive dialogue between the government and civil society on an issue which is arguably the most sensitive of all.

Consultations are then held with relevant segments of civil society—typically including business leaders, newspaper editors, religious leaders, academics, nongovernmental activists, chambers of commerce, professional bodies—to test the interest and the feasibility of forming a national chapter imbued with the TI philosophy and approach. An important aspect of the latter discussions is to identify prospective leaders of a TI chapter who would be seen as independent of government, as being above politics, and as being individuals of outstanding character and probity.

The TI team normally concludes with a final round of talks with government leaders. A report is then prepared, assessing the impressions gained by the mission and the prospects (and where appropriate the preconditions) for an effective move against corruption and this is shared with both the government and leaders within civil society. On this basis, last year TI teams visited Bangladesh, Benin, Mali, Russia, South Africa and Uganda, with follow-up missions to Ecuador.

"Islands of Integrity"— the Anti-Bribery Pact (ABP)

The second essential feature of TI to be summarized here, is its evolutionary approach, the effort to establish "Islands of Integrity". This concept reflects the recognition that in view of widespread corruption it is difficult for individual firms or even exporting nations to take the first step in ending corruption; they fear that their competitors will continue to bribe and get the contracts.

The problem is too great for it to be swept away in a single blow, as witnesses countless failures around the world. Systemic corruption has to be dismantled systematically. We looked for ways in which government might proceed, step by step, in a gradualist way which would involve the private sector and build the requisite degree of confidence that the rules were changing for everyone and at the same time. TI has therefore initiated attempts to arrange, in well defined markets, a pact among competitors to stop corruption simultaneously, by entering into an Anti-Bribery Pact (ABP).

1994 saw the initial implementation of this mechanism in the energy sector of Ecuador. The Vice President announced—at the occasion of the first Annual Meeting of TI in Quito—that in future all enterprises wishing to do business with the public sector in Ecuador would have to enter into a mutual solemn pledge not to engage in any corrupt practices to obtain contracts.[12] This would apply to all firms, local and international, and to all types of government contracts—although initially it was intended to focus on selected large public development projects.

Ecuador has made a start in implementing these steps. Major corporations were briefed and requested to sign the anti-bribery pact. The government pronounced its side of the pledge in the form of a letter, signed by the Vice President, in June 1993. It instructed its procurement officials "to require all bidders in projects involving international procurement of systems, equipment, or services to submit a signed statement that they will not offer or give a bribe to any public official in connection with such bids".

The firms where expected to sign their acceptance of this pact as a corporate commitment, substantially in the form of a letter with the pledge that the firm:

"(a) will no offer or give bribes or any other form of inducement to any public official in connection with its bid;

(b) will not permit anyone (whether its employee or an independent commission agent) to do so on its behalf;

(c) will make full disclosure in its bid of the beneficiaries of payments relating to the bid (both already made and those proposed to be made in the event of the bid being successful) to any person other than an employee of the corporation but including any bonus payments which may be made to employees (such disclosures being made under terms of commercial confidentiality if the corporation so requires), and,

(d) will formally undertake to issue instructions to all its employees and agents or other representatives in Ecuador directing them to all times comply with the laws of Ecuador and in particular not to offer or to pay bribes or other corrupt inducements to officials (whether directly or indirectly)."

It was expected that both the Chief Executive Officer and the Executive of the local subsidiary, if any, place their names on this pledge. The reason for this was to create a strong personal, psychological commitment to break the corrupt culture which has over time entered the business methods of many companies. Therefore the ABP does not rely merely on legal commitments—the legal prohibitions against bribery already exist in Ecuador as they do in other countries—but to create an effective attitude of transparency, a sense of mutual trust and confidence between the public and the private sectors and among the competitors themselves.

The intention of the government was to make the signature of the ABP a general legal requirement for all bidders competing for public contracts. However, the wording of the proposed Presidential Decree raised a few legal issues. Therefore, the legal requirement to sign the ABP was not firmly established and its first application was on a voluntary basis.

As it happened the four bidders for a large Refinery Rehabilitation Project, estimated to cost the equivalent of US$160 million, considered this mechanism to be in their mutual interest and all signed voluntarily. The procurement process for this project has been successfully completed. The next stages will be monitored carefully, not least by Transparencia Ecuador, the Ecuador Chapter of TI.

The government and Petroecuador in a board meeting in February 1995 decided that the ABP will again be included in the required bidding documents for an Oil Pipeline Project, costing about US$ 600 million. In the meantime the legal snags in the enabling legislation, for making the ABP a binding requirement for all Ecuadorian public procurement, have been settled and the legal reform for making the ABP compulsory for all public contracts in Ecuador is under preparation.

It can be expected that in addition to the de facto impact, there will be significant legal sanctions connected with the ABP in terms of invalidating the contract, damages for the State and competitors, loss of bid security etc., if the ABP is found to be false or to have been violated. This will hopefully give credibility to this instrument on which competitors can rely when they refuse to offer bribes.

TI is promoting this concept in other countries. If this idea works, it can serve as a model for other countries and other situations. In fact, it may even serve as an integral part of present efforts to implement the OECD Recommendations, which may also depend on a gradualist, confidence building approach for global implementation.

Escaping the Prisoners' Dilemma

Corruption is akin to drug addiction: Once you start, it is hard to stop. Many proponents of the relativity of corruption ethics are merely rationalizing what they feel they cannot stop. They would rather be straight but they fear if they stop, and their competitors continue, they will lose business. This is a classic prisoners' dilemma—but there is a way out of the trap.

The solution lies in a coordinated system of gradual reduction of corruption. This paper singled out two practical and concrete approaches to achieving such coordination: building coalitions and the use of Anti-Bribery Pacts. They are interrelated. The gradualist approach proposed by TI under the concept of building "Islands of Integrity" is at the same time a specific part of the overall integrity systems and a strategic tool to bring about global coalitions. It can, as a "confidence building measure" bring in the support of those exporters and exporting nations who fear losing contracts. These fears act presently as formidable deterrent for many firms and their home governments.

The present time offers an opportunity for change. At the international level a number of initiatives are underway. The OECD is recommending a coordinated approach against bribery to its members.[13] This is a breakthrough, but by no means a singular event. Many OECD- and non-OECD member countries, and their leaders in the public and in the civil sectors, are keen to build international coalitions against corruption.

At the Summit of the Americas in Miami in December 1994, 35 democratically elected heads of governments of the Western Hemisphere shattered the taboo by actually having an honest discussion on the issue of corruption at the highest level. A first indication of a major change in Africa came with the Regional Ministerial Conference Against Corruption held in Pretoria, South Africa, in November 1994; the conference established a Ministerial regional group to monitor corruption and to foster creative efforts to contain it.

At the European level significant initiatives are afoot at the European Union and the Council of Europe. The International Chamber of Commerce has resumed its work to revive its Code of Conduct and make it operational. For the international development agencies corruption has become a major element of their "good governance" agenda and the new World Trade Organization is also considering initiatives to include corruption as restrictive trade practice into its purview.

An important precondition that this common effort will succeed is the shedding of the myth of moral acceptability of corruption in the South. It is the recognition that "in no society—North, South or East—is it acceptable to the people for their leaders to feather their own nest at public expense", as General Obasanjo points out: "Once this simple truth is widely accepted, more meaningful social and economic development will follow."

On this basis a more transparent, a better world can be built.

---

[1] *Olusegun Obasanjo, "Positive Tradition Perverted by Corruption"*, Financial Times, 14 October 1994

[2] Lord Young in BBC World Report, 17 May 1994 ; for very similar positions by prominent German politicians, see: Antwort des Parlamentarischen Staatssekretärs Dr. Kurt Faltlhauser, 16 January 1995; Presseverlautbarung Nr. 2515 der F.D.P. Bundestagsfraktion, Bonn, 24 June 1994; Minister Rexrodt, ARD: Berichte aus Bonn, 13 January 1995

[3] As recent events have shown, this is indeed what they do in Rome.

[4] In using the terms "North-South" I mean, in a nontechnical sense, on the one hand, a group of highly developed industrialized states and, on the other hand, a very diversified group of states, that are economically and socially in transition, including the developing countries, mostly in the South, but also the countries in transformation in the East; many of the issues discussed

here apply in the East as well.
5 E.Werner Külling, Krebsübel im Süden, mitgenährt vom Norden: Entwicklungs-Killer Korruption, Helvetas Partnerschaft 138/1994, p. 8
6 For a fascinating description of the cultural and historic factors affecting corruption in Italy, see Werner Raith, Thesen zum Vortrag bei der Friedrich-Ebert-Stiftung, 12 January 1995
7 Wolfgang Schaupensteiner, Bekämpfung von Korruption und Wirschaftskriminalität —was muß verbessert werden? Presentation of 17 February 1995, Friedrich-Ebert-Stiftung
8 Professor Pater Rupert Lay S.J. in "Einem Stern folgen—Welche Ethik brauchen Manager?", Das Sonntagsblatt, Nr. 7—17 February 1995, p. 18
9 see Paul Gregory in the Observer, 16 October 1994 on the Gordon Foxley Case, UK.
10 see British Aerospace, Austria; Mannesmann, Norway; Augusta, Belgium
11 For a summary of the experience with the US Foreign Corrupt Practices Act (FCPA) 1977 see Fritz Heimann, Ungestraft bestechen? in: Entwicklung und Zusammenarbeit, 1994/12, p 326 ff.
12 see Press Release of 1 April 1994 and initial announcement by the government of Ecuador in June 1993.
13 see Recommendation of the Council of the Organisation for Economic Cooperation and Development (OECD) of May 1994 on "Bribery in International Business Transactions".

Ednan Agaev

NORTH-SOUTH: THE NEED FOR A CO-OPERATION STRATEGY

The end of the Cold War and of the East-West confrontation helped to free the intellectual potential of the world's policy-makers and political analysts and to focus their attention on the challenges which during the last decades remained among the "second-ranking" priorities.

Instead of disarmament and prevention of global nuclear conflict, world politics is now mainly concentrated on the "trade wars" and the stability of the financial markets. Simultaneously, the inertia of the old thinking drives towards searching for a new enemy. Combination of those two trends results in transforming the multinational deliberative and negotiating fora into battlefields, dominated by rather harsh rhetoric. Corresponding terminology is emerging like "civilized countries", "aggressive exports", "subversive economies", "fortress Asia" and so on. Some people tend to draw the line between the different cultures, going sometimes as far as predicting the clash of civilizations.

The relatively optimistic visions of the first post-Cold War days when the international community preferred to talk about growing interdependence and the plans for a stable world order and harmony have been overshadowed by tough egoism packed in the slogans of priority of the national interests.

The collapse of Communism made unnecessary the strict block discipline as well as submission of the specific national interests to the so-called higher interests of the common security. National interests are becoming now the main rationale of the foreign policies of states. Unfortunately, in some cases the perception of the national interests tends to be selfish and opposes the ideas of interaction and interdependence.

Meanwhile, the modern world is a world of emerging powerful groups of countries sharing the same economic, financial and trade interests. The ideological alliances are giving place to commercial and economic partnerships. Unlike their ideological predecessors, new alliances are based on purely pragmatic concerns excluding in principle the possibility of the client-type relationship. This trend in general is a positive one. A real partnership is solid if it is built on the deep mutual interests and doesn't depend on the political conjuncture. But at this point exactly comes into the play the internal contradiction of the "mutual interests" perception. Narrowly and selfishly perceived national interests prevent from establishing a large, efficient international system capable of regulating the differences and to reconcile the inevitable conflicts of interest. "Fortress Europe" attacks fortress "Asia", and vice versa, blaming each other for unfair, or, worse, "uncivilized" trade policies. Structural changes in many of the national economies—and as a by-product crisis of specific industries—make protectionist governments to adopt tough protectionist measures. A protectionist economy unfortunately is feeding xenophobic psychology and national egoism. National interests are thought to be better protected if the interests of the others are somehow neglected.

Selfishness on the national level is extending to the group level. At the final point, it reaches the ultimate line of division—North-South.

On the both sides, the mutual irritation is accumulating. The North sees in the South a potential threat to its stability and prosperity. The South regards the North as an arrogant user rejecting any possibility of a fair deal. The eternal antagonism of rich and poor is aggravated by the differences of cultures and psychologies. The rich ones claim that every prosperity is self-made and nobody should expect free lunches or gifts. The poor ones, on their turn, are insisting that they are denied the very chance to improve their desperate situations since all the instruments of the world politics and global economy are controlled by a handful of states.

The problem of course is not a new one. But in the Cold War era the former West and East trying to consolidate their respective positions on the global scene of competition were eager to provide the so called Third World with generous aid conditioned only to ideological or political loyalty. Now nobody seems to be really interested in maintaining a rather expensive ideological friendship. The new principle is "do it yourself". Furthermore, in a time of tough budget restraints the former rich friends are demonstrating not only total deafness to their onetime loyalists, but even a growing degree of hostility. The North is giving birth to the theories of "threats to the civilized world", imposes a penetrative control over developing societies, insists on the preservation of strict rules regarding the access to new technologies and so on.

The South, for its part, instead of readjusting to the new realities and paying more attention to domestic problems—first of all, to the problem of modernising the political systems, which in a vast majority of countries can hardly be helpful for a sustainable development -, tries to impose changes on the existing multilateral mechanisms in order to make them "more balanced", as if they were in fact decision-making bodies. Sometimes the South chooses, to put it mildly, doubtful ways of self-expression. The initial opposition of an important number of developing countries to the indefinite prolongation of the Nuclear Non-Proliferation Treaty (NPT), for example, resulted only in mutual frustration and suspicion. Another example of wrongly designed tactics is a crusade to reform the United Nations with the declared aim to make it more democratic.

A stable international security is a cherished baby of the politically "big" powers. They still need to get used to the situation where nobody really (except for themselves, perhaps) is challenging that stability. Still in the mood of dedicated warriors they suspiciously regard the world map looking for a potential troublemaker—sometimes such "bad guys" appear in the personality of dictator rulers and then all the powerful machine of international ostracism is directed against them. But one or two dictators are not a formidable enough challenge. The theories of "islamic nuclear danger" or of "an international terrorist plot" look far more attractive. They could be used as an excellent excuse to continue or even increase the military expenditures of the Cold War days.

In other words, mutual misunderstanding and misperception generate an atmosphere of tension. To avoid further aggravation which may develop into a new line of division the modern international community needs a cooperative strategy. The North must accept the diversity of the world and the impossibility of isolating itself from the problems of the South however unpleasant they may appear. The South for its part must acknowledge that its destiny mainly depends on its own and on an optimum combination of political and economic reforms.

In practical terms this will mean stimulation of the development of the politically, economically and socially sound societies. Tough recommendations imposed on the developing countries result in many cases in a total neglect of the social aspects. The aim should not be an impeccable budget or financial stabilisation. The Mexican crisis taught a hard lesson: financial stability and economic growth are extremely fragile unless they are accompanied by an adequate political and social environment. The main threat is coming not from the absence of any economic results. Nowadays, with the exception of Africa, practically the entire developing world is in a rather dynamic economic trend. But the spectacular growth of GNP still does not allow to consider them as developed countries, since they continue to face the same or even worse social problems they had 20 or 30 years ago.

The final objective of the cooperation strategy should be the development of civic societies in the developing countries, having modern and stable democratic political systems, human-oriented economics and predictable foreign policies. Achievement of this goal demands however resources, not only financial but also political and moral. The models of societal organisation should not be imposed, but grown taking full account of specific national and cultural traditions.

The adherence to the commonly shared ideals of the civic society would help to engender a better mutual understanding or even a solidarity irrespective of cultural differences. And despite the inevitable conflicts of national interests an emergence of a new dividing line can be avoided.

Peter Anyang' Nyong'o

THE CHALLENGE OF NATIONAL LEADERSHIP AND DEMOCRATIC CHANGE IN KENYA

Introduction

It has been painful, almost heartbreaking, to realise that Kenyans may be moving to a permanently cynical attitude that no politician can rise above his or her ethnic limits. This is particularly so since the young generation of politicians, particularly some of the "Young Turks", may finally be revealing to Kenyans what they really are: simple run of the mill Kenyan politicians.

Following the recent acrimony in the Kenyan mass media, it is difficult to argue against this cynical attitude. Yet if some of us do not analyze the situation and explain to Kenyans what is going on, we shall be failing in our duty. I still do believe that there are genuine nationalists among us—but I may be frightfully mistaken. I believe that democratic change is still on the agenda if we have committed national leaders.

First, I think it is wrong to make a general statement that no politician can rise beyond ethnic prominence to become a genuinely national leader with a national outlook in day-to-day politics. Thomas Joseph Mboya was one such leader, so was Ronald Gideon Ngala, Joe Murumbi, Argwings Kodhek and Josiah Mwangi Kariuki—Jaramogi Oginga Odinga still stands out as an eminent nationalist—always ready to take principled stands even when they go against the popular sentiments among the Luo people who propelled him to national leadership. Such was the case in the S.M. Otieno saga.

Second, national outlook in politics, though partly a subjective quality cultivated by an individual who has certain intellectual and philosophical views of the world, is also a function of the objective and material conditions under which politicians—as ordinary human beings—operate.

We are all born into one ethnic community or the other; there is very little we can do about this. We speak our mother tongue, sing our music, quite often marry into our ethnic group and finally stand for Parliament where we are known best. These are objective conditions which can only change through a long historical process. There is very little we can do to change them through our subjective willpower even if we wanted to. And were we to do so, not all of them can be changed at once. These objective and material conditions will usually require some conscious effort on the part of all of us to respect cultural differences and to realise that being different does not make any of us superior or inferior to the others.

Third, let me emphasize that it is much easier to be an ethnic chauvinist than a nationalist in Kenyan politics today. Why? Because since 1970, Kenyan politics has been organised unashamedly on ethnic lines. Yet true leadership comes not from conforming to easy options but from confronting difficult ones. When the Kenya People's Union (KPU) was formed in 1966, it included among its ranks politicians from all parts of Kenya: Oginga Odinga, Bildad Kaggia, Munyua Waiyaki, Oduya Oprong, J.D. Kaliand and many others. Through state repression and fear-mongering, the Kenyatta regime deliberately turned some away from opposition politics tempting them with easy options; KANU then projected the image that the KPU was simply a Luo affair.

The cost of being a nationalist

This allegation was never tested in an open democratic election. In the meantime, access to resources and positions of power were denied those who gave the KPU political support, the government thereby began to entrench the tribalisation of Kenyan politics. Without an opposition political party to check the behaviour of the government in the 1970s, powerful Kikuyu politicians used their closeness to Kenyatta to enrich themselves using the state machinery. A few others from other ethnic groups also benefited. J.M. Kariuki opposed this; he was murdered in cold blood. Koigi wa Wam were openly criticized this ethnic economic chauvinism; he was run out of the Rift Valley into detention. Ngugi wa Thiongo was vociferous in his writings against these betrayers of the national cause; he was sent to learn good manners in detention. Micere Mugo mobilised the youth to resist this culture of ethnic greed; she could never sleep peacefully in her house. In other words, it was very difficult for a Kikuyu to be a Kenyan nationalist in those days when the likes of Kihika Kirnani were the supremos in politics. It was much easier to succumb and join "the cheering crowd" who saw it as the opportunity for the House of Mumbi to eat. Yet a few, like Micere Mugo, resisted and stood for their principles. It was not easy, but they did resist and paid dearly for it in terms of material comfort, job security and even personal health.

Right from the beginning of this regime, Moi knew that his greatest opponents were GEMA leaders. He dismantled GEMA as an organization, put its leaders into disarray through the politics of "carrot and stick" and started to mobilise the other ethnic elites behind him on an anti-GEMA platform. To replace GEMA chauvinism, he introduced an anti-GEMA chauvinism—following "Nyayo". Within no time, state corporations were being defrauded of billions of Kenyan shillings to enrich a small Kalenjin elite—and their political touts—around Moi's presidency. It again became much easier to become a Nyayo follower than to criticize this wanton rape of the Kenyan economy to enrich a few individuals just because others did so under Kenyatta! Sick logic, isn't it? Bishop Alexsander Kipsang Muge opposed tills and ended his life in a mysterious car accident. Robert Ouko's murder is a puzzle yet to be explained.

An all powerful President is undemocratic

When FORD was formed, our hope was that we could take state power and use that power to transform the political culture of this nation on democratic lines. First, it is because we have a highly centralized Presidential system of government that competition for the presidency—seen as the centre for dishing out wealth and resources to the ethnic group which captures it—becomes so vicious. If the power of the President is reduced and dispersed by strengthening other institutions like Parliament, the Public Service Commission, the National Investments Commission and so on, people will not be so crazy about who becomes the President. If we have a President as Head of State, a Prime Minister as Head of Government and a Vice President as heir apparent to the President, the centre of power will be so diversified that no one ethnic group would hold others hostage to the whims of its chauvinists because "it has the presidency". If the President, the Vice President and the Prime Minister held office for a fixed term of six years and the President is not allowed to run for another term, people would take turns and a fairer system of access to power would exist. If jobs and resources were distributed rationally by public institutions and not by one man sitting in State House, there would be a fairer system which all Kenyans would learn to respect and not fear as they do the presidency today.

National convention and constitutional reform

Second, if the Constitution is changed and the Rule of Law more systematically observed, we shall have less room for tribal or chauvinistic politics. For example, our electoral system is all wrong. Single constituency representation can easily lead to a minority government ruling this country after a multi-party election. As it was said during the "Nairobi We Want" Convention, we also need proportional representation. This is why some of us have been calling for a National Convention to give Kenyans the opportunity to air their views about this "Kenya We Want", but do not have. We shall then talk about the institutions and processes that will promote a national outlook among Kenyan politicians and in the Kenyan political establishment, as opposed to the present peddling of ethnic fears as a basis for making political coalitions and alliances. After all, constitutions are products of conscious political and social engineering, national aspirations, cultural ideals and historical possibilities in the evolution of society. What we have now as a constitution embraces burdens from our past; we are under no obligation to bear these burdens indefinitely.

Individuals and social groups who are beneficiaries of these burdens that we bear will of necessity be opposed to the National Convention Idea. They will cite all kinds of legal technicalities, constitutional bottlenecks and what have you. The word "convention" is a noun derived from the English verb "to convene", which means to come together to discuss something—of a political, religious, cultural or economic nature. A group can also convene simply to celebrate.

But when we are calling for a National Convention, we need to state what form it will take, how it will be organized, who will attend, its agenda and the extent to which its decisions will be binding on society, the government, Parliament, etc. The fact that we are not yet clear about these issues does not mean that calling for a National Convention to discuss "The Kenya We Want" is a futile exercise. It is even a greater demonstration of logical inaptitude to oppose the National Convention idea "because it is not provided for in the Constitution" as the Attorney General would want us to believe. The Constitution guarantees freedom of assembly and of expression; it thereby guarantees the freedom to convene and discuss, recommend, propose or suggest constitutional changes necessary for the "Kenya We Want". In any case, the process towards a National Convention had already been started last year, under the chairmanship of Bishop Henry Okullu at the Second Symposium in Limuru. A Working Committee, of which I was a member, drew up plans for a National Convention. Those documents are still valid.

Ethnic caucuses can be a drawback

I do not think that our problems as a nation can be solved by political formulas worked out by elite politicians caucusing on a purely ethnic agenda. Whatever ethnic gains were made under both Presidents Kenyatta and Moi, no proper redress can be carried out by installing yet another President who will simply ensure that—his people eat—while he is in power. A more frightening project is that of people wanting to resume where they left when Moi came into the picture! That is why it is very important that we identify as our national leaders people who are truly ready for qualitative change and democratization. These people should be true in word and deed. The word comes in the way they address national problems; the deed comes in their political life as we Kenyans know them.

Transparency, leadership and sacrifice

All of us in the forefront of Kenyan politics today must therefore be ready for a great deal of scrutiny by the public. Some harsh words will be spoken against us—some fairly and some totally unfounded. But we must be prepared to put up with the difficult question that Jesus posed to Peter and John: "can you be baptized with the baptism with which I am baptized?"—Can we be prepared to work voluntarily for the nation, to seek to do good, and yet to be subjected to the most scathing criticism by the same public as Jesus was? Can we struggle so hard to bring about multi-party politics and yet be deprived of the material comfort that it has brought some people who, by mid last year, thought they would go into exile when FORD comes into power?

We should not be angry; we should not chew our insides with regret. We should be happy that the process of change has started; a revolution is in the offing. Like all revolutions, it can also suffer from a counterrevolution turning the clock back. We have both forces at play now—the forces of change are trying to forge ahead against a strong wall of resistance from those who would like to turn the clock back. With enormous resources at his disposal, Moi is the standard bearer of these reactionary forces. They lure, they cajole, they frighten, they blackmail and they even appease those opposed to them.

Democratization a process, not an event

The forces of change must be strong. We must see the struggle for democracy as a process not an event; a long marathon relay race and not a sprint. We must therefore espouse more the goals and ideals we set ourselves at the beginning and not the social recognition and material comfort that might have followed accession to public office had we won the elections. In any case, by sticking to that which is right, upholding the good, promoting justice and supporting the afflicted, we shall get social recognition from the right quarters: from the ordinary Kenyan people who are very badly hit by inflation, corruption, mismanagement and the arrogance of power the *wapende wasipende* (whether they like it or not) syndrome in the Kenyan Government.

Are Kenyans "salt lickers"?

It may take months to get there, but we must continue using every opening that the democratization process gives us. We must not be adventurous; nor should we think that qualitative changes only come as a result of certain apocalyptic events. History shows us that strikes, civil disobedience, demonstrations and other forms of insurrection can bring qualitative change only if they are part and parcel of a process set in motion by a social movement resident in the womb of people not merely imagined in the minds of some elites.

One reality that we shall have to accept about the Kenyan masses is that they can easily be detracted from an important national political agenda by being made "to lick salt". The Moi regime has perfected this art; some of Moi's erstwhile critics inadvertently follow his footsteps by creating salt licks for their followers very much away from the track on which the race for democratization is being run. What do I mean?

Those of us who have looked after cattle know very well that cattle love salt; all herbivores do. But though no herbivore will pass a salt lick without stopping, it is a foolish herdsman who sends his cattle to the lick first thing in the morning; salt is to cattle what pudding is to man. It is not the main food; it is a supplement.

The reason why I say Kenyans can easily be detracted from the national political agenda by being made to lick salt is that they can be persuaded that an isolated job given to one of their kind brings them "development" rather than the lengthy struggle for democratization whose outcome is still uncertain. A few leaders whose loans are paid off by the incumbent regime will easily abandon opposition politics since "their problems have been solved".

No main meal; just salt-licking, and Moi will win them back one after the other. This is the counterrevolution referred to earlier. What can we do about it?

Bad leadership breeds bad people

Let us not moan about it, nor should it turn us into cynics. But let us recognise it for what it is: part and parcel of the political sickness of this nation following two or so decades of retrograde, corrupt and inept political rule. When people in public office espouse no principles, aspire to no ideals, excel in nothing but immorality and maintain power by repression and not popular consent, one must expect some sheep-like behaviour from the oppressed and dehumanized.

To overcome these pitfalls in the national conscience of our people we must continue to be determined in our struggle to democratize society. We must always be resolute to achieve our goals of decency, justice, respect for human rights, government by rule of law and not presidential arbitrariness and a dignified and free nation. We must be determined; we must be resolute.

Determination is our strength against corruption

Determination is always the source of strength in any movement for social change; and resoluteness always the essence of struggle. But our determination and resoluteness for progressive change in Kenya is being hampered by corruption. Corruption is the scourge of the Kenyan nation. It comes in many forms. It can be blatant but it can also be subtle. What is obvious, however, is that it has led to the wastage and misuse of our resources—natural, human, financial and managerial. State corporations are the worst offenders in corruption. They are rotten to the core.

This nation cannot be left to be ruined by corrupt politicians and government officials forever. We must be determined to fight corruption so that Kenya can develop. Without the Goldenbergs of this world, there would be no need for Structural Adjustment Programmes—there would be no inflation either. A corrupt government cannot organize or run democratic elections. A corrupt government cannot keep any decent promise on the face of this earth.

That is why the Moi government has cheated this nation throughout its very disappointing period in power.

But we cannot fight corruption successfully if we do not have lawmaking and law enforcement systems which are free from corruption. Those of us in politics must organize our political parties well.

What does it mean to belong to a party?

It means you are party to something. In FORD-Kenya, we are party to the principles and ideals stated in our Manifesto, the Charter for the Second Liberation. That is what makes us different from other political parties. We must practice those principles. We must fight corruption at any time. We must fight the major enemy—the Moi regime. We must not fight among ourselves however self-righteous an individual feels. We can correct contradictions among ourselves within the party.

Leadership

When you are a member of a party, you must accept to be led. Good leadership always stands out—because it is by example and humility: it is not bulldozed. A good leader accepts he is wrong when he makes a mistake. A good leader is an open and not a closed person. You cannot be a bully and expect to lead the masses. You must be an accessible person, and a person who listens to the high and mighty, as well as the low and humble.

Our opposition political parties in Kenya today are bedeviled with "too many stars who do not want to get off the screen. We have a problem which sophisticated English calls the primadonna syndrome; i.e. those who feel they are leadership material want to lead all at once—none of them wants to follow the other. They don't even want to recognize historical facts and the popular mood, both of which are important in shaping the circumstances under which a particular leader emerges.

Nobody among the primadonnas seems to want to deny himself, take up his cross and follow the mission of liberating this country from political oppression and economic exploitation. This is the key issue today. It will still remain the key issue tomorrow with Moi as the President, Saitoti as the Vice President, Biwott wielding power everywhere and the KANU establishment as firm as the mimosa tree.

There is work to be done. Let's do it—now!

III. Africa's Development Challenge

Chief Emeka Anyaoku

THE IMAGE OF AFRICA

In contributing to this book I do so on two main counts. Firstly, I pay tribute to General Obasanjo's contribution to African progress in our time. In particular, I wish to recognize his exemplary legacy to political development in Africa as the first, and so far only, military head of state to voluntarily relinquish power and return his country to a democratically elected government.

I want also to pay tribute to General Obasanjo's contribution to Commonwealth affairs. As Co-Chairman of the Commonwealth Eminent Persons Group to South Africa in 1986, he played an important role in reinforcing international pressure on apartheid South Africa which ultimately accelerated the progress towards a multiracial democracy in that country.

The continent is engulfed by economic collapse, war, famine, AIDS and malaria which may bury hopes of freedom, peace and prosperity—that was the picture of Africa painted by a London quality newspaper on 29 July 1991. And it is the way you might come to think if you relied solely on the general image purveyed by what Lord Jock Campbell once aptly described as VIPs—Very Itinerant Pundits—who generally depict Africa, especially black Africa, as an area of economic and environmental disaster, a land of instability and dictatorship. That view is far from being the whole truth. But, like any myth, it is not wholly wrong either. Let me explain.

It is of course true that most of the period since African countries achieved their independence has been marked by a great deal of political upheaval including no less than 40 attempted and successful military coups d'etat. In a number of cases, the upheaval has ended in outright civil war, conflicts some of which are still in progress. The consequences in places such as Ethiopia, Somalia and Sudan have been disastrous in creating thousands of refugees and worsening the effect of nature-induced famines.

But it is equally true that the projection of Africa in the Eurocentric world as a region of stagnation if not outright retrogression is based essentially on historical prejudice. There is nothing new in notions of racial superiority of this kind. The Greeks, we all know, looked down on the Romans and everyone else as lesser beings. The Romans in their turn took a similarly exalted view of themselves and their civilisation in relation to the Britons, the Gauls and other subject peoples. And it remained so down to the European conquest of the 19th century and the resulting Eurocentric world view in which Europeans appeared as the lords of human kind.

The point is made in a very telling manner by the historical evolution of the word "barbarian". According to the Shorter Oxford English Dictionary, the word first meant a non-Greek; then later a non-Roman; and when these two supremacies vanished, it came to designate a non-Christian and later still, in the age of the Renaissance, a non-Italian.

But where the prejudice of the ancients stemmed largely from ignorance, that of our modern pundits stems in the main from a mixture of motives, not the least of which is a reluctance to acknowledge that, for all its afflictions, independent Africa has some achievements to its credit and is working even in inauspicious circumstances to secure its future. There is more to Africa than wars and famines. However real the present difficulties, there are good grounds for Africa's hopes of freedom, peace and prosperity.

The socioeconomic achievements of independent Africa tend to be overlooked in the interest of sensational reporting. The extent of the achievements can be seen by comparing the position at independence with the position in subsequent years using the usual indicators of the quality of life. In the field of education, for example, only a very small percentage of the population could read and write. In places such as Niger, Mali, Sierra Leone and Senegal, to name a few, as many as 80 per cent of adults could neither read nor write. From this poor foundation, Africa set out to win the war against illiteracy. By 1985 the situation had improved considerably with the result that the number of adults who could read and write had risen to 48 per cent. This improvement was particularly marked in countries like Nigeria, Ghana, Tanzania and Botswana.

The achievement was even more remarkable in the education of women. Again, let me mention one or two figures. In 1970 only 17 per cent of adult women could read and write in Sub-Saharan Africa, i.e. black Africa as a whole. By 1985, the number had increased to 38 per cent. In some cases, the increases were quite dramatic. For example, in the same period, the number of women who could read and write from 18 per cent to 88 per cent in Tanzania; from 47 per cent to 77 per cent in Zimbabwe and from 44 per cent to 69 per cent in Botswana.

Another area where independent Africa has made great strides but which is not often reflected in much of what we read in non-African publications is public health. At independence, the infant mortality rate was generally very high—284 children out of every thousand died before the age of five. In some cases, the rate was in excess of 350 per thousand. However, this depressing picture steadily changed for the better in the years following independence. By 1988, the infant mortality rate had fallen by more than 100 per thousand in many countries, including Burkina Faso, Benin, Malawi, Nigeria, Cameroon, Zambia and Gabon.

Even in the more difficult area of economic growth, there have been notable advances. Between 1965 and 1973—that is before the onset of the oil crisis—a number of African countries experienced an average annual growth rate of over 4 per cent. These included Malawi, Kenya, Lesotho, Côte d'Ivoire, the Congo and Gabon. A few averaged even higher growth rates. Nigeria registered an annual growth rate of 5.3 per cent, Swaziland 5.8 per cent and Botswana a staggering 9.3 per cent.

For most African countries, this period of economic buoyancy came to a close at the end of the 1970s, by a crisis which continues to this day. Rising prices of oil and manufactured imports, the continuing fall in commodity prices and, not least, mistaken policies in the past, are the principal reasons for Africa's economic crisis. But I do not want to dwell on this. Let me instead spell out briefly what Africans themselves have been doing to climb out of the economic through.

The economic crisis led to a serious rethinking of the development paths which African countries had hitherto followed and which had contributed to their present predicament. It was generally agreed that these past policies and strategies had resulted in unfulfilled promises and that far from advancing Africa, they had in some cases made it even more vulnerable to external pressures. So when African leaders met at their Lagos summit in 1980, they decided that the realistic way out of their problems lay in the adoption of what they called "a far-reaching regional approach based primarily on collective self-reliance". By this they meant promoting through regional groups a greater degree of trade and economic cooperation among African countries.

Already a number of regional economic groupings had emerged: the Economic Community of West African States in West Africa (ECOWAS) in 1975, the Southern African Development Coordination Conference (SADCC) in 1980; and the Preferential Trade Area for Eastern, Central and Southern African States (PTA) in 1981. It was accordingly decided at the Lagos meeting that these regional economic organisations would form what one might call the building blocs for a pan-African common market. The next major step in this journey was taken in June 1991 at the last Summit of the Organisation of African Unity (OAU) held in Nigeria's new capital city of Abuja. At Abuja, African leaders signed a treaty establishing an African Common Market to come into force early in the next century.

There are of course those who see precious little that is new in these emerging economic groupings. Such people point to the fact that, in colonial days, the continent was more integrated economically than it has been since. Such critics either forget or conveniently ignore the fact that the old, regional arrangements were intended to meet the needs and demands of a different epoch and a different order which invariably tied Africa's economic life to the needs of the governing European metropolis. Independence created its own needs which had to be met in new ways.

Colonialism in Africa was essentially a process that began with carving-up and dividing the continent at the 1884/85 Berlin Conference. The consequent horse-trading by the European colonial powers paid little regard to Africa's old national or ethnic loyalties. As a result of this, the pressing priority after independence was to build the political unity of the continent on the basis of the new political boundaries. It was also clear that to pursue an active policy of regional integration before Africa's new nations had experienced their newly won independence and sovereignty would have ended in chaos. In Africa as elsewhere, nationalism had to come before internationalism; independence before interdependence. Indeed, it is because the current policy of African economic integration has been allowed to grow out of a common acknowledgement of its necessity, that we have the best assurance of its viability.

In the meantime, no less than 40 African countries are undertaking far-reaching domestic economic reforms or economic restructuring. These reforms are being pursued in the face of considerable difficulties. I have already referred to the problem of the continuing fall in commodity prices. For example, at the time of independence a country like Tanzania need to produce and sell 7 tons of sisal in order to buy one tractor from Europe; seven years later, the same tractor required 35 tons of sisal for its purchase. For African commodity producers—and most African countries are commodity producers—this means producing and selling more and more for less and less by way of economic return. And now these huge disadvantages are made worse by competition from Eastern and Central Europe for the available international investment capital.

Structural adjustment usually entails great hardships for the population at large but especially so for the disadvantaged and the vulnerable. To sustain structural adjustment programmes therefore calls for considerable political courage; and the fact that the great majority of African governments have nonetheless sustained the programmes shows an unwavering resolve to come to grips with their economic problems. Those who decry Africa's economic performance would do well to bear these considerations in mind.

What of the recurrent coups, wars, abuses of human rights and other afflictions which are said to threaten Africa's hopes of peace and prosperity? The extent to which Africans are determined to realise their hopes of peace and prosperity is often not adequately reflected in the international media, some of which occasionally imply that the continent might benefit from a new round of management from abroad. We must never forget that, whatever its apparent practical benefits, colonial rule, by the nature of human history and experience, had to come to an end. The job of developing the continent had ultimately to be undertaken by Africans and on African terms. In this connection, it was always clear to all Africans of sense that making a reality of independence would be no easy task. That is why in spite of all the coups and civil conflicts, nowhere in Africa have people sought or will ever seek the return of colonial rule. Instead, the clamour was for independence and is now for multi-party democracy in which there will be genuine popular participation and effective checks against abuse of power.

In the past year alone, the cause of multi-party democracy has gained considerable ground. In more than 15 countries, including Angola, Mozambique, Nigeria, Zambia, Sierra Leone, Togo, Côte d'Ivoire, to name some of the more prominent examples, multi-party politics has either been restored and elections held or preparations for the return of multi-party politics have been far advanced. Some commentators have attributed this resurgence of the democratic movement in Africa to developments in Eastern and Central Europe. It is simplistic to suggest that it is the breakdown of Communism in Europe that has inspired Africans to campaign for multi-party democracy. The rejection of one-party or military rule in Africa is wholly an internal African judgment on 30 years of Africa's history since Independence.

Another noteworthy dimension of the new democratic movement in Africa is that it has in most cases not been driven by elite groups merely wanting their own turn to control state power. In many cases, the movement has been started by trade unions, as was the case in Zambia, or by students, as happened in places like Côte d'Ivoire and Benin. In these instances the students and trade unions alike had no difficulty in enlisting opposition to one-party rule and support for democracy among armies of the unemployed especially in urban and industrial areas. Africa-wide, a number of grassroot organisations such as the Sudan Council of Voluntary Agencies, the Ghana Federation of Business and Professional Women, the All African Conference of Churches in Kenya and the Tanzania Environmental Society have helped to shape the agenda of the pro-democracy movement.

In February 1990, over 500 such grassroot organisations from all over Africa met in the Tanzanian city of Arusha under the auspices of the United Nations Economic Commission for Africa. Their deliberations identified the absence of democracy in Africa as being primarily responsible for the political and socioeconomic crisis of the continent and concluded that unless there was genuine popular participation in the running of society and economy, neither development nor transformation could be expected.

Whether from below or from above, there is a clear consensus in Africa on the essential need for democratisation in the interest of political stability and orderly socioeconomic development. There are now clear indications that, politically, something fundamental is taking place in Africa. It involves a clear break from the recent past and, all considered, is a great advance for democracy and decency. As in the case of the economic changes underway, the strength of this emerging political transformation lies in the way it has evolved—not imposed from outside but grown naturally and organically from within.

Africans are only too well aware of the enormity of the tasks before them. They know that democracy is a desirable goal; but they also know how exceedingly difficult it is to secure, especially in countries made up of different and long-established ethnic groups. Similarly, they know that while real improvement to their economic condition must ultimately depend on their own efforts, they cannot hope to succeed if they have to contend at the same time with such hostile external factors as having to service a crippling debt burden; earning less and less from exporting the commodities on which their economies depend; and having to suffer steadily worsening terms of external trade.

But whether it is politics or economics, Africans approach their afflictions with the optimism and the conviction of a happy outcome. That is why they are eager for non-African commentators, especially those in the Eurocentric world, to interpret and project Africa's circumstances with greater objectivity and less condescension and despondency than is generally the case. Africans ask for no favours in the reporting of their affairs. They ask, for example, that civil wars and other human tragedies in Africa should not invoke vocabulary that is different from that used for similar tragedies elsewhere such as describing the casualties of European civil wars as being "killed" while those of African civil wars are being "slaughtered".

To sum up, all that Africans ask for is that their strengths and weaknesses should be viewed and interpreted with the same degree of realism and understanding as is applied to other peoples and regions of the world. After all, we should not forget that all human life began some four million years ago in Africa.

Robert S. McNamara

SUB-SAHARAN AFRICA'S DEVELOPMENT CRISIS[1]

No African statesman has done more to try to stimulate other African leaders to address the fundamental economic and social problems of their nations—particularly the problems of the most disadvantaged—than General Olusegun Obasanjo. And yet, as my statement below indicates, there is much more to be done by all of us. I submit the statement in honor of Olu—a man I admire immensely—on his 60th birthday.

Sub-Saharan Africa is heading towards an inevitable tragedy. And no one can prevent such an outcome except the African leaders themselves.

Much has been written about the growing marginalization of the region in recent years. The evidence is grim. Among all the areas of the world, Sub-Saharan Africa has the lowest life expectancy, the lowest literacy rate, the highest infant mortality, and the highest population growth rate. Nearly one-half of the region's population lives below the poverty line. The story of the area's growing economic marginalization has been told so often—and in such graphic detail—that I need not belabor the point.

What is more disturbing, however, is the fact that, in many respects and certainly relatively, the situation is getting worse, not better. Over the last three decades, the share of Sub-Saharan Africa has fallen from around 2 per cent of global GNP in 1960 to around 1 per cent in 1990; in global trade, the share has declined from 4 per cent to 1 per cent during the same period. Throughout the 1980s, per capita income has declined in 19 African countries[2]. In several countries—such as Cote d'Ivoire, Gabon, Niger and Nigeria—per capita income in 1990 was only one-half to three-quarters of what it was ten years earlier. Can one imagine the depths of human despair when wholly inadequate incomes fall to about half of their previous levels and when there is little prospect of a significant increase during the next decade? In fact, the latest estimates of the World Bank show that, even on fairly optimistic assumptions, Sub-Saharan Africa will not reach by the year 2000 its per capita income level of even 1980 —miserable as it was.

We are already witnessing the slow descent of the region into social confusion and political anarchy. Several countries are beginning to disintegrate from within. Ethnic and regional conflicts are erupting as fierce battles develop over declining incomes, diminishing jobs and reduced socio-economic opportunities. In the last three years, there were at least ten domestic conflicts within Africa, each lending to more than 1,000 deaths. Somalias and Rwandas are only an early warning of the events yet to unfold—unless we act in time.

And the real action lies in the hands of the African leadership. It is convenient to find an external alibi for every internal problem of Africa today. It is tempting to recall the injustices of colonialism, the brutality of the slave trade, the dark shadows of a receding past. It is easy to suggest that more liberal doses of foreign assistance will turn around the economic destiny of Africa. But let me say as a friend of Africa, as someone who feels the African tragedy deep in his bones: none of this will be determinative. African problems are structural ones. And they require African solutions.

The first task before the African policy makers is to recognize that it is only they who can rescue Africa from its current dilemmas. It would be courageous to admit that no one from outside obliges Angola, Somalia and Ethiopia to spend twice as much on arms as on the education and health of their people. They do it themselves. No one from outside forces Cameroon to lose more budgetary resources every year from the losses of its inefficient public enterprises than its total oil revenues. This is its own choice. And no one from outside orders Mali and Sierra Leone—two of the poorest nations of Africa—to spend over 80 per cent of their limited health budgets on urban hospitals rather than on primary health care. The decision is theirs.

It is time to be brutally frank with ourselves. African problems require courageous decisions within Africa. External alibis won't help. We are all anxious to mobilize worldwide financial support for African development. I have spent a great deal of my own energies and time on this effort. But all this is marginal in the overall context of Africa. No one can deliver an African turnaround from the outside. It requires fundamental reforms within the region.

Let me share with you a few of my ideas about the nature of these reforms, though I would reiterate that a workable plan can only emerge from African leaders themselves.

First, the rapid population growth rate in Sub-Saharan Africa must be slowed down. This growth rate was 2.8 per cent during 1960-92 and is expected to accelerate to 3.4 per cent during 1992-2000. A demanding target will be to reduce the average population growth rate to 2.2 per cent a year over the next 30 years. Even under this scenario, the population of Sub-Saharan Africa would be over 1.2 billion by 2020 and it would not level off much below 3 billion. Admittedly, a population growth rate of 2.2 per cent a year for the next 3 decades is ambitious. It would require a reduction in the total fertility rate from about 6.7 children per woman to 3.6 by 2025. This means that nearly 50 per cent of African married couples would then be using effective contraception instead of 15 per cent at present. It also means that all African leaders must quickly commit themselves to effective family planning programs. And they must also recognize that population growth is a development issue as well as a clinical problem. Any effective policy must create the underlying conditions for fertility decline—particularly expansion of basic education, especially for girls; economic independence of women; and rising income and employment levels.

Second, Sub-Saharan Africa needs substantial investment in human development. Of the 47 countries in the region, 41 are in the bottom half of the low human-development category, according to the UNDP's 1994 Human Development Report. About one-half of the adult population of Sub-Saharan Africa is illiterate. The mean years of schooling for adults above 25 years of age are only 1.6 years. The average life expectancy is only 51 years—24 years lower than in the industrial world. Most social indicators are a shocking reflection of the diminished value of human life.

There are no magic formulas to reverse this situation. It will take great patience, major financial investments and time. Overall, investment in social services must increase, it should be spent more efficiently, and most of it should be earmarked for basic services of primary health care, basic education, safe drinking water, essential family planning services and nutrition programs for the severely malnourished. Such expenditures are small at present. For instance, they are only US$2 per person per year in Tanzania and US$6 in Nigeria. All Sub-Saharan African countries should formulate long-term human development strategies and commit their political energies and financial resources to implementing those strategies.

Third, none of these investments, on the scale required, will be possible and no reforms will ever succeed unless the pace of economic growth is accelerated and the process of economic policy reform and adjustment continued. In everything from exchange rate management through investment in education and agriculture, the lessons of failed or inadequate policies in Africa stand out. One of the most telling indications of poor policy frameworks has been Africa's declining competitiveness in world markets. Certainly, the external environment has not been kind to Africa with the fall in commodity prices, oil shocks, high interest rates and so on. But a hostile external environment is not the main reason for Africa's poor economic performance. As shown in the table below, the region's disappointing GDP growth compared, for example, with growth in East Asia, has been associated with a very low level of domestic savings and a very low level of investment.

Per cent of GDP

	Africa	Asia	
Concessional aid (early '90s)	6-8%	1%	
Rate of investment ('88-'92)	17%	31%	
Domestic savings ('88-92)	14.5%	22%	(India)
Cumulative capital flight ('71-'90)	80%	15%	(S. Asia)
Income growth per capita per year ('88-'92)	-0.2%	+1.9%	(S. Asia)

In recent years, South Asian economies have been growing at nearly 2 per cent per capita per year, compared to Africa's -0.2 per cent. A major factor contributing to the higher Asian growth rate has been a rate of investment, as a percent of GDP, nearly twice the level of Africa. It is often said that Africa's low rate of investment is a function of inadequate flows of external financial assistance. But Africa, as a percent of GDP, has been receiving seven times as much external aid as Asia. Africa's investment problem can be traced to a totally inadequate domestic savings rate and inefficient use of its financial resources. India's domestic savings, as a percent of GDP, are about 50 per cent higher than the level in Africa. Even more disturbing, the incremental output generated by Africa's investment has dropped dramatically from 31 per cent of investment in the 1960s to 2.5 per cent in the 1980s.

To contribute to an increase in domestic savings, Africa must further reduce fiscal deficits. I am aware that there is a contentious debate going on today about the nature and content of structural adjustment programs in Africa and about the harsh conditionality of World Bank and IMF loans. I believe that there is considerable room for improvement on all sides. Why, after all, should budgets be balanced on the backs of the poor rather than on the backs of the rich? Why must food subsidies to the poor be cut ahead of interest and credit subsidies to rich landlords and industrialists? Why must education and health expenditures be slashed in preference to military expenditures? Who makes the final decisions? And when there is so much waste and corruption and inefficiency, does it require a genius to figure out how to move toward balancing national budgets without unbalancing the lives of poor people or future generations?

Fourth, I am deeply disturbed about the waste of scarce resources in many of the countries of Sub-Saharan Africa on high levels of military expenditure. This military spending has increased steadily from 0.7 per cent of their combined GNP in 1960 to 3.5 per cent by 1990. This is the only region where, during the last 30 years, the ratio of military spending to social spending has not declined but risen: from 27 per cent in 1960 to 43 per cent in 1990. Many of the poorer nations are spending large amounts on their armies rather than on their people. Three countries in the region—Angola (20 per cent), Ethiopia (13.5 per cent), and Mozambique (13 per cent) -- devote more than 10 per cent of their GDP to military expenditures, at a time when 3 million people face starvation in Angola, when 50 per cent of the population in Mozambique lives below the poverty line, and when nearly two-thirds of the population in Ethiopia does not have access to a simple basic necessity like safe drinking water. They are not alone in diverting funds from the poor to military establishments. According to the 1994 Human Development Report, Nigeria purchased 80 battle tanks from the UK in 1992 at a cost that could have immunized all of its 2 million unimmunized children and provided family planning services to nearly 17 million out of the 20 million couples who lack such services.

It is for African leadership to decide today what are the legitimate needs of their national security and what are the competing claims for their human security. The evidence from the past is clear. Those nations which spent too much on arms and too little on human development were neither able to protect their territorial security nor the welfare of their people. Somalia spent five times as much on its military as on education and health in 1980 and the international community added to the problem with external supplies of arms. On the other hand, Botswana invested only one-fifth as much in arms as in the education and health of its people. Today, its adult literacy rate is 75 per cent, its life expectancy 60 years, and its average GNP growth rate was over 6 per cent during 1980-92.

This is a time to move away from excessive expenditures on military establishments. In the post-cold war era, global military spending has been declining by nearly 4 per cent a year (i.e., since 1987). But the poorest region of the world, Sub-Saharan Africa, continues to spend over $8 billion a year on defense. A few years ago, an international study commission, chaired by Helmut Schmidt and including such senior officials as Pierre Trudeau and General Obasanjo, suggested that any poor country spending more than 2 per cent of its GNP on military should be penalized in aid allocations. Based on published data, such a policy would immediately affect 21 countries in Sub-Saharan Africa. It may be necessary to start with a more moderate goal and at a more gradual pace—but a start should be made. The international financial institutions should focus on this issue and make it a part of their policy dialogue. And the OECD nations should support the recent proposal of the Administrator of UNDP, Gus Speth, who has called for "a phasing out of all arms trade and military assistance to Africa over the next three years".

Fifth, let me mention briefly a spreading menace that does require defense, though of a different kind. I am referring to HIV/AIDS. According to the latest estimates, the cumulative number of HIV-infected people in the world is now around 15 million, of which 9 million (60 per cent) are in Sub-Saharan Africa. The rate at which AIDS is spreading in Africa can frustrate all our well-laid development plans. I mention this problem specifically since it is receiving so little effective attention in Africa. I believe that this is an avoidable tragedy if national and international policy makers devote sufficient attention to it at this stage.

Finally, let me turn to outside support for Africa. In focusing so much attention on the domestic agenda of reform in Africa, I do not mean to imply that continued external assistance is irrelevant. It is essential. But it will not be justified unless internal reforms are carried out simultaneously. In fact, in 13 Sub-Saharan countries, aid already represents more than 20 per cent of their GNP—namely, in Mozambique (115 per cent), São Tome and Principe (108 per cent), Guinea-Bissau (59 per cent), Equatorial Guinea (51 per cent), Tanzania (48 per cent), Cape Verde (42 per cent), Gambia (36 per cent), Zambia (30 per cent), Burundi (26 per cent), Uganda (23 per cent), Malawi (22 per cent), Ethiopia (20 per cent), Chad (20 per cent). But in none of these countries has it made a decisive difference. What has been decisive are the domestic policies.

While we must continue to ensure that the poor countries of Africa receive liberal amounts of concessional flows—along with appropriate debt rescheduling—it is important to emphasize again two fundamental points: First, aid is no substitute for trade: Sub-Saharan Africa is almost falling out of the world markets. With 10 per cent of the world population, Sub-Saharan Africa has less than 1 per cent share in global trade.

Sub-Saharan Africa must diversify its exports and improve its export competitiveness. At the same time, world markets must accommodate more of Africa's exports. Second, aid money must be more intelligently allocated and more efficiently spent. Donors should question whether it is wise to continue to allocate less than 10 per cent of their aid to human development in Sub-Saharan Africa when resources for human development constitute the region's greatest need. And they should consider, as well, whether it makes much sense to support, through technical assistance, 100,000 foreign experts in a region which in a 5 year period (1985-90) lost an estimated 60,000 of its own technicians by emigration, for want of adequate opportunities at home.

Let me conclude with by emphasizing again the theme of my remarks: There is no dearth of analysis today on what ails Africa. Many scholarly treatise have been written. Many professional reports have been prepared. What is missing is a political commitment on the part of many of the leaders of Africa—a recognition that it is their responsibility to turn their countries around to move them from a specter of impending tragedy to a story of hopeful change. If they step forward—with courage and decisiveness—I believe the international community will support their every step. That certainly is my hope—and my prayer.

---

[1] I am grateful to Mahbub ul Haq, Special Advisor to the Administrator of UNDP, for assistance in preparing the text and tables of this contribution.
[2] I will use Africa and Sub-Saharan Africa interchangeably in this text.

Per Pinstrup-Andersen

FOOD SECURITY IN SUB-SAHARAN AFRICA

This paper is a tribute to General Olusegun Obasanjo for his great contributions to the promotion of agricultural development and reduction of food insecurity in Africa and in the world. Among many such contributions, only one will be mentioned here: His constructive and effective participation as a member in the International Advisory Committee of the 2020 Vision Initiative for Food, Agriculture, and the Environment. The Initiative benefited greatly from his vision, wisdom, and dedication to the cause of alleviation of food insecurity, malnutrition, and other human misery.

Introduction

Food insecurity and malnutrition is widespread in Sub-Saharan Africa. About 200 million people, which is about one-third of the population, are reported to be food insecure and 30 million of Sub-Saharan Africa's preschool children are underweight. There were almost 10 million more underweight preschool children in 1990 than in 1980 despite only a marginal increase in prevalence rates, a vivid reminder of the population dynamics in this region. Projections indicate that the number of food insecure may increase to 300 million by 2010.

Sub-Saharan Africa produced considerably less food per capita at the end of the 1980s than at the beginning and net cereal imports account for about 25 per cent of total cereal availability in 1988-90.

Agriculture's poor performance matched the overall economic performance as reflected in an annual decrease of about one percent in per capita incomes during the decade of the 1980s. Yields of major food crops remain substantially lower in this region than elsewhere. Area expansion has thus far been a major source of growth in agricultural production; during the 1980s, there was a 28 per cent increase in area under cereals in Africa, but only a 12 per cent increase in yields. As cultivable land becomes more and more scarce and as the economic and environmental costs of expanding into marginal land rise, yield increases will have to be the major source of agricultural expansion. Already, an estimated 22 per cent of Africa's vegetated land suffers from human-induced soil degradation, half of which is caused by overgrazing and another quarter by agricultural activities. While some yield increases have been obtained for maize, the other important staples in Sub-Saharan Africa have experienced little or no yield improvements in recent years. Despite its poor overall performance, agriculture remains a very important sector in the region, contributing about one-third of the GDP and employing about 75 per cent of the labor force.

Development strategy and assistance

If Sub-Saharan Africa is to overcome its poverty, food insecurity, and malnutrition in a sustainable manner, national governments must make this the overriding goal of development and industrialized countries and international assistance agencies must make a long-term commitment to the transfer of resources to the region over and above those needed to deal with emergencies.

Eradicating food insecurity in Africa must be the central pillar of development efforts. There is no easy or inexpensive way to do it. It will take much time and money and solutions designed for local problems and conditions. Famines, food insecurity, and poverty are manifestations of collective failures that have complex origins and require complex solutions.

Famine and food insecurity are not just humanitarian concerns, they are development issues. The conceptual wall between relief and development must be breached. Famine intervention often costs as much as long-term development initiatives and divert resources that could be better used for these long-term efforts.

In the long run, eradication of hunger and the threat of famine will result from successful development, as opposed to relief, activities. This requires programmes that raise incomes and alleviate poverty for the most vulnerable, or famine-prone, groups. It is the failure of national governments and donors to allocate resources toward sustainable poverty alleviation in Africa that is the reason for existing food insecurity and the continued resurgence of famine.

Designing and implementing a strategy for broad-based sustainable growth and development requires national capacity that is in short supply in most countries of the region. Although donors paid much lip service to the need for strengthening such national capacities during the 1980s, very little external assistance was provided for such purposes. Instead, donors occupied an increasing role in national decision-making through the specification of conditionalities for obtaining assistance. At the same time, reduced project financing resulted in less technical assistance previously tied to the design and implementation of development projects. Conditionalities imposed from outside the country may be justified to get access to external assistance and to correct externalities including political economy factors adverse to the poor. But they are very poor substitutes for effective national capabilities to design and implement sound development strategies and policies.

The role of the state

While it is clear that the state has played an inappropriate and excessive role in the economies of most countries in the region, it does not follow that the state has no role to play in the future. On the contrary, the state has an extremely important role to play to facilitate effective and efficient private-sector activities, including agricultural input and output markets, and to assure investment in the production of public goods. Failure to recognize the new role of the public sector and strengthen its capacity to execute this role within the African reality could possibly be as costly for the poor as past excessive and inappropriate activities of the state. Relying exclusively on the private sector and leaving the market to its own devises in countries with very poor infrastructure, inappropriate institutions, and underdeveloped human resources is a prescription for disaster based on lack of understanding of the conditions necessary for markets to operate efficiently and justly.

Future national development strategies and related external assistance should place high priority on identifying the appropriate roles of the public sector during the adjustment period and beyond and on the strengthening of the capacity of the public sectors in Sub-Saharan Africa to identify and assume such roles. This does not imply an increase in the size of the public sector. Rather, it recognizes the importance of the state to support and facilitate a development model based on the private sector by identifying what the public sector should and should not do.

In most countries of Sub-Saharan Africa, accelerated investments in the creation of public goods are essential for broad-based development, which in turn is essential (although not usually sufficient) for sustainable alleviation of poverty, food insecurity, and malnutrition. Such investments are urgently needed to create and maintain rural infrastructure such as roads and transportation infrastructure, financial institutions, and information; and to enhance primary education, primary health care, family planning, nutrition, and other measures to enhance the human resources. Investments in human resources are justified both on their immediate welfare effects and the longer-term productivity effects.

The role of agriculture and agricultural research

Agriculture is central to economic growth and development, particularly in the least developed countries. Agricultural growth and development must be vigorously pursued in Sub-Saharan Africa and supported by external assistance for at least three reasons:
- to successfully and in a self-sustaining manner alleviate poverty through employment creation and income generation in rural areas, which is where the majority

of the poor are located;
- to meet the growing food needs and fill the widening food gap driven by rapid population growth and urbanization; and
- to stimulate overall economic growth.

In most of the Sub-Saharan African countries, agriculture is the most viable lead sector for growth and development and most of the countries are unlikely to experience acceptable rates of overall economic growth without first or simultaneously experiencing rapid agricultural growth.

Investment in agricultural research must be accelerated if the countries of Sub-Saharan Africa are to assure future food security for their citizens at reasonable prices and without irreversible degradation of the natural resource base.

Sub-Saharan Africa, which desperately needs appropriate technology to support productivity increases in agriculture, has only 42 agricultural researchers per million economically active persons in agriculture and 7 researchers per million hectares of agricultural land (Pardey, Roseboom, and Anderson 1991). This compares to 82 and 32, respectively, for all developing countries on the average. During the 1960s, the number of agricultural researchers in Africa grew at an annual rate of 9.1 per cent (Pardey, Roseboom, and Beintema 1994). The growth rate decreased to 6.1 per cent in the 1970s and 3.5 per cent during the 1980s. The rate of growth in African agricultural research expenditures dropped even more, from 6.6 per cent during the 1960s to a negative 0.3 per cent during the 1980s. In 1961, Africa's agricultural research expenditures were 0.36 percent of the agricultural GDP. They increased to 0.58 per cent in 1971 and to 0.84 per cent in 1981, but during the 1980s they dropped to 0.55 per cent (Pardey, Roseboom, and Beintema 1994).

In addition to raising yield levels, research resulting in tolerance or resistance to adverse production factors such as pests and drought, research leading to biological and integrated pest control, and research to develop improved varieties and hybrids for agro-ecological zones with less than optimal production conditions, all reduce risks and uncertainty and enhance sustainability in production through better management of natural resources and reduced environmental risks and should be expanded.

Accelerated agricultural research aimed at high-potential areas will reduce pressures on fragile lands. Future research for these areas must pay much more attention to sustainability than in the past to avoid a continuation of extensive waterlogging, salination, and other forms of land degradation. However, a continuation of past priority on high-potential agro-ecological zones is inappropriate and insufficient to achieve the goals of poverty alleviation, improved food security, and appropriate management of natural resources. The relative allocation of research resources to high-potential areas and areas with fragile lands, poor rainfall, and high risks of environmental degradation must be changed in favor of the latter. A large share of the poor and food insecure reside in agro-ecological zones with high risks of environmental degradation. In low-income developing countries, poverty, rapid population growth, low agricultural productivity, and poorly-defined ownership and user rights to natural resources are the major causes of land degradation, deforestation, and inappropriate use of water. Attempts to meet basic needs for survival in the short run take priority over longer-run sustainability.

The low priority given to research to develop appropriate technology for these agro-ecological zones in the past is a major reason for the current rapid degradation of natural resources, and high levels of population growth, poverty, and food insecurity. Much more research must be directed at the development of appropriate technology for these areas. Outmigration is not a feasible solution for these areas in the foreseeable future simply because of the large numbers of poor people who reside there and the lack of alternative opportunities elsewhere. Strengthening of agriculture and related non-agricultural rural enterprises is urgent and must receive high priority.

Declining investment in agricultural research for developing countries, including those in Sub-Saharan Africa, since the mid-1980s by both developing country governments and international foreign assistance agencies is inappropriate and must be reversed. While privatization of agricultural research should be encouraged, much of the agricultural research needed to achieve food security, reduce poverty, and avoid environmental degradation in developing countries is of a public goods nature and will not be undertaken by the private sector. Fortunately, while private rates of return may be insufficient to justify private-sector investment, expected high social rates of returns justify public investment. The major share of such investment should occur in the developing countries' own research institutions (NARS); there is an urgent need to strengthen these institutions to expand research and increase the probability of high payoffs. The recent decision by the World Bank to allocate US$500 million annually over the next five years to loans for developing-country NARS is a much welcome initiative.

The centers under the auspices of the CGIAR have a well-defined role to play in support of the work by NARS, namely to undertake research of a public goods nature with large international externalities and to strengthen the research capacity of the NARS and networking among NARS, international centers and research institutions in the industrialized nations.

Failure to expand significantly agricultural research in and for Sub-Saharan Africa will make food security, poverty, and environmental goals elusive. Lack of foresight today will carry a very high cost for the future. As usual, the weak and powerless will carry the major burden, but we must all share the blame for inaction or inappropriate action.

Citations

Pardey, P. J. Roseboom, and J. R. Anderson, eds. 1991. *Agricultural research policy: International quantitative perspectives*. Cambridge: Cambridge University Press.

Pardey, P., J. Roseboom, and N. Beintema. 1994. *Agricultural research in Africa: Three decades of development*. Briefing Paper No. 19. The Hague, Netherlands: International Service for National Agricultural Research.

TWINS SEVEN – SEVEN
The Farmer That Cares To Feed The Poor People Is In Bondage. HELP!! Africa Freedom Is In Bondage, 1995

Ellen Johnson Sirleaf

THE LEADERSHIP DIMENSION OF AFRICAN DEVELOPMENT

Introduction

Some forty years ago, Sub-Saharan Africa was at the threshold of a new era. The Second World War had just ended, returning soldiers and shaken nations looked to a new life. More importantly, there was general agreement that the time was ripe for the final thrust towards political emancipation after four centuries of contact with Europe which had resulted in human slavery, colonial rule and the orientation of African economies to serve the raw material needs of the North. In less than one generation, the irreversible force towards independence which was unleashed led to the virtual political emancipation of the continent. In 1957, Ghana became the first country to attain independence and within the next 14 years, more than two thirds of all the African colonies had been liberated.

A major factor in the pace of emancipation was the quality of political leadership in Africa. The Nkrumahs, the Azikwes, the Keitas, the Kenyattas, and the Margais were—irrespective of their weaknesses and in some cases subsequent failures—true leaders of their time. These were people who provided vision and hope to their people, men who commanded the respect of the rank and file of the countries' population; leaders who could motivate and channel the energies of the masses toward a clearly defined goal.

These vanguards of political liberation were men and women who were committed to their people and saw the independence of their countries as their chief objective. It is important to note that each of these leaders was democratically elected by their people to power. They were perceived as honest and accountable: the choice of the people. In other words, there was a mechanism for the identification and selection of the best leaders.

More than anything else, they were pan-Africanists. In the words of Nkrumah, "... *the independence of Ghana is meaningless unless it is linked to the total liberation of Africa*". Today, with the collapse of the apartheid system, the dream of Nkrumah is about to be fully realized, 36 years after they were spoken.

Not only was the quality of African leadership at the highest level of state affairs, but a good many of the countries could boast, albeit of limited number, of first class civil servants and teachers. Even at the community level leadership was not lacking and lawlessness was virtually alien to the continent. The "palava house" or town and village meetings provided a forum to air out differences and flush out policy and programmes. Yes, we were poor, but we were proud Africans! And we were made proud by our leaders!

Leadership and progress

The quality of leadership was a major ingredient not only in the progress made at the political front, but a key factor in the unprecedented burst of improvement in all social and economic indicators in the 60s and early 70s. The present crises all over Africa should not blind us to the rich heritage of progress made by Africa over the decades of the late 50s to the early 70s, progress almost unparalleled in such a short period in any region of the world.

Indeed, few regions in the world, at a similar stage of development, made such rapid social gains for their people as did Africa in the 1960s and 1970s. Tens of millions of jobs were created. The provision of education and health services expanded and the development of physical infrastructure such as roads, transport and telecommunication network—sorely neglected during colonial times—were aggressively pursued. The 1967-74 years were a period of particularly successful growth for Sub-Saharan Africa, with average annual GDP growth rate registering just under 6 per cent. By 1980, primary school enrolment had nearly doubled from 41 per cent to 79 per cent, and under 5 mortality rates dropped from 300 per 1,000 in 1960 to 200 by 1980 and 164 by 1990.

Decline in Africa

But the progress was not sustained and, by the beginning of the 1980s, the decline in both social and economic areas had reached crises proportions in most parts of Africa. Signs of decline were prevalent everywhere. Growth rates of GDP for Sub-Saharan Africa which averaged 5.9 per cent in 1965-73 dropped to 2.5 per cent over 1973-80 and 0.5 per cent in 1980-87. Similar declines took place in all sectors—agriculture, industry (where it was most precipitous), manufacturing and services. As a result, general consumption which was growing at a historic high of 9 per cent per annum in 1965-73 started to decline at the rate of 0.7 per cent per annum in 1980-87. Gross domestic investment rates which had averaged 9.8 per cent in 1965-73, turned totally around, with Sub-Saharan African countries disinvesting at an alarming rate of 8.2 per cent between 1980 and 1987.

With population growth rates rising sharply from an average of 2.6 per cent in

1965-73 to 3.1 per cent in the 1980s, the average African was no better off in 1990 than s/he was in 1960, in terms of income per head.

One cannot but recall the glories of institutions like Fourah Bay College in Freetown, Sierra Leone, and its corresponding ones like Legon in Ghana and Ibadan in Nigeria which were hallmarks of centres of excellence but became symbols of decay as they struggled with meagre resources to train our young people.

Conflicts, emergencies and leadership

Nowhere was the decline most evident as in the area of conflict and associated emergencies. The most devastating consequence of Africa's leadership crisis is the serious humanitarian situations that we find in Angola, Liberia, Mozambique, Somalia, and pockets of other African countries. I submit that the main ingredient in these destructive civil wars and the dire human conditions which they create is selfish, dishonest and poor leadership.

The consequences are gruesome. Today, it is estimated that there are six million refugees in Africa representing a third of the world's refugee population. In addition, an estimated fifteen million have become internally displaced. Successive emergencies have affected millions and moved the focus of international assistance from development to humanitarian giveaways. In West Africa, the prolonged conflict in Liberia has left over half of that country's population exiled or displaced and has generated thousands of refugees in the subregion. The recent problems in Togo have added another 200,000 or so distressed.

The figures in terms of lost lives are equally horrendous. For example, since 1983, it is estimated that 1.3 million southern Sudanese have died as a direct result of civil war. Multiply that by the atrocities and sufferings in Angola, Mozambique, Liberia, etc., and the figures become mind-bogging. With the deaths and suffering came famine and loss of economic activities. For example, the headline-catching famines in Ethiopia, Sudan and Mozambique in recent years were the direct result of civil wars and conflict more than lack of rain. This is supported by the fact that in 1992 despite a one-in-a-century kind of drought in Southern Africa, there were no pictures of starving children. There, peace, quality political and technical leadership continue to avert disaster. Man-made rather than natural factors constitute the fundamental cause of emergencies in Africa.

Equally important is the diversion of development assistance to meet humanitarian needs when leadership breaks down and parochial, personal and partisan interests dominate. All the evidence points to declining development assistance to Africa in the 1990s. The available statistics show that official development assistance to the poorer African countries fell from US$16.9 billion in 1990 to US$15.4 billion in 1991 and the trend is downwards. A World Bank donors' meeting to raise US$8 billion for adjusting African countries over 1994-96 yielded US$5.5 billion. At the same time, intervention in civil conflict in one African country alone has absorbed over US$2 billion in less than two years and over the continent as a whole humanitarian assistance and peace keeping averaged over US$3 billion per annum on very conservative estimates.

Time would not allow me to recount the insecurity, the heart breaks, the rapes, the tortures, etc., that have accompanied the breakdown of leadership and civil wars. Besides all these, there is the high cost of rehabilitation and reconstruction.

Decline in leadership

One of the main characteristics of the post-independent history of Africa was the failure of the vanguards of liberation to transform themselves into or set the pace for the emergence of development leaders. The subsequent deterioration in the quality of leadership on the continent followed their demise. The decline is evident in the areas of vision, identification of leaders and in their nurturing and training.

A. Loss of Vision

The visions exhibited by many leaders in Africa in recent times is but a shadow of what drove the struggle for independence. Over the years, focussed vision was replaced by dispersion and diversion of goals; long-sighted goals, strategies and programmes for development were replaced by myopic or short-term economic policies; examples being deficit financing to support politically determined projects, overvaluation of currencies, inefficient regulation of domestic and foreign trade. Leader after leader exchanged the inclusive social, political and economic policies for partisanship, tribal allegiance and generally exclusive tendencies. Pan-Africanism and the strife for subregional and regional integration was traded for crude nationalism. A classic example was the breakup of the East African Economic Community.

B. Deterioration of the process of leadership identification

Not only was the vision of leaders lost, blurred or narrowed, but with that came serious deterioration in the process of leadership identification. That occurred imperceptibly. First, there was concentration of power. State after state moved away from political pluralism to one party system, authoritarian regime or outright dictatorship. The mechanism for testing and proving leadership through competition and participation was replaced by party affiliation, nepotism or tribal affiliation. Excellence was no longer a criterion.

This deterioration in the process of leadership identification re-enforced statism in economic management. The result is history: lack of transparency and accountability, outright greed and corruption. When the leaders lost the confidence of the governed, they resorted to oppressive measures, divisive tendencies and other measures to retain power. Under such conditions coup d'etats, as a means of ceasing state power, became the norm rather than the exception.

At the technical and functional levels in public administration, the same process of dilution of quality and leadership took place.

C. Deterioration in nurturing and training of leaders

With the narrowing of the vision and the deterioration in the identification of leadership it was only a matter of time before the natural process of the nurturing and training of leaders would be undermined, the process which encouraged the nurturing of leadership through decentralization and participation from the grassroots at the county, city and community levels.

Many representing the best leadership replenishment stock expressed their lack of confidence in this new form of statism by migrating to the North, thus further compounding the leadership crisis. Many who remained reacted by saving abroad, causing serious capital flight. The fact that even some of those in the leadership resorted to stashing funds in overseas banks is an indication that they themselves had no confidence in the system over which they presided.

The challenge of development today

The challenge of development in Africa today is how to generate the kind of leadership that would lift our countries from their present state on to a path of sustainable human development. That would entail several fundamental actions which combine differently under different situations.

In countries involved in civil war and emergency situations, the first line of action is peace, a peace that kills the fires of war and limits humanitarian emergencies. Without peace one cannot truly think about development. The effort of African nations at the subregional and regional level through instruments such as the OAU should be singularly aimed at lasting peace. However, let us be clear that there is no substitute for, no external force or action that can replace the commitment of national leaders to finding lasting solutions to national problems.

For others, the path towards regaining the quality of leadership lies in creating a new vision that conforms to the development challenges of today; fostering a mechanism that allows for the identification and nurturing of leaders and putting in place institutions, both formal and informal, for the training of leaders at the political and functional levels.

a) **A new vision:** In a search for a new vision, the challenge is to revive the African dream. For far too long, Africans and their partners have talked in terms of the negatives of African development. Progress made so far is scarcely heard. The renewal of the African dream requires a new sense of positive thinking, about what is feasible with the continents' human and natural resources, about what it takes to expand the continent's competitiveness and potential, about what represents the hope for future generations.

But hope requires a sound foundation for transformation into action. This leads to the need for an authentic African development paradigm of sustainable human development, a paradigm which will have behind it the leadership force similar to the force that propelled our countries into political independence. Let me suggest that, as a first step, each of the African countries needs to conceptualize a new vision of the future based upon a consensus derived from the participation of the peoples in its formulation. Then we need to draw up national long-term perspective strategies that elaborate the attainment of these strategies in, say, 25 to 30 years. We need these strategies to become the rallying point for national optimism and the central points for national involvement.

b) **Identification of leaders**: What are the chances of such leadership emerging? Contrary to what my analysis may suggest, I believe that the forces that would produce such leaders are already unleashed. The peoples of Africa are already expressing their dissatisfaction of the failure of leadership, sometimes with great risks to their lives and safety. In more than two dozen countries, there has been demand for accountability and transparency leading to political changes.

The crucible for producing development leadership is through trial and error, allowing for political pluralism, opportunity to test and change leaders who do not meet the aspirations. I believe the peoples of Africa will demand this. I believe, albeit, the chances of reversals—the trend is irreversible.

Of course there are other issues to address such as the mobilization of human and material assets for national development. Domestic savings must be mobilized and allocated efficiently to engender growth and development for Africa, to go to work for Africa. The national self-confidence which comes with self-reliance must be nurtured, recognizing that dependency (on external aid) saps our pride and potential.

c) **Capacity Building**: Mobilization also means the development of human resources. Here, let me mention three dimensions: first, the rehabilitation of human development infrastructure—basic education, water and sanitation, etc.; second, improvement in domestic conditions to arrest the brain drain and encourage the return of Africa's skills and third, an aggressive programme of technology development to meet the challenges of a modern world.

In the struggle for better leadership, the cities with sizable numbers of our socially deprived, will be the testing ground. Thus, the metropolitan administrations will be at the centre of the storm, will become the cutting edge for reform and progress.

But none of this will happen unless the requisite leadership is in place. By *development leadership*, I mean leaders characterized by: vision, understanding (of the leadership problem), perception, courage/selfishness; in short, leadership, not rulership, the ability to mobilize, to motivate people and to manage resources.

Metropolitan governance

While the rural sector remains still dominant in most of our countries urbanization is definitely on the increase. In West Africa, there has been a massive shift of population to cities so that today there are several cities with populations in excess of one million. These numbers are on the rise. Thus, although we must try to expand the range of services to the rural population, the reality is that our region cannot escape the global trend towards greater and greater concentration of populations that will be living in the cities, a population projected, in the early 21st century, to represent more than half of the world's population.

In West Africa, as elsewhere, these urban centres have become the melting pot of various ethnic cultures, the nodal points of national economies and increasingly, as we move from mono-crop economies to industrialization, the major source of national incomes. Most significantly, the urban centres which were the cradle of political agitation for independence will remain the starting points of movement towards greater participation and better governance.

The cities in West Africa, like cities in other developing countries, are particularly significant because they reflect the tensions, the dichotomies and the prospects of national development. It is where the impact of the rapid population growth is most evident. The "distressing symptoms of urban overload such as traffic and pollution problems, declining standards of basic services, rising crime rates and thorny minority issues" are most evident. Our urban areas constitute a mosaic of wealth and poverty, places where modernism and tradition crash; places where the jet and the donkey arrive at the same time.

The management of urban centres, therefore, poses all the political and managerial challenges of African states. The quality of urban leadership, of modernized governance cannot be overstated. And the choices are obvious with differing consequences. It is a choice between competence and incompetence, a choice between participation and centralization; a choice between better governance and self-serving oligopoly.

Nowhere do our people feel as disenfranchised and bypassed as in urban areas. This is partly because, unlike the rural areas, they are most dependent on central services—transportation, urban schools and health centres, water services, etc.

I want to suggest five imperatives of urban development if the cities of West Africa are not to turn into huge urban slums but rather become the rallying points of sustainable development in the 21st century.

1. The imperative of quality urban leadership and management

If our cities are to meet the challenges they would face then the quality of leadership and metropolitan administration must be improved. Mayors would be required to provide vision, motivation and the guidance in an increasingly complex situation. The same skills required of national leaders would be expected of them. New York City's budget is bigger than every state in America except California and New York State. What that means is that the Mayor of New York must be of the quality of the best Governor or even the President. What is true of New York in America is equally true of Lagos, Accra or Freetown. This is a fact often missed and that is why Mayors of our cities are not accorded the same or even higher honour than the average Minister of State. The quality of leadership, however, would depend on the quality of the overall management capacity of the city. The accountants/treasurers, the personnel administrators, etc., must be of the highest calibre. City administration cannot function with political appointees and second rate staff. The pay and incentive structures must be such that the best would be attracted.

2. The imperative of better metropolitan governance

It is all too easy to talk about lack of transparency and accountability of national administration. But if we are honest with ourselves, we would admit that many city administrations are fraught with the same criticism, including corruption, as those levelled at Governments. Part of the reason why our cities are in such financial straights is that the traffic warden arrests offenders for his "chop money" or daily ration; the town planner allows all sorts of structures anywhere for a few bucks, etc.

That leads to the second factor of improving the environment for the private sector. It is well known that the most unstable, corruption-prone part of our generally weak legal system is the administration of justice in urban areas. We live in a part of the world where a land bought and paid for is not yours until you have your building on it; where urban planning regulations are flaunted with impunity; where government agencies proliferate with rules and regulations. That would require improved coordination mechanism of delivery systems, clear identification of areas of authority, review of laws and regulations dating back to colonial days to simplify and streamline them and swift administration of justice.

It is not a matter of choice. The growth of our urban centres require actions to improve metropolitan governance. We have to radically transform city administration to be more transparent and more accountable on the one hand and to improve the administrative and managerial capacity through recruitment of high calibre staff and training on the other.

One area where we need to move rapidly and which could be the target of assistance from the central government and international agencies is improving the technological climate of metropolitan administration. Traffic and environment monitoring in our cities, for example, can no longer be done without the requisite computers, systems and the help of modern technology in general.

Our cities have grown without a corresponding increase in administrative and management capacities. Most metropolitan administrations still inhabit the same buildings of the colonial city administrator. There is an urgent need to upgrade the level of urban administration and management.

3. The imperative of decentralization

One of the facts of life in our cities is that most people are far removed from those who govern them. This is because our cities have expanded without a modicum of decentralization. The borough system that has characterized urban centres in the metropolis of the North are critically nonexistent in Africa. The greatest imperative of urbanization in West Africa is decentralization.

Decentralization, inter alia, would:
(i) strengthen local government and administration;
(ii) enhance the sense of ownership of urban programmes and promote self help;
(iii) improve revenue collection and reduce the dependence on central government to finance urban services;
(iv) allow the addressing of peculiar problems of the suburbs, such as those in the poorer neighborhoods;
(v) enhance accountability and transparency;
(vi) effect greater scope for the exercise of leadership skills.

A key complement to decentralization is participation. There is no point in decentralizing to people who are hand picked by Mayors. People must be free to choose their leaders and be actively encouraged to participate in policies and programmes that affect their lives. One cannot be asked to elect a president or a parliamentarian if they cannot elect their councillor.

An important aspect of participation is the encouragement of private initiative. In West Africa, the idea of private sector in providing health services, education, transport, etc., is not new. But the centre has often looked at these initiatives with suspicion. The importance of improving metropolitan governance would require active encouragement of civil society to share in these and to enter into other sectors hitherto reserved for central authority monopolies such as garbage collection and provision of infrastructure. Sustaining our cities would demand active promotion of public/private sector partnership and a *sine qua non* to encouraging private sector participation is firm administration of justice. Law and order or jungle law. We cannot have it both ways.

4. The imperative of physical and environmental planning

It is a fact that as our cities grow and as urbanization increases in Africa, urban planning and environment management will assume greater importance. Urban squalor is a fact of most West African cities. There is no doubt that the rapid growth of urban centres has outstripped the ability to provide services. The cities, as political, economic, social and cultural activities, have attracted young and old alike. These have contributed in no small measure to the environmental degradation, poverty, transportation problems and the springing up of shanty towns around metropolitan centres.

Unfortunately, the situation could only grow worse unless positive steps are taken to reverse the phenomenon. Urban planning has to be prospective in that it anticipates events decades down the road; firm in the sense of being based on environmental and scientific principles, and not whimsical in the sense of it depending on the integrity and wishes of planners. Urban planning requires firm laws and regulations to be effective and the challenge is greatest in our part of the world where family ties, friendships—simply put connections—often override judgement and national good.

I believe that decentralization and better governance would, in turn, help to resolve the problems of urban planning and environmental degradation. People must be able to hold others accountable, they must be made to understand the cost of pollution and be made part of the solution.

5. The imperative of urban finance

I have left to the end a topic which is foremost on the minds of not only Mayors but national administrators. As a former Minister of Finance I know the pain of being presented with unlimited needs on a shoe's strap budget.

Financial capacity of municipal governments is severely limited which, in turn, constrains their ability to extend social services to inhabitants. This is particularly true as central government's support has weakened, with the economies going into crises management.

At the same time, the metropolitan centres would be increasingly called upon to raise the bulk of the resources they would need through local taxes, user charges, tax sharing with central government, investment by the private sector and limited subventions from the centre. In other words, metropolitan administrations would have to be effective cost centres, raising resources and using them efficiently, rather than as channels of centrally allocated resources.

I do not have all the answers to the financial problems of metropolitan areas. However, the following suggestions will go a long way towards that end.

First, there is need for decentralization of not only decision-making, but finances from the centre—national government—to the region and the cities. In particular, in a situation where a city is taking care of about a tenth or more of the total population of a country, as is the case in many West African nations, an equivalent proportion of national revenues should be directed at the metropolitan area concerned to be managed locally. One way to do so would be to give a region status to certain cities.

Second way to find the money is an improved tax collection by the cities themselves. It would be surprising if there is any city in West Africa, which is currently collecting 50 per cent of the local taxes and user charges which have been legislated. Why that is not happening is partly technical in the sense of lack of statistics, good monitoring systems, etc., and partly due to the governance issues I alluded to earlier. These have to be tackled.

The management of the municipal resources is a key element in improving city management. Decentralization means the development of a sense of financial autonomy in the long run with a simultaneous increased accountability. To accomplish this, one might consider the creation of municipal banks whose major task would be:
- to receive funds from different sources destined to municipal projects (central government allocations, tax and other revenues, etc.);
- to initiate and to study municipal projects and to oversee their implementation; and
- to collect revenues for the cities and to mobilize additional resources through mechanisms such as redeemable stocks, municipal bonds, etc.

The long term objective of this suggestion is to gradually reduce the cities' over-dependency on central governments and develop a sense of financial autonomy and improve the management of municipal resources in the long run.

Thirdly, with decentralization and greater participation, some of the services now undertaken by the metropolitan administration at great loss could be reduced. I have in mind things such as urban transportation, garbage collection, etc. Of course, it will ever remain the responsibility of the city administration to set standards and monitor delivery, but without necessarily having to provide the services themselves. People pay for services provided by the private sector for example, while the tendency is to look to central administrators as Father Christmas.

Babafemi A. Badejo

THE ASSOCIATIVE SECTOR AND THE POOR IN AFRICA

"I believe that if in Africa we cannot reach the moon, we should be able to reach our mouth and our stomach, reach our body and our neighbour and touch our environment for sustenance."

Olusegun Obasanjo

Preface

There are a number of quotable quotes that had been associated with General Obasanjo over time. This quotation, like some others reflects the duality of the simplicity and fundamental nature of the Obasanjo praxis.

For a former Head of State in any African country, Obasanjo's simplicity is unique. Many a time, he is on the wheel either in Abeokuta, Ota or Lagos without what I may refer to as the "accouterments of an Emperor" normally associated with holders or former holders of high public office on the African continent. This style that was tagged low profile while he was Head of State has continued to date. It is not unusual to meet General Obasanjo at any airport in the world struggling with his luggage looking like any other African peasant farmer. Of course, this situation has his own problems at times. Chief Femi Olopade once recounted how this simplicity was a problem at the Miami International Airport. Olusegun Obasanjo had flown from Cuba into the airport without a diplomatic passport in the early Reagan years. Asked where he was coming from and who he was, he stated that he was a Nigerian farmer coming from Cuba. When asked what he went to do in Cuba, he responded that he went at the invitation of Fidel Castro. Of course, the Americans wanted to know if he went to teach Castro farming or the other way round. The frustrated officer that could not deal with the candor started rummaging through Obasanjo's luggage and personal effects. At a point when Obasanjo would not allow a reading of his personal files, he refused to cooperate further. Seeing the American official agitated, Chief Olopade had to intervene by informing a superior officer that a diplomatic row should be avoided because the person probably being considered a Castro agent was Nigeria's former Head of State.

This simplicity in life style, some people have argued, is bad because a former Head of State should not be carrying his luggage around airports in dresses that give the impression he is really a peasant farmer. But then, there is a fundamental message in this practice. It is refreshing to find a departure from the African situation where wealth is often flaunted in the face of the wretched of the earth whose wretchedness is mainly a consequence of the corruption and bad management of the leaders.

The problem of leadership on the African continent is one that General Obasanjo has been seriously concerned with. Not only has Obasanjo written a lot on bad leadership and chose specific opportunities to castigate some examples of bad policies by bad leaders in Nigeria and Africa, he has tried in practice to give leadership. The Murtala/Obasanjo brief period in Nigerian history is one that will continue to be visited with some nostalgia. More importantly was the steering of the Nigerian state towards democratization in 1979. This development remains novel when one puts the tenacious hold of African leaders on power into proper perspective.

Out of office, Olusegun Obasanjo set about the institutionalization of the training of leadership for the continent. Inspired by the wisdom of the late Chief Simeon Adebo and the devotion of a number of other people, the Africa Leadership Forum continues to carve a niche for itself.

Introduction

Poverty alleviation and overall human development efforts in Sub-Saharan Africa remain at a crossroad. Despite the post-independence attempts at the realisation of development in Sub-Sahara Africa, development continues to elude the majority of the inhabitants of this region of the world and poverty remains endemic. In the last three to four decades, Africa has not been short of consultants who at one time advised that the solution is for African governments to undertake wide ranging investments and to build a viable public sector under authoritarian regimes or the "modernizing armies".

More recently, that is, along the waves of the 1980s, the advice has been the need to privatize government owned enterprises and allow the reign of market forces under democratic multi-party governmental arrangements. Though the privatization pressures have been adopted in many Sub-Saharan African countries for about a decade, the subregion continues to harbour a major share of the poorest people in the world. Whatever indices one cares to examine, the situation is not salutary for Sub-Saharan Africa and more importantly prospects for the realisation of rapid human development and the alleviation of poverty for the majority of the people appear worrisome.[1]

Given such a desperate situation efforts continue in seeking solutions that can ameliorate mass poverty. One of the responses that blossomed in the 1980s was the clear articulation of the role that Non-Governmental Organisations (NGOs) can play in the nudging of the poor towards mass alleviation of poverty. In this study, we reiterate the role that a variant of NGOs that are referred to as "people's organizations"[2], has been playing in the alleviation of mass poverty in Africa.

The associative sector[3]

Concerns for developmental planning in Africa has, for some time vacillated along a continuum of a private sector- or a public sector-dominant orientation with respect to the production arrangements. In the case of the former, the initiative for the production of economic goods and services was to be left in the hands of individual or corporate entities. The State was only expected to provide the environment for national and international capitalists to grow so that their efforts in expanding the economy can trickle down to the poor. In some instances, such efforts of the State involved the nurturing of big enterprises into profitability before handing them over to the strong and entrenched interests in society irrespective of whether such interests are foreign or domestic.[4] The failure of such massive big business efforts to ensure the reduction of poverty and the growth of smaller household entities led to the recognition of the role of micro-businesses that are tagged the "informal sector" or better still the informal economy. It is important to note that the so-called informal sector is not a sector in contradistinction to the private sector. The so-called informal sector operates within the rules of private capitalism.[5]

The public sector orientation has involved the State in the active role of production. The logic of this position was that the State in Africa at independence had more resources to foster economic growth. Furthermore, the State it was thought, would be in a better position to ensure equity. The strengthening of the State it was felt would lead to the overall improvement in the lot of the weak and the not so powerful who are bound to loose out in an unbridled unleashing of market forces. But the persistence of poverty on the African continent and the continued marginalisation of the very poor raise questions on the adequacy of the State as an instrument for the alleviation of mass poverty. Whatever additional reasons that could be discernible in justifying the role of the State in the production process are presently not at issue. The fact is that the current position in the international power structure—and hence the present intellectual fad—is the pressure on the State to divest from the production arena.

The emphasis that was at different times placed on both the private and public sectors in independent Africa did not just flow from "rational" economic thought and decisions. Both outlooks can be seen as flowing from a political and ideological primacy that the post-Colonial State in Africa won over civil society at independence.[6] Just as democratisation was seen in terms of a top-down effort in the realisation of a benevolent State apparatus at the expense of popular movements,[7] so also the logic of production of the poor in many popular associational[8] forms were regarded as outmoded.[9]

The debate on whether the poor occupy a transitional phase in Africa, or that the persistence of poverty in Africa so far is a result of a failure to incorporate the rural areas into the logic of capitalism[10], is beyond our purview. Suffice it to note, however, that the barrenness of the assumption that the logic of the production arrangement that had suited the purposes of the poor constitute a transitional phase in the movement from tradition to modernity has led to recent concerns on the need to build on the indigenous.[11] This present preoccupation it must be understood involves a political struggle against the State which—even though weak in the African formation—continues to tower above the rest of civil society.[12] The situation on the African continent as Mamdani and others suggest has involved the building of the State with the State later trying to build a nation out of civil society.[13] The State in such an experimentation has naturally marginalised as many of the structures in civil society that enjoy reasonable autonomy from the State. The marginalisation process has involved the incorporation, monitoring, benign neglect and outright dismantling of some of the structures of civil society. So, in order to build on the indigenous, in Africa, it is important to realise from the onset that such an effort necessarily involves the rolling back of the State from the total space it currently occupies vis-a-vis civil society. A number of analysts have examined the possibilities that a rediscovery of popular movements in civil society can bring about in the struggle towards democratisation in Africa.[14] In this article, however, our focus is on the possibilities that such an emphasis on popular movements can bring about in reaching the very poor that are normally left out in State-centred development planning efforts and the unleashing of market forces.

The logic of the associative sector

It is essential to examine some of the characteristics of the organizational efforts of the poor and/or for the poor. The organizations of the poor have involved popular reactions of people who as a communal or primary group recognize the weakness of individual or nuclear family efforts to solve personal problems that are identical to existential problems faced by others in the same geographic environment.

The fact that many a NGO of the self-help variant operates on the basis of ascriptive attributes like consanguinity, ethnicity, age-sets, kinship etc. raises questions on the validity of the general assumption that voluntariness is one of the characteristics of NGOs. There are NGOs that are voluntary organizations just as there are those that people automatically belong to because of the circumstances of their birth. For instance, a city dweller is automatically a member of his "hometown association". He may choose not to pay his dues or attend meetings. But some circumstances like burial ceremonies of his relations or his return home on retirement etc., provide the opportunity for the people of the hometown to collect a backlog of his dues. But it is important to note that such sanctions vary among communities.

Face to face interaction within a natural spatial environment is important. Such spatial consideration may at times be reinforced with affect or other primordial attachments flowing from consanguinity or some feeling of common descent or other similar identity of interests. Within such a face to face interaction, it is possible for every member to understand the strengths and weaknesses of one another. And on the basis of such a knowledge some specialization in the role to be played by each individual is arrived at.

An essential outgrowth of the face to face interaction is the development of trust in one another and the institutions that are historically developed by the people by themselves for themselves. It is important that the institutions are not imposition by people who think they know what is good for the poor.[15]

Production in this situation has a limited focus. It is the existential consumption realities of the people that dictate what is to be produced and the quantity. Thus, production is on a small scale for use-value rather than exchange value.[16] Expansion can take place if the people themselves realise the need to expand instead of having the need to expand imposed from above in order to meet the needs of the State. For instance, as Ake pointed out, the imposition of various taxes on the poor with a requirement to pay in cash (rather than in kind as was the case prior to colonisation) forced many a people in Africa into cash crop production and drove some off the land into wage labour.[17] And the inability of the poor to meet their food needs have always resulted in band-aid efforts that would have otherwise been unnecessary.

The organizational structure is simple, and very democratic. There is a high degree of flexibility in procedural matters. The possibilities of rigid rules that are difficult and complex to comprehend by the operators and members are absent. The rules are informal, impartial and easy to understand by all participants.[18]

Production by individuals and families take place in association with the efforts of other individuals and families in a rotating cooperative arrangement. Such associative effort could be in the provision of labour, capital or credit for production.

More importantly, the organizational efforts of the poor for production are participatory. Each beneficiary is involved in deciding on goals to be achieved and the processes for achievement. And as a number of studies have shown, participatory efforts that are "bottom-up" strategies are not only cost-effective and efficient they are also qualitatively sustainable.[19] This is so because the self-help arrangement takes place in a one-to-one cordial relationship in such a manner that it becomes a way of life. David and Yvonne Robinson describe this aspect of self-help thus:

"Self-help helping ... takes place in the context of friendship. There is no distinction between the treater and treated. All have problems. All are helpers. The distinction between helping and being helped, problem solvers and problem sufferers, problem-solvers and friends are lost. Self-helping merges into the everyday life of the self-helping group member. Self-help, in fact, becomes a way of life."[20]

The spirit of a communal orientation[21] whose roots can be found in rural Africa continues to rear its head in the cities. This communal affect has led to the growth of "ethnic associations" or "hometown associations" in the cities with such associations not only providing succour for the migrants among themselves but, in addition, maintaining a close relationship with the ancestral geographic areas of origin.[22] The efforts of these associations continue to be the only means through which most infrastructure for the betterment of the lives of the poor gets to many a rural area in Africa.[23]

The efforts of the primordial nongovernmental associations either in the original form in the rural areas or in the more recent forms in the cities operate under an associative logic that is different from the logic of either the private or public sectors. And it is for the recognition of the vital role that these organizations play and continue to play in the lives of the majority of people on the African continent that we make the case for the recognition of the African economic development possibilities as inadequate without a focus on an additional sector. This additional sector of focus in the production process in Africa we choose to tag the "associative sector." Such an associative sector is one in which the NGOs of the grass-roots organizations or the "hometown association" variants are dominant as instruments of human development and the alleviation of mass poverty.

The impact of the associative sector in Africa

Labour-pooling or mutual help production arrangement are very common in Sub-Saharan Africa. The arrangement manifests itself in two basic forms in spite of some minor differences. A farmer in undertaking some major task like ploughing or the construction of a homestead could request for the labour of other farmers. A day or some days are set aside for this purpose. On the appointed date, the farmer on whose project the others are to work provides food and drinks for everyone and he is assisted on his individual project without paying for the labour services of others. The food is not seen as payment for it is given and taken in a spirit of sharing. It is understood that any of the farmers who are involved in such an arrangement could call for the services of every other person at another time. This arrangement is called *nhimbe* in some parts of Zimbabwe.[24] Among the Yoruba people of Western Nigeria it is called *owe*.

The other form that labour-pooling mutual help takes is when farmers as age-sets, friends, kinship groups etc., mutually assist each other on a rotating basis by preparing the individual farms of one another for the cultivation of various crops. The arrangement here is a little more formalized and it is called *jangano* in Zimbabwe[25], *nnoboa* in South Eastern Ghana[26], and *aro* among the Yoruba.

The role of labour pooling in many parts of Africa in the pre-colonial and colonial times has been documented.[27] In more recent times, however, efforts have been made to build on these indigenous institutions to develop new institutions to carry out developmental tasks in society. For example, with respect to labour-pooling, the Naam Groups—*Groupements Naam*—represent a revival of a similar concept for the execution of community projects in Burkina Faso. The Naam groups involve the pooling of the labour of young men together to undertake productive activities that include planting of millet, cotton, sesame and peanuts in the rainy season and environmental protection, soap and textile making etc. during the dry season. The needs of the groups are met through the proceeds from their activities and generated surplus is reinvested in developmental activities.[28]

A variant of labour pooling for community work among the Akan in Ghana known as *nkabon* was, on the eve of independence in Ghana, successfully extended to the provision of many health stations, school buildings and teaching in Ghana through the harnessing of contributions in labour services or money contributed in lieu of labour by adults in a community. Though some of the projects embarked upon received some external assistance in situations where requirements could not be locally sourced, much of the effort was on the initiative of the people guided by the age-old wisdom of the institution of the *nkabon*.[29]

For Liberia, Seibel and Damachi document the role of community work groups that have existed over time. As they stated: "Informal community work groups are formed among some groups in Eastern Liberia: Young men gather informally to perform farm labour or community tasks; these are peer groups based on the traditional age sets."[30]

The *Harambee* experiment in Kenya has been documented.[31] As Keller noted, the rooting of the school movement on the age-long idea of pooling together at the clan level for the achievement of community purposes account for the relative success of the *Harambee* school movement.[32]

Aside from labour-pooling, more popularly known to the literature is the role of self-help NGOs at the grass-roots level in the provision of savings and credit to their members. In many parts of Africa, grass-roots savings and credit arrangements are very popular among the poor. The richer or middle level people at times partake in this credit delivery and savings mobilization arrangement by forming their own separate groups. Membership is really determined on the basis of what an individual can afford to contribute. So, individuals form groups with people who have similar levels of income and choose one of their members that has over time been known to be trustworthy to keep the money contributed and make disbursements to the membership as necessary. But then, an individual can be a member of many groups once he can meet the contribution requirements of each group. The savings and credit self-help NGOs are called various names: *esusu* among the Yoruba people of Western Nigeria; *susu* in Ghana[33]; *ibimina* in the Kivuye commune in Northern Rwanda[34]; *tontines* or *njangis* in Cameroon[35].

Seibel and Damachi document some successful attempts and an unsuccessful attempt to develop on the *esusu* concept in order to ensure the delivery of credit and the mobilization of savings in the rural areas of southern Nigeria.[36] In situations in which the age-old traditions of communities were followed, it was possible to boost credit delivery and savings mobilization using a cooperative concept. But it is instructive that in an experiment that was meant to scale up in which a commercial bank literally took over the control of a "modernised" form of the *esusu*, the result was a resounding failure.[37] The age old trust and confidence that the people had in their organization which allowed them to see the money contributed and lent for individual uses as "our money" was lost to the impersonal rules of banking which equally meant a perception of the money being lent as "their money."

In Cameroon the *tontines/njangis* are very popular. Nchari suggests that some 50 per cent of the Cameroonian population is organized in *njangis*.[38] The *njangis* membership control the management of their affairs and only elect a management committee from their membership on an annual basis. The efforts of *njangis* have resulted in many productive investments by individuals as well as an ability to build homesteads and send children to school. In addition, some *njangis* as associations have invested in vehicle transportation, construction of halls and purchase of chairs that are rented out to people for various ceremonies.[39] Haggblade goes further to point out that many African enterprises in urban areas in Cameroon are financed by *njangis*.[40]

The second variant of grass-roots self-help associations as we noted earlier are those referred to as "Hometown Associations". For many an African, the concept of hometown is important. The hometown is not the place of birth or that of resident for many an African. It is the place to which an individual's ancestry is traced which at times is referred to as one's root or place of origin.

Cosmologically, for a number of Africans there is a binding union between the dead, the living and the unborn. This cosmological wedlock with the ancestral home has in modern times provided an exclusive self-help arrangement. Individuals whether as businessmen or as professionals who left their hometowns or villages for the cities or are born and reside outside their hometowns/villages continue to owe an obligation to see to the improvement of their villages even when they are not residents there.[41] Such obligation is discharged in the form of contributions under the auspices of various hometown associations for the provision of various facilities for the upliftment of the social life of villagers (who are relations) who continue to eke out a living in the villages. Some of the efforts in this respect go towards the provision of welfare and socioeconomic facilities like, schools, electricity, pipe-borne water, town-halls, churches and mosques etc. as associations. Some associations do in fact embark on direct production activities. And even individuals within these groups are under pressures to embark on what Guggler refers to as conspicuous investment like building houses to maintain a desire to one day return.[42] It is important to note, however, that such buildings provide improved quality of shelter for kinship members who occupy many rooms in such buildings free from the payment of rent on the understanding that such residents will provide simple day-to-day cleaning efforts.

In providing facilities for their place of residence, the hometown associations involve the residents of their villages in participatory development. While the "sons and daughters" of the village residing in the cities or abroad contribute in cash, the village residents are not just recipients, they contribute labor and other material resources that are within their power to dispense. We could take some illustrative examples of this phenomenon.

Joel Samoff[43] provides information on the role of the Kilimanjaro region indigenes who were city residents in actively contributing to the goal of providing private secondary schools in the Kilimanjaro region in order to accommodate the graduands of the universal primary education that the Tanzanian government could not provide for. It is interesting that the effort that Samoff described took place when the central government had dissolved local governments. With the efforts of the local organizing committees and indigenes in the cities, Kilimanjaro was able to open one secondary school in each division as the national policy sought to open one in each district (a division is a subdivision of a district). Thus, by 1984, Kilimanjaro which had 5.6 per cent of the national population could boast of 26 per cent of all the secondary schools in the country. Kilimanjaro had 11 per cent of national government-provided secondary schools and 42 per cent of the total privately-provided secondary schools in the country.[44] The Tanzanian government was initially indifferent to the various local organizing committees which were informal and unrecognized by the law. But as Joel Samoff noted, once the local organizing committees started collecting funds and started meeting State officials over land-use approvals, curriculum, etc. they received *de facto* recognition and in due course, the State itself started recognizing the need to reintroduce the local government system. Samoff argues that it is this popular initiative that resulted in the reintroduction of local governments in Tanzania.[45]

Joel D. Barkan et al. provide three successfully interesting cases of hometown self-help NGOs from Western Nigeria.[46] These were the *Otan-Ayegbaju Progressive Union* which was founded in 1930 by a railway clerk from *Otan-Ayegbaju* to provide support for this rural community through personal contributions that were used to pressure the colonial government for the provision of matching grants for the execution of various projects like schools and electricity. Despite its ups and downs, the *union* remains in existence and one of its most recent achievements was the provision of a 25-bed hospital for the rural community. This hospital project became a four-way partnership involving the union, the World Health Organization, the state government and a Federal government teaching hospital. Similar achievements were recorded by the *Fiditi Progressive Union* founded in 1934 and the *Egbe Omo Ibile Awe* which was founded in 1912.

In the case of *Egbe Omo Ibile Awe*, the effort has in fact gone beyond the provision of socioeconomic support institutions. This self-help group in 1982 incorporated Awe Development Corporation (A.D.C.) as a "development agency" that can easily tap into funding from far and wide. Unlike the parent body, ADC is run like a business organization with a 15 member board and with a central planning committee made up of professionals. What is important, however, is the fact that profit is socially owned and utilised for the improvement of the community.

Some problems

In the current embrace of the desire to build on the indigenous, there are some problems that need to be pointed out and consciously thought through as this sector develops. Samoff, Keller and Enemuo[47] all call attention to the fact that self-help efforts, as a result of spatial differences in resource endowments, could aggravate spatial inequalities. This is more so the case when efforts of grass-roots self-help associations or the hometown associations variant are rewarded by the State by way of matching grants.[48] It may be desirable that matching grants be provided on such a basis that equity comes into focus. Thus, the level of development of each spatial area of the country could be a separate concern in the process of revenue allocation in such a way that each more dynamic area is not discouraged from the self-reliant orientation in improving the common lot of the village. While resources from the State can and should augment the communal efforts of people it should not become a means of discouraging the highly participative and sustainable self development efforts of people themselves.

As civil societies become more vibrant in Africa, conscious efforts need be made to guard against the current desires for an incorporation of areas that presently remain relatively unincorporated by the logic of individualistic private accumulation. The issue here is that the efforts of the State to define its goals as the goals of the people constitute a return to some of the earlier problems that are still being confronted to date. An illustrative example could be found in the desire of the Nigerian State to set up Community Development Associations (CDA) in various villages. The intention of the government in this direction was to "improve the nation's foreign exchange position by obviating the need for food and raw materials imports and thus conserve foreign currency and also earn it by producing surplus; raise rural income and purchasing power and thus widen the market for local industries; and improve rural welfare by providing industry socio-infrastructural facilities and thus curb rural-urban drift..."[49] The problem here is that the State is beginning to set goals for civil society in order to realise its own desires. To what extent are these goals foisted from above congruent with the desires of the people themselves? This question should constantly be in focus.

Even then, care must be taken in receiving aid either from the State or the external environment. Aid in any form could imply an alteration in the basic characteristics of the associative sector. And such alterations not only result in a disjointed orientation for the erstwhile vibrant organizations, they could actually sound the death knell of some of the efforts. For example, the requirements for the receipt of aid involve such things as writing project proposals and keeping accounting records in ways that conform with the set designs of the aid-giver. In certain situations, the grass-roots self-help associations are not "sophisticated" enough for some of these demands. This results in the need to hire "experts" who are not in any way attached to the ways of the people other than seeing themselves as salaried workers. This new reality pushes aside tested and trusted members of the community who had always served as leaders. In some instances, vices like corruption and stealing of communal resources—that the people did not partake of before the arrival of aid—get imported.

A number of analysts have also called attention to such points of tension between NGOs and the State like the need to register. Governments present this need as a coordination requirement for NGOs operating in its territorial space and NGOs see it as choking monitoring by a bureaucracy.[50] Mamadani, for instance, is concerned about the substitution of popular accountability for bureaucratic accountability once popular social movements are being monitored by the State.[51] There is, thus, the need to develop civil society in such a way that organizations in the associative sector are accountable to civil society as they have been over the years rather than to the State.

Conclusion

The associative sector is an important part of the complimentary operation of the African economic structure as a three sector arrangement. The associative sector operates under a logic that is abhorrent to private capitalism and constitutes an irritant for the government controlled public sector.

In examining the associative sector it is possible to focus on the role of a wide range of NGOs in society. However, we have been particularly interested in the role of grass-roots face-to-face organizations in the rural areas of Africa and those of city-based hometown associations that cooperatively ensure the remittance of a portion of the urban income to the rural areas in order to put a number of self-help socioeconomic structures into place.

In spite of the demonstrated relevance of the two variants of the NGOs that we have looked at in Africa, it is important to note that the associative sector is not in a place to eradicate poverty from the African continent. At best, the associative sector is in a position to ameliorate the viciousness of poverty without consuming an equivalence of the massive drains that governmental and donor programmes tend to constitute. The fact of the matter is that, to date, there appears to be an irrelevance of both the private and public sectors to the problem of degradation of existence in rural Africa. The relevance of this sector, however, goes beyond savings. Operations of the associative sector are also participative and highly sustainable.

Even if it is "certain" that the communal spirit in Africa will wither away, there is the need for responses that integrate this orientation—that remains dominant for now—into the developmental efforts on the African continent. But then, such planned integration must not continue on the yardsticks for incorporation into the capitalist world system that has remained a major part of the African problem.

---

[1] See, UNDP, *Human Development Report 1992*, (New York: Oxford University Press, 1992). In particular, see a picture of the trends for Africa in Box 3.1, p.40.

[2] See, David C. Korten, *Getting to the 21st Century: Voluntary Action and the Global Agenda* (West Hartford, Connecticut: Kumarian Press, Inc., 1990), especially, Chs. 9 & 10.

[3] The idea of the "associative sector," we owe to Koenraad Verhagen, *Self-Help Promotion: a challenge to the NGO community* (Amsterdam: Royal Tropical Institute, 1987). At page 20, Verhagen defines the associative sector as: "a complex of self-help organizations and their coordinating or federative bodies which together constitute a distinct sector of the economy, different from the conventional, profit-oriented private sector as well as from the government-controlled public sector. Associative organizations/enterprises and their membership normally interact commercially with organizations/enterprises belonging to the other two sectors and as such are an integral part of the economic system."

[4] On Nigeria, for instance, see, Sayre Schatz *Nigerian Capitalism*.

[5] For a treatment of the characteristics of the informal economy, see, Hernando De Soto, *The Other Path: The Invisible Revolution In The Third World*, (New York: Harper & Row Publishers, 1990). See also, Peggy Antrobus, "Women and the Informal Sector: Priorities for Socially Sustainable Development," *DEVELOPMENT: Journal of the Society for International Development*, 1992:3, p. 55.

[6] For a detailed explication on this theme, see, Mahmood Mamdani, "State and Civil Society in Contemporary Africa: Reconceptualizing the Birth of State Nationalism and the Defeat of Popular Movements," *Africa Development*, Vol. XV Nos. 3/4, 1990; Claude Ake, "Sustaining Development on the Indigenous," in *Background Papers: The Long Term Perspective Study of Sub-Saharan Africa*, Vol. 3, Institutional and Political Issues, World Bank, 1990, pp. 7-21; Rajesh Tandon, "Civil Society is the First Sector," *DEVELOPMENT: Journal of the Society for International Development 1992:3*, pp. 38-39 and Peter P. Ekeh, "The Constitution of Civil Society in African History and Politics" in B. Caron, A. Gboyega and E. Osaghae (eds.) *Democratic Transition in Africa* (Ibadan: CREDU, 1992), pp. 187-212.

7. Mamdani, *ibid.* and Ekeh, *ibid.*
8. Our usage of association in this piece is not restricted to the those usages that limit the term to only voluntarily joined organizations. Our usage is not focused only on the mode of recruitment and whether the organization is inclusive or exclusive. Our usage embraces all organizations irrespective of the mode of recruitment that focus on the cooperative efforts of individuals within groups (some of which groups may emanate from primordially exclusive recruitment patterns) to embark on the goal of human development in civil society outside the logic of individualistic private accumulation.
9. Ake, *op. cit.* and Tandon, *op. cit.*
10. For instance, see, Akin L. Mabogunje, "Eradication of Poverty," paper presented at the Africa Leadership Forum Conference on Eradicating Poverty in Africa, Ota, Nigeria, July 27-29, 1992.
11. See, *ibid.*
12. Michael Bratton, "Beyond the State: Civil Society and Associational Life in Africa," *World Politics*, 41 (3), pp. 407-429. On how successes by primordial associational groups in ensuring the spread of development could and actually threatened entrenched interests of the manifestations of the power of the State, see, Ake, *op. cit.*, pp. 10-11.
13. See, Mamdani, *op. cit.*, and Mahmood Mamdani, "Democratic Theory and Democratic Struggles," Paper presented to the CODESRIA General Assembly, February 11-14, 1991, Dakar, Senegal; Ekeh, op. cit.; Jean-François Bayart, "Civil Society in Africa," in Patrick Chabal, ed., *Political Domination in Africa: Reflections on the Limits of Power* (London: Cambridge University Press, 1986).
14. For instance, see, *ibid.*
15. See, F.J.A. Bouman, "Indigenous Saving and Credit Associations in the Third World; a Message," *Savings and Development, Quarterly Review*, no. 4/1 (1977).
16. See, Ake, *op. cit.*
17. See, Claude Ake, *A Political Economy of Africa*, (Essex: Longman, 1981).
18. A number of efforts have shown that formal rules with which the poor are unfamiliar has tended to make it difficult to reach the poor when the poor are the targets of policies. For instance, see, M.J. Esman, "Development Administration and Constituency Organisation," *Public Administration Review*, Vol. 36, 1978, pp. 166-172 and Delmos J. Jones, "The 'Community' and Organizations in the Community," in Leith Mullings (ed.), *Cities of the United States: Studies in Urban Anthropology* (New York: Columbia University Press, 1987), p. 118.
19. See, David Marsden, "What is community participation?" in Richard C. Crook & Alf Morten Jerve (eds.) *Government and Participation: Institutional Development, Decentralization and Democracy in the Third World*, (Bergen: Chr. Michelsen Institute, 1991), pp. 29-50; Michael M. Cernea, *The Building Blocks of Participation: Testing Bottom-up Planning*, World Bank Discussion Papers, No. 166, 1992 and Dharam Ghai, "Participatory Development: Some Perspectives from Grass-Roots Experiences," *Journal of Development Planning*, No. 19, 1989, pp. 215-216.
20. David and Yvonne Robinson, *From Self-Help to Health*, (London: Concord Books, 1979), p. 79.
21. Ake, op. cit., rightly makes the point that Africans unlike Europeans operate more on the basis of communal rights than individual rights. See, pp. 9-10.
22. On the cosmological wedlock between the African in the city and his hometown, see, Babafemi A. Badejo, "Nongovernmental Organizations," A Background Report prepared for *Human Development Report, 1993*, October 1992, p. 11.
23. *Ibid.*, pp. 11-13.
24. See, Lovemore M. Zinyama, "Local Farmer Organizations and Rural Development in Zimbabwe," in D.R. Fraser Taylor & Fiona Mackenzie, (eds.) *Development From Within: Survival in Rural Africa* (London & New York: Routledge, 1992), p. 49.
25. See, *Ibid.*
26. See, George J. S. Dei, "A Ghanaian Rural Community: indigenous responses to seasonal food supply cycles and the socio-environmental stresses of the 1980s," in Taylor & Mackenzie, *op. cit.*, p. 69.
27. See, for instance, Lord Hailey, *Native Administration in the British African Territories, Part III* (London: His Majesty's Stationery Office, 1951) and Audrey Smock, *Ibo Politics: The Role of*

Ethnic Unions in Eastern Nigeria (Cambridge, Massachusetts: Harvard University Press, 1971).

[28] See, ECA, *Guidelines... op. cit.*; Robin Sharp, "Who's helping whom?" Perspectives, No. 7, 1991/92 and OECD, *Voluntary Aid for Development: The Role of Non-Governmental Organizations*, 1988, pp. 47-48.

[29] Hans Dieter Seibel and Ukandi G. Damachi, *Self-Help Organizations: Guidelines and Case Studies for Development Planners and Field Workers—A Participative Approach*, (Bonn: Friedrich Ebert Stiftung, 1982), pp. 100-101.

[30] *Ibid.*, p. 52.

[31] See, Ake, *Building on the Indigenous... op. cit.*; and Edmond J. Keller, "Harambee! Educational Policy, Inequality and the political Economy of Rural Community Self-Help in Kenya," *Journal of African Studies*, Vol. 4, No. 1, Spring 1977.

[32] Keller, ibid., pp. 92-93.

[33] See, Jacob Songsore, "The Co-operative Credit Union Movement in North-Western Ghana: Development agent or agent of incorporation?' in Taylor & Mackenzie, *ibid.*, p. 83.

[34] See, ECA, *Guidelines on the Role of Non-governmental Organizations in Participatory Rural Development in Selected African Countries*, ECA document no. ECA/SDA,IRD/90/1.2(d), pp. 10-11.

[35] See, ibid., pp. 9-10 and Anthony Nforba Nchari, "Cooperatives as Decentralized Socio-Economic Institutions: The Case of Cameroon," in Ladipo Adamolekun et. al., *Decentralization Policies and Socio-Economic Development in Sub-Saharan Africa*, (Washington, D.C.: Economic Development Institute of the World Bank, 1990), pp. 65-74.

[36] Seibel and Damachi, *op. cit.*, pp. 103-107.

[37] *Ibid.*, p. 107.

[38] Nchari, *op. cit.*, p. 67.

[39] See, *ibid.*, pp. 68-70/

[40] See, Steve Haggblade, "Africanization from below; the Evolution of Cameroonian Saving Societies into Western Style Banks, *Rural Africana*, no. 219, 1978.

[41] For a thorough examination of this phenomenon that is based on an empirical inquiry with respect to the *Ibo* people of Eastern Nigeria and comparative references to other areas of Africa, see, Josef Guggler, "Life in a Dual System: Eastern Nigerians in Town, 1961," *Cahiers D'etudes Affricaines*, Vol. XI, No. 43, pp. 400-421.

[42] See, *ibid.*

[43] Joel Samoff, "Popular Initiatives and Local Government in Tanzania," *The Journal of Developing Areas*, 24, (October 1989), pp. 1-18.

[44] *Ibid.*, pp. 6-9.

[45] Though Samoff sees the reintroduction of the local government as a positive reaction of government, it is possible to reinterpret this action as part of a general fear of popular initiatives by State bureaucrats. Local governments in such a situation become an avenue to control popular initiatives.

[46] Joel D. Barkan, et. al., " 'Hometown' Voluntary Associations, Local Development, and the Emergence of Civil Society in Western Nigeria," *The Journal of Modern African Studies*, Vol. 29, No. 3, 1991, pp. 457-480.

[47] Samoff, *op. cit.*, Keller, *op. cit.*, and Francis Chigbuo Enemuo, "Communal Organizations, the State, and Rural Development: The Political Economy of Community Self-Help Efforts in Anambra State, Nigeria," Unpublished Ph.D. dissertation, University of Lagos, Lagos, November 1990.

[48] See, Enemuo, *ibid.*

[49] See, *ibid.*, pp. 1-2.

[50] See, Badejo, *op. cit.*, pp. 21-23.

[51] See, Mamdani, "Democratic Theory..." *op. cit.*

Pierre Claver Damiba

INTRODUCING CULTURAL FACTORS INTO DEVELOPMENT IN AFRICA

"Serve Africa first!"

When I boarded that evening the British Airways 747 flying from London to Harare, my neighbour in business class was unknown to me. He was dressed yoruba style and I noticed his naked feet in his shoes. He was very relaxed though quite pensive. After I took my window seat, he greeted me:

"How are you, brother?" he said;

"Fine, thank you, Sir," I responded.

Until the take off, he was busy thinking and at the same time completely at ease. I was more and more intrigued by my elder brother so simple and so dignified and I wondered who he could be. When dinner was served, he came from his deep meditation, reluctantly, I must say, to have a slight meal with plain water. Then he looked me in the eyes and, somehow amused, he said:

"Wouldn't I be right if I guess that you are one of our African brothers based and working somewhere in the North, and jetting in and out of Africa?"

"Correct! You are absolutely right!" I replied.

"Please", he carried on, "don't forget Africa! It is Africa that needs you, not the North! Serve Africa first!"

This was my first encounter and dialogue with General Olusegun Obasanjo, some ten years ago; and his strong reminder to me still echoes in my memory: "Serve Africa first"...and wherever! I consider the "General" a true African leader because he is well rooted and profoundly committed to the achievement of Africa's substantive partnership with the rest of the world. By creating the Africa Leadership Forum he has shown his strong desire to get at all levels in Africa leaders endowed with competence, integrity and commitment. General is a man of consensus and of honorable compromises; he is a true statesman and, above all, a peacemaker. Isn't he amongst those peacemakers blessed in the Bible "for they shall be called the children of God"?

This contribution on Culture and Development in Africa is in homage to General Olusegun Obasanjo's commitment to both African culture and development, more specifically since development is also another name for peace. I happen to know that this subject is General's preferred and well travelled territory. Peace indeed is a harmonic atmosphere that enables prosperity to occur in terms of both quantitative and qualitative progress for each person, for the entire society and for humankind. This paper provides general comments on approaches that could enable a more effective interplay between culture and development in Africa, as true servant of peace.

The reinforcing interaction

My starting point is that culture defined as a "whole complex" by Unesco should not be the function of development since the "cultural corpus" preexists to development as the seed to the plant; it is an endowment inherited at the very inception of life. The genius for survival of our ancestors was a cultural wealth; the way they apply it for example for hunting was already a process of development. Culture should then be viewed as the prime mover of life individual and collective endeavours. It is rather development that should be function of culture. In my view, it is development that is a "factor" and even a "fact" and an "expression" of culture. Indeed, development should be viewed as a construction engineered by culture. It is culture that proceeds as an inner, endogenous energy and provides the humus-bearing ground to development.

Between culture and development there is of course a cross-pollination, a reinforcing interaction. The methodological issue is how to make development a true servant of culture and more specifically how to achieve this reinforcing interaction. One way of handling it would be to identify the determinant parameters for a "development-servicing culture", like school and audiovisual, and to ensure that they will perform this function, or to review the performance of a sector such as agriculture against the impact of cultural values. Another way would be to highlight the key values that matter for the society, the ethics that have helped the group to survive and to ensure their preservation; in that respect the Japanese and the Jews could be cited as successful examples. Design and implementation of National Cultural Assessments (NCA) could serve as both diagnosis exercises and means to take stock of the major cultural values, knowledge and practices and to update them as appropriate. They should also serve to promote within the society the necessary interactive and consultative process in such priority areas as culture and development. Moreover, this paper provides comments on the tragic breakdown of the cultural harmony in Rwanda and its relation with development. The paper also refers to the management "A l'Africaine" in the search for methodological insights and prescriptions. These investigations plead for an urgent need to carry out further research to support the design of relevant approaches in that area of culture and development.

Culture engineering development

"Culture may now be said to be the whole complex of distinctive spiritual, material, intellectual and emotional features that characterize a society or social group. It includes not only arts and letters, but also modes of life, the fundamental rights of human being, value systems, traditions and beliefs", as stated by Unesco. This broad definition and interpretation has become the conventional and shared wisdom on culture as a complex totality.

Indeed, culture is not a sector of the total economy, the microculture compared to the macro-development. However there is a reality of cultural "atomization" exemplified through the creation of ministries of culture and the often reduction of culture to traditional dances and songs at the airport to salute political VIPS, or traditional artifacts as gifts to the same personalities. Moreover, often forgotten are references to those basic cultural values which in the traditional Africa have nurtured, inspired and ruled the devolution of power, the settlements of conflicts, the family security and the social solidarity.

Culture is like the "soul" of a human being while development is the body. Culture energizes the visible and the invisible self of an individual and his interactions. It is the common "soul-of-reference" for the society. Culture as the "soul of life", is kept alive through a complex interaction between an array of factors and players. Culture is not an "ad-on" or an "afterthought" of development; it is ingrained in the human seed/gene from the very beginning, it is an original human/inner endowment; it begins as a silent heritage and is carried over from generation to generation. It is, indeed, part of the human biological "software". It develops and grows differently, depending upon individual endowment, social environment, collective memory, technological stages, etc. which it constantly keeps influencing. Civilisations as forms of culture can disappear but culture itself always transcends individual and collective death. Paul Valery stated that "civilisations are bound to die." Yes indeed, but not culture, because civilisations are only mere contingent and historical expressions of culture. Development can die like civilisation but culture never passes away, since it is a constituent of human nature. The issue is a fundamental one. It is associated to the Cartesian paradigm that is: "I think therefore I am" and the related debate. I am of the school which states that "I am therefore I think". In the relation between culture and development, culture is the "I am" and development the "I think". Culture is essential; it precedes, makes possible, generates development which is existential; culture and development in turn influence each other through an interplay process.

In the interaction between culture and development, one question is indeed what development is referred to? Is it the Western model for its sustained success, its high pressure on the daily life of the majority of people including those outside of the developed world, or its capacity to dominate through technological and military advance, information and trade? In that context, if culture is the soul of life, then development with which it interacts cannot necessarily be but itself servant of the soul of life. And the very purpose of development is to serve culture, to provide an enabling atmosphere for culture to play its creative and supportive role vis-a-vis development. It is not surprising that some people equate development with peace although, personally, I would have rather equated, first and foremost, peace with culture, as development should only be their outcome. Development is the civilisation engineered by peace and culture.

It is the "intersection" of culture and development that should create the culture of development and the development of culture. Development that represses the soul can hardly take off not to mention be sustained. Culture that hinders development is bound to remain a primitive and an infant one. The destiny of humankind in the Universe is indeed, to exploit what is in nature, to develop what is uncovered; it is why development can be considered as an "added-value" by human beings not only to Nature but also to themselves. If development leads to a decrease in the capital of values together with an increase in material goods, then this kind of development cannot be sustained. As it is well known "science without conscience leads to the ruin of soul". In other words, development achievement without conscience can only lead to the ruin of culture. This is the reason why the conscience and concern for culture and their related analytical and research work should provide the very humus-bearing ground for development as an added-value.

Development "servicing" culture

Within the framework of an holistic approach to culture, the methodological issue could be addressed, partly, in identifying critical determinants or in capturing the cultural interactive process, at some stages of human individual or collective developmental behaviour. What are the key factors or major sources of the interplay between culture and development? They would constitute critical elements, and suggest not new but basic directions to support the necessary dialogue, between those engaged in rethinking development planning and those directly affected by the changes that will take place. I have selected the following four "operators" and key determinants: mothers, adults and society, audiovisual and school. They could be used to build scenarios, masterplans, to help revisit strategies and programmes for an effective interaction between culture and development. The interplay between these parameters, would also help focus on the very intersection of culture and development.

The first determinant factor and source of culture is the mother. The interaction of a human being with his mother, the "motherly care", is a critical factor of culture and it is this interaction that prepares the ground for further human growth and development. In the beginning is the mother. She is the first to prepare and cultivate the "cultural humus". She is the prime channel of culture to the baby, the teacher of the first bio-cultural class; and the impact and legacy of this baby-curriculum on human behaviour is decisive indeed in terms of its impact on future developmental behaviour. We can extend the concept of mothers as "individuals" to the concept of family, as the "extended mother", the cultural cradle of any human being and even human society. One cannot address the methodological problems of culture and development by bypassing the "mom" as she is, ab initio, a major piece in the culture and development interaction. Influencing mothers, educating them, focusing on them as the first major source and pillar in this interaction, should be a critical part and a priority of any new pedagogy that aims at bringing about the expected creative tension and effective interplay between culture and development.

The second determinant factor are adults and society. President Julius Nyerere, in a famous statement, said that: "children in the precolonial Africa, learnt by living and doing... education was thus informal; every adult was a teacher to a greater or lesser degree ..." This context provides a "symbiotic process" through which culture is acquired for the survival of individuals and communities; the survival constraint as energized by culture, is the phenomenon whereby one can read the interaction between culture and development. "Work or play, rites and ceremonies were all day-to-day opportunities for learning, from motherly care to lessons from the hunter-father, from observing seasonal changes to watching familiar animals, or listening to tales told by elders and chants of the tribal shaman" (cf. Report of the International Commission on the Development of Education, "Learning to be", Unesco, Paris 1972). The methodological issue here is not to introduce cultural factors into development but rather to observe "culture at work" and for us to learn from the real lives of millions of people who have been "learning by living and doing and for whom living and learning were synonymous". "Adults" and "Society" by and large, provide natural and uninstitutionalized forms of learn and of culture and development interaction, in the traditional Africa.

Audiovisual is a large window through which the world-Americanized culture has fed and transformed many people's minds and finally has succeeded to exclude them from their inner being and culture, their own environments, and continues to do so. How could an audiovisual system which deliberately tells the stories of foreign cultures, help endogenous development attempts become successful? Several actual experiences tell the stories of the impossible development in such conditions.

Here is an anecdote which is symptomatic of the cultural traumatism and alienation of millions of African men and women. A young lady, 28 year-old, employee in a beauty salon, in Abidjan, completely illiterate, used to explain in forceful details the scenario and the content of two American series (soap operas) that used to play on the television. These were "Dynasty" and "Dallas" which had invaded almost all African televisions; she was so addicted to these shows that she ended up identifying herself with some of the actors/actresses; she had her role model, her supermen and superwomen etc. It has become her universe, her "Weltanschauung." This young woman raised and brought up in her remote village where she had no access to audiovisual, overnight found herself confronted with the "so-called" urban/modern life and had become driven by and greedy of a by-product of a culture totally unknown to her. This case is widespread throughout Africa, illustrating the brainwashing power of dominating cultures through the audiovisuals and the strong projection of development models in the imagination of these people.

The values and morals depicted in such shows are completely foreign and often irrelevant to those she, as an African, has been taught. Yet, by watching and literally swallowing those shows, indigestible though they are, she has come to believe that

Western culture is the culture by excellence, the reference. The girl ended-up "borrowing as hers" the Western system of values for family life, for social relations, for problem-solving and over and above as a dream for social achievements. All these culminate for her in buying Coca-Cola and ripped-up jeans as well as additional videotapes of the same sort to nurture her newly-acquired cultural virus. And most of the time the African economies cannot respond to the newly acquired needs, this in turn generates frustrations and the profound desire to emigrate to Europe or the United States. Unfortunately, they are millions upon millions of Africans with culturally-dominated consciousness including in the most remote recesses of the Continent.

The school is reputed to get culture servicing development. And in the interaction between education and culture, one would have expected a perfect match. Indeed, education is supposed to deliver the cultural engine and to enable, through the dispensation of proper knowledge, the achievement of economic development. The school was established as a powerful machine-tool in the relations between culture, education and development. But experience has shown that the school in Africa has largely failed to service development as it did in Japan. The irony is that the school in Africa has shown itself to be an "infernal machine" of exclusion, not only because of its elitism and the number of dropouts but also because the school does not vehicle African culture and savoir-faire. It delivers instead straight-jackets to make its beneficiaries play the game of the dominating cultures of the developed economies. Africa still has to rethink the development paradigm in order to get it flow from the inner wealth of its people or firmly grafted to their specific self being.

Inculturation of management

The interaction between management and culture is a well traveled road, in management sciences and practices. In effect, management is the best reflection of culture and in its interaction with the latter, it provides also the ground for further expansion of culture. In Africa, this interaction has failed to bring about the expected endogenous and sustained growth and development. With respect to management, African public and private managers, business professors and academicians "have jumped into the bandwagon" of the styles and practices of the dominating cultures in the United States and Europe. Indeed, in three decades of independence, the African countries, by and large, failed to effectively manage their huge natural endowment, to the extent that absolute poverty reposes on absolute wealth. Most of the management practices used by African managers so far, have proved to be nothing more than straightjackets hindering them in the running of institutions, public services, private companies, and even their personal businesses. It is why the time is ripe for the "in-culturation" of management in Africa in particular, through proper organization of management research.

"Very little is known about what African managers are called upon to do in their everyday work." Against this statement made by African and non-African scholars on that matter some universities propose a methodological approach that calls for the establishment of an African management research network to address management research questions in Africa. Some of the key questions could be summarized as follows: "What creates successful managers in Africa? What systems and styles do they operate? How are they effective? What are the major barriers to high quality performance? What typology should we use to categorize different managerial structures, particularly in the public administration system? How efficient is the policy formulation process in key sectors like agriculture, transport, health and education? How effective are private sector managers in African subsidiaries of international corporations, by comparison with their counterparts in other parts of the globe? Until we begin to answer some of these questions with substantive research, our understanding of African management will remain sketchy and much sought after improvements in managerial performance will be elusive."

It is expected that a network could be established to produce research data and materials on African management that would help improve the knowledge base and allow the policy formulation process in business and government to be better informed. It would also encourage African researchers to build indigenous models for understanding the African situation and to develop empirical studies drawn from the African experience. The basic and underlining option of this research program is the in-culturation of management, in other words, the achievement of a management "a l'Africaine".

The breakdown of cultural harmony in Rwanda

The Rwandan crisis is a tragic illustration of the dramatic consequences that occur when the cultural corpus of a society and the living harmony, i.e. the state of development, it supports and energizes, are broken down. Time International of 16 May 1994 provided relevant analysis and information which are largely used here.

A century ago the Tutsi cattle lords and the Hutu farmers were living in "symbiotic harmony" whereby a Tutsi king used to rule over the country and the Hutus used to keep the Tutsi clothed and fed. "They were a reasonably contented rural society" and "there was no hatred between the two groups. That came only with the colonial system" (Basil Davidson).

The breakdown of this living harmony was engineered indeed, by the European colonization, German and Belgian, who introduced their notion of racial hierarchy; in particular, the Belgians upheld the dominance of the Tutsi. As a consequence, the years of colonialism essentially destroyed the social and political structure and accepted values that had kept tribal peace for centuries and the related state of development. The colonisers paved the way and provided the foundations for the tribal-hatred based slaughters, witnessed in 1994. Indeed, in the absence of agreed common and constructive values, the irrationality of hatred dictates counter values, whereby vengeance breeds counter-vengeance that can easily be fuelled and manipulated, for the worse, by ethnic sentiments or external elements "when there is a rupture of authority, that creates a situation which is apocalyptic by nature and leads to fear and anguish" (Prof. François Constantin). The 500,000 death toll of the 1994 cultural war in Rwanda, measures the abysmal nature of the national breakdown. This Rwandan case, illustrates, if it were, two points with respect to the relation between culture and development.

First of all, when the European stumbled into Rwanda a century ago they applied the well known principle of "divide and rule". As colonisers, they were determined to weaken the indigenous social fabric and they used military domination and malicious manipulations as well. Secondly, in the Rwandan context, one should have expected, as per the conventional wisdom, that successful economic development would have provided stability and justice, as billions of US dollars have been spent for the economic growth and development of Rwanda. At some point in time, Rwanda even qualified as a good "pupil" and highly rated disciple of the Bretton Woods institutions. However, it was clear that such development achievements were "built" in a profound cultural disarray and disharmony. It was a window dressing economic success story. Whereas the very prerequisite for development to succeed should have been to focus, first and foremost, on the rehabilitation and reconstruction of the lost cultural harmony which would have allowed to restore the cultural fabric and the "symbiotic harmony" as a peaceful terrain for effective development to grow. On the contrary, the Government of the late President Habyarimana increased ethnic tensions, by creating a sense of tribal solidarity, by establishing racial identity cards, etc. Hence, the governance of independence worsened the colonial practices, instead of building a nation freed from the colonisers' practices and deep-rooted in the "symbiotic harmony" which the population had already experienced.

The need for National Cultural Assessments

There is not a single African country which has carried out the priority requirements of cultural assessment at independence and prior to any further development undertakings. National or sectoral plans, structural adjustment or major reform programmes are prepared and implemented without proper cultural assessments. Instead these countries are only giving lip-services to culture; they are playing with culture through the changes of names, the imposition of dress codes such as "abacos" and alike; they organise traditional dances ("animation culturelle"); they make policy statements and create still-born cultural institutions; national constitutions are often borrowed from such countries as UK, USA, France, with no reference to the time-tested practices and the traditional wealth regarding the devolution of power, the settlements of conflicts, the family relations etc. By so doing, Africans have been "playing the appearances" of in-culturation while the reality of the cultural soul is dying. Meanwhile Africa is being invaded by the "by-culture" and its related byproducts of the dominating nations. African civilisations are dying and the remaining culture is being more and more impoverished. In that context, more Rwandas are to fear in the near future.

National Cultural Assessments (NCA) are proposed as an approach to support an effective interplay between culture and development. Such NCA are not meant to harvest the variety of cultural artifacts, but rather to identify and shed light on the core of the cultural corpus that characterises the society concerned. They should allow to tackle emerging cultural issues and to respond to such questions as "what cultural values when by-passed can make development projects and programs succeed or fail?". As we can see, the NCA should be an interactive and consultative process within a longterm perspective and affected by a transgenerational concern; the followup and necessary updating of their findings can help prevent the breakdown of African nations and the recurrence of tragedies like the Rwandan one.

Culture as the undied

In this endeavor to identify relevant approaches, there is a risk of wounding or marginalizing culture for the sake of development, by striving to put it into boxes or to translate it into guidelines, systems and models. However, since a minimum of structured guidance is unavoidable, one should keep in mind in dealing with culture and development, that culture should be kept as a living soul and development as its successful achievement.

Finally, culture should be the bedrock from which cultural springs would flow and water the African development endeavours. It is from this premise that relevant ingredients could be designed for a successful social engineering. Methodological scenarios including the parameters highlighted here, require certainly further debates and research for improvements. Management being the very nexus of culture the related research network proposed above could be another approach worth exploring in support of the inculturation of Africa's development. Also, the proposed National Cultural Assessment may prove to be a useful tool insofar as it remains a democratic vehicle and not a tool for political domination and repression. Through the NCA process and based on its core-findings, cultural constitutions, for instance, could be worked out to provide cultural frames of reference for the African nations' endeavours in all sectors.

The very source of culture is the people, and today the majority of the people in Africa are excluded from education which is the critical determinant of development. However today's excluded majority is tomorrow's agent of change, hence they are already the alphas and the omegas of culture and development. Let us move from the syndrome of "we" the leaders and "they" the people, to be democratic enough and to be no more and no less than the people.

Ola Balogun, a Nigerian film producer, beautifully highlights in his movie "River Niger" the undied memory of his Yoruba ancestors; they are still alive amongst the living, within the families and in the villages where they continue to attend and have their say in meetings as well as their place in various celebrations. This means that culture should never die. "Culture is the Undied." Therefore, African people should more than ever pray the "Undied", their ancestors, the spirit of Africa, for a panafrican cultural rebirth which only would engineer an endogenous development.

Thomas R. Odhiambo

THE MILITARY DIMENSION OF THE AFRICAN SCIENCE ENTERPRISE

Just over 900 years ago, the great Islamic physician, Al Asuli, writing in Bokhara, divided his pharmacopoeia into two: the first into "diseases of the rich", and the other into "diseases of the poor". The Nobel Laureate Abdus Salam, writing in 1963, related this pharmacopoeitic classification to the capacity to understand and utilize science in the modern context, and did so in rather poignant words:[1]

"If Al Asuli were alive today and could write about the afflictions of mankind [today] ... he would again plan to divide his pharmacopoeia into the same two parts. Half his treatise would speak of the one affliction of rich humanity—the psychosis of nuclear annihilation. The other half would be concerned with the one affliction of the poor—their hunger and near starvation. He might perhaps add that the two afflictions spring from a common cause—the excess of science in one case and the lack of science in the other."

The difference then between the "have's " and the "have-nots" is not simply that of the possession of crude material wealth; rather, it lies in the degree to which the one commands the knowledge and skills arising from scientific research and technological development (R&D), whereas the other has no such command.

The account written in 1470 A.D. by a young astronomer from Kandhar, who left his village to go and study and undertake research at the then famous observatory at Ulugh Beg in Samarkand, writing to his father in Kandhar, illustrates the deep anguish that can pursue a young scholar who dares to leave his agrarian and military life behind to acquire the new vistas that science can open up to a searching mind:[2]

"Admonish me not, my beloved father, for forsaking you thus in your old age and sojourning here at Samarkand. It is not that I covet the muskmelons and the grapes and the pomegranates of Samarkand... I lost my native Kandhar and its tree-lined avenues even more and I pine to return. But forgive me, my exalted father, for my passion for knowledge. In Kandhar there are no scholars, no libraries, no quadrants, no astrolabes. My stargazing excites nothing but ridicule and scorn. My countrymen care more for the glitter of the sword than for the quill of the scholar. In my own town I am a sad, a pathetic misfit."

There is no doubt that the passion for knowledge is deep and enduring in Africa—in spite of the five centuries of transcontinental slavery and imperial colonization that started contemporaneously with the scientific greatness of Samarkand in the East. For instance, between 3.2 and 10.1 per cent of the gross national product (GNP) in different African states is devoted to education and training; and the various governments expend between 16.0 and 27.5 per cent of their national budgets on education and training at all levels. Yet, the rate of illiteracy among the 15 year olds and above is horrendously high, ranging between 42.5 and 67.1 per cent.[3] It is difficult for one to envision how a modern, knowledge-intensive production and marketing can flourish in a continent that has so far developed its human capital so scantily and so belatedly. Even in the new post-apartheid South Africa, which has been touted as a possible engine for economic growth in the Southern African region, 14 million of the 28 million black South Africans cannot read; and 1.5 million black children get no schooling at all, in the midst of 82,000 school places going begging in erstwhile white-segregated schools.

The spectre of the poor, particularly the urban poor, in Africa is becoming a major threat to the body politic and family life; and the erosion of the resilience of the society to meet the contemporary challenges of development is real. Robert Kaplan, in a recent article, gives Cote d'Ivoire as an illustration of the looming revenge of the "urbanized peasants", which will constitute at least 62 per cent of the country's population by the end of the current decade.[4]

Because of lack of an obvious force to maintain order, a weak cluster of political parties, a leaden state bureaucracy, and a population that is at least 50 per cent non-Ivorian, Kaplan avers that there exists no sense of nationhood that would obviate the need for such enforcement. Kaplan goes further, and talks of the state facing "a possibility worse than a coup: an anarchic implosion of criminal violence—an urbanized version of what has already happened in Somalia. Or it may become an African Yugoslavia, but one without mini-states to replace the whole", yet getting the government overthrown by stone-throwing adolescents. Consequently, Kaplan envisages that this internal conflict illustrates the looming cultural conflict which is likely to sweep Africa and other Third World countries in the next two decades, rather than the ideological conflicts that dominated the five decades of the Cold War, or the nation-state conflicts that pervaded the first half of this century.[5]

Foreign intervention, and less so foreign aid, is unlikely to provide a sustainable solution to this poverty and development conundrum. Foreign aid is an invention of this century; no economic or social development has occurred before on the basis of foreign aid. Indeed, some public affairs observers consider that foreign aid has brought into existence the concept of "third world" or "the South", in contrast to "the first world" or "the North". They argue that the singular characteristics of the Third World are not poverty or economic stagnation or exploitation, nor are they defined by brotherhood or skin colour or geographical location. The core taxonomic element is that of official development aid or foreign aid: "The concept of the Third World and the policy of official aid are inseparable. Without foreign aid there is no Third World."[6]

In this context, it can be argued that foreign aid is by and large detrimental to the broad-based progress of those countries that achieved their political independence after World War II. In most cases, this type of aid, which began with United States President Harry Truman's Point Four Program in 1949, is not only not a prerequisite for economic and social development, it can actually impede it.

"[Foreign aid] diminishes the people of the Third World to suggest that, although they crave material progress, unlike the West they cannot achieve it without external doles... External donations have never been necessary for the development of any country anywhere."

Indeed, if the developing countries have to maintain an aggressive competitiveness in both the domestic and global markets, while maintaining a healthy economic partnership with the industrialized countries wherever they are in the world, they must take full cognizance of the fact that the overwhelming majority of resources required for national and regional development emanate from their own sources, as Smuckler and Berg (1988) so clearly state:[7]

"Contrary to the general impression, the Third World itself finances the vast bulk of development in the Third World. Aid programs contribute altogether only about 10 per cent of the Third World's total development investment. Foreign talent and financial resources often provide an impetus that would otherwise not be present. The primary contribution foreign donors can make is quality assistance, since quantity, by any measure, is modest compared to total investments and problems addressed."

The quality brought about by some instances of foreign development aid is done violence to by the military aid that is so contrary to the spirit of sustainable development.

Military aid, and military trade, is not an option for development in Africa—or any part of conflict-prone areas of the world.

Military aid and trade

Trade in covert arms, mostly of conventional small arms, is worth anything from US$ 1 billion to 10 billion a year by estimates produced by the Stockholm International Peace Research Institute (SIPRI). The official, government-related trade is estimated to be even larger: in 1992, it amounted to US$ 18.5 billion; in 1987, it was far larger than this hefty sum, totaling US$ 46.5 billion, and reflecting the fact of the many proxy wars then current from Angola to Afghanistan, from Nicaragua to Mozambique. In 1993, there were 30 or so major conflicts in Africa and the rest of the world that attracted both covert and government military cross-border trade.

It is estimated that Sub-Saharan Africa spends some US$ 1 billion a year on arms purchases. This is a heavy burden on a region whose total external debt stock in 1993 amounted to US$ 199 billion, and whose GNP is a mere US$ 291.2 billion. Principal repayments on these debts alone cost the region US$ 4.97 billion a year.[8] Thus, Africa cannot afford the massive arms it is purchasing, when it no longer has external armies to fight, and no comparative advantage in fighting other people's wars.

Africa needs a peace dividend of its own—savings from the large outlays that have been expended to expand the armed forces, the equipment at their disposal, and the conflictual areas and incidences in which they have been engaged since the early 1960s. Indeed, one can begin to consider it as axiomatic that security and suitable social and economic progress are interlinked. This linkage was clearly seen by the Organization of African Unity (OAU) Summit of African Heads of State and Government, meeting in Abuja, Nigeria, in June 1991, during which they considered the so-called Kampala Document which had been steered by General Olusegun Obasanjo, in his capacity as Chairman of the Africa Leadership Forum, and put forward at a meeting in May 1991 in Kampala, Uganda, to recommend the launching of a Conference on Security, Stability, Development and Cooperation in Africa (CSSDCA). The OAU Summit acknowledged, for the first time ever, that "there is a link between security, stability, development and cooperation in Africa", based on some of the considerations of the Kampala meeting:[9]

"The concept of security goes beyond military considerations. It embraces all aspects of the society including economic, political and social dimensions of individual, community, local and national life. The security of a nation must be construed in terms of the security of the individual citizen to live in peace with access to basic necessities of life while fully participating in the affairs of his/her society in freedom and enjoying all fundamental human rights... This security of the African people, their land and property and their states as a whole is an absolute necessity for stability, development and cooperation in Africa."

This sentiment is strongly entrenched in three of the seven general principles enshrined in the Kampala Document:

1. Every African state is sovereign, and respects the rights inherent in the territorial integrity and political independence of all other African states.
2. The security, stability, and development of every African state is inseparably linked with that of other African states. Consequently, instability in one African state reduces the stability of all other African states.
3. The erosion of security and stability in Africa is a key cause of its endemic crises, as well as a principal impediment to the creation of a sound economic and cross-border cooperation.

The regional and national conflicts, as well as ethnic and racial confrontations have spelt out another dimension of Africa's wretchedness during this century. To foster and defend the policy of apartheid, the just-eclipsed old South Africa had developed and become a significant arms producer and exporter. To ward off geopolitical supremacy in several African states, leaders have frequently resorted to erecting ethnic barricades around their new-found communal laager. We cannot live out our lives in secure cocoons, as elites, letting the abject poverty, now threatening to become endemic in the continent, just take its own historical course. We must all become deeply involved in its resolution, as Edward Mortimer, in an article in the *Financial Times*, warns the elite in Africa, as well as in other developing regions of the world:[10]

"[The privileged elite of global capitalism] increasingly have to spend its time in a kind of air-conditioned, heavily defended ghetto—since large areas of most big American cities...are already little safer or healthier than the anarchic, Aids-ridden shantytowns in which so many Africans now live their short and miserable lives."

The epoch-making formal act of self-determination that was acted out in Eritrea in 1993, and the unprecedented act of moral restitution that was accomplished in early May 1994 in South Africa, are a singularly fitting symbolism of the death of the old, conflict-weary, ethically abused Africa, and the rise of a new, future-oriented continent that is eager to find its own place in the sun.

The 41st Pugwash Conference held in Beijing in September 1991 on the theme "Striving for Peace, Security, and Development in the World," stated it extremely well, as if it was entirely focussing on Africa's wars of want and conflict:[11]

"After decades of frustration and disappointment, history has given our generation a decisive and perhaps fleeting opportunity to rid future generations of the scourge of war and poverty. Time has also made our task more urgent and success more vital".

We must convert our predilection to conflict and war, to a culture of security and development.

Military conversion

One hears of stories of the entrepreneurial and self-survival instinct that has begun to engulf the ex-Soviet military establishment in recent months. Weapons factories which used to manufacture nose cones for missiles are now making artificial hip joints; Yak-141, the only supersonic vertical takeoff jet in production, is being converted to civilian use especially for difficult terrains and off-putting climates; and an extraordinary technology exhibition displaying over 600 products from the Soviet military-industrial complex was shown to the outside business world for the first time in May 1994 at the Washington Convention Center. It is this type of wholehearted military conversion that needs to be initiated among the African persons in uniform and the weapons of destruction that fill up military stores and ordinance inventories.

Almost every African country—except perhaps tiny Djibouti and the Seychelles—has built up enormous armed and paramilitary forces that are grossly in excess of what they can justifiably require for external defence or internal security. Already the economic liberalization and structural adjustment programmes sweeping through the continent have thrown these military recruitment policies under severe strain. Firstly, few countries have worked out a systematic demobilization plan that would address the problem of creating new economic opportunities for the demobilized soldiers, or retrained them adequately to reenter into ordinary civilian life. Secondly, the industrial-business community has not taken advantage of the skills, both technological and logistical, of these vigorous and disciplined youth to transform them into nuclei of industrial production and management. And, thirdly, Africa has not yet deliberately tested the feasibility of converting military equipment, usually robust and precise, to productive civilian uses. Vast potentials are locked up in this enormous offensive equipment, in these standing armies, and in the trained personnel obliged to quit the profession of killing ones own biological species.

This is the time to design a long-term programme of military conversion in all the three senses that have just been characterized. The Research and Development Forum for Science-Led Development in Africa (RANDFORUM), which started operating from its headquarters in Nairobi, Kenya, in August 1992, is planning to launch a think-tank group—the Trans-Africa Science, Security, and Development Associates (TRASSDA)—later this year to address military conversion and the associated problems of technology-dominated development. These issues are likely to prove Africa-specific, although the purely hardware engineering conversion questions are largely generic in character.

The rationale for initiating the difficult process of military conversion in Africa is that the dramatic changes in the global economy and geopolitics since the beginning of this decade have essentially transformed the realpolitik of the world, and that Africa cannot isolate itself from this power transition. The justification for Africa's own military conversion programme is that consciously building a harmonious society is the best guarantee for a strong and secure society. David Halberstam, in his book *The Next Century* has said it very well, when talking about American obsession with military weaponry:[12])

"[Most] people talking about national security [in the United States] were ill equipped to do so because they had lost touch with the country, that national security was no longer an index of weaponry (essentially a missile and tank count), if it ever really was, but a broad array of factors reflecting the general state of national wellbeing. It included the ability of a country to house its people, to feed them, to educate them, to provide them with opportunities in keeping with their desires and education, and to instill in them trust and optimism that their lives were going to be valued and fruitful."

Through TRASSDA and similar initiatives, the bristling array of Africa's armed forces should have been transformed, within the span of a single generation, into a quickening array of producers, marketers, and distributors.

---

[1] Hassan, A. and Lai, C.H., editors (1984), Ideals and Realities: Selected Essays of Abdus Salaam; Singapore: World Scientific Publishing Co. Pte. Ltd.

[2] see Hassan/Lai, op. cit.

[3] see United Nations Educational, Scientific and Cultural Organisation, World Education Report; 1991; Paris

[4] Kaplan, R.D., The Coming Anarchy; in: Atlantic Monthly, February 1994, pp. 44-76

[5] see Kaplan, op. cit.

[6] Bauer, P.T. and Yamey, B.S., Foreign aid: what is at stake?; in: The Third World: Premises of U.S. Policy; revised edition (W. Scott Thompson, ed), San Francisco: ICS Press, pp. 135-155

[7] Smuckler, R.H. and Berg, R.J., New Challenges—New Opportunities; 1988, East Lansing, Michigan: Michigan State University
[8] World Bank, World Debt Tables: External Finance for Developing Countries. Vol.I: Analysis and Summary Tables, 1993, Washington, D.C.
[9] Africa Leadership Forum, The Kampala Document: Towards a Conference on Security, Stability, Development and Cooperation in Africa; 1991, Abeokuta, Nigeria
[10] Mortimer, E., A blot on the map, Financial Times, 11 May 1994, p.14
[11] Johnson, L.V., Report on Working Group 1: World Peace; Pugwash Newsletter 29/1991, pp 74-76
[12] Halberstam, D., The Next Century; 1991, New York: William Morrow and Company, Inc

Jean F. Freymond

AN AGENDA FOR THE COMING YEARS

After a certain age, birthdays are primarily occasions to reflect on past achievements. Olusegun Obasanjo belongs to the very few who on his birthday challenges us to consider what is still to be accomplished and when he might provide the needed leadership.

Mankind has embarked on a rather rare journey through an era of transition. The XXth century is over. It ended on the 10th of November 1989 with the fall of the Berlin Wall, the way the old regime came to a close on the 14th of July 1789 with the capture of the Bastille. The XXIst century has yet to begin, let alone be shaped.

This is not the first time mankind has faced such a challenge. History is an arrow that unfolds in stages in an irreversible direction. It proceeds in a discontinuous manner, in congruence with the laws governing the evolution of Earth and living matter which consistently displays a propensity towards more complexity, adaptation, integration and fortuity. A threshold separates stages, characterized by the disappearance of old structures and the emergence of new ones of a higher order of complexity. These thresholds resemble abrupt jumps. They are crossed with all the difficulties of degeneration and the pain of childbirth in a laborious transition that can spread over years, if not decades. We are right in the middle of such a transition.

Technological advances as driving forces

Our age is in many respects driven by advances in technology. Transportation is more rapid and inexpensive. Increasingly, people move back and forth. They mingle like never before. Headways in telecommunications, low costs of phone calls, facsimiles and the rapid spread of electronic mail systems allow people to be in direct contact and instant communication. The globalisation of television, satellites and satellite dishes, and radios reaching every corner of the planet result in public opinion being better informed—and sometimes—informed at the same time as the decision-makers. People are more aware of others' culture, life styles and problems and of the ways in which these problems are solved. Live and visual coverage mean that citizens can no longer be "told stories" the way it used to be.

Popular discontent, the call for participation and the development of civil society

Technological changes have resulted in more transparent societies. This transparency—to which the media and judges have also much contributed—has revealed misfunctioning and inadequacies in public institutions, behaviours considered as ethically unacceptable and abuses on the part of some office-holders. It has led to disenchantment towards the state, indeed at times cynicism and rising eccentrism. Erosion of trust in the political establishment is mounting; unethical conduct is less tolerated than before; requests for more transparency and public participation are multiplying. Democracy still is essentially a system where power to decide and to run a country is delegated to elected representatives. People increasingly call for this power to be shared and for a democratization of democracy. They also join forces and coordinate efforts within nongovernmental organizations (NGOs) of which the number and influence have exploded over the past decades. NGOs constitute a cornerstone of civil societies. Everywhere they are becoming forces which states have to reconcile with and with which they have to enter into close and constant dialogue.

Formal social and political structure adjustments to technological changes have yet to take place

Adjustments in social and political structures commensurate to technological transformations have so far not taken place. Social and political structures have barely evolved. Sometimes they continue to be rooted in centuries old approaches and concepts, some of which certainly remain valid. Their functioning mirrors their functioning 30 to 40 years ago. Formal structures of power and decisions are still largely pyramidal, at a time when networking rendered possible by technological changes has become a dominant feature of society.

A complex world in which increasingly everyone is in charge

Over the centuries, societies have grown more complex. Today's world has reached such a stage of complexity that single individuals or small circles of decision-makers can no longer be effectively in charge of all and of everything. States also are bypassed by events and unable to master many situations. Although they persist pretending to be in command, numerous dimensions of the problematic escape their control and often their understanding. The shape of events depends increasingly on millions of individual and independent decisions which citizens take every day all over the planet. This has prompted some to say that we live in a world with no one in charge. Would it not be more appropriate to speak of a world where everyone is in charge and co-responsible?

ELEMENTS FOR AN AGENDA

Education as a priority

A world where everyone is in charge signifies a massive effort in education; and first an *education in good citizenship and ethics*, so that public opinion can move beyond the mere expression of its discontent, confrontational approaches and the defense of narrow sectorial interests. Education should concentrate on rendering understandable the complexities of our time, as well as mapping in a simple way the period through which we are going. Education might occur in families, which should again be given a central place in societies. This implies parental and grand-parental education. It should also happen in schools and within the entire system of formal education, which presupposes the education of the teachers.

Education should also take place through the media, which suggests questioning its increasingly populist rationale, based on audience rates which govern decisions on what the public will hear and see. It also implies perhaps a finer definition of the role of media in society, where its educational responsibility might be made more explicit.

Education finally should be a major responsibility of NGOs.

Developing effective public leadership

Despite the trend towards a world where everyone will be in charge in one way or another, some will be always more in charge than others. Public leaders are more required than ever. There is also a need to restore faith in the holders of public offices. Public leadership has thus to be examined, modes and criteria of selection rethought, and continuous educative processes of leaders put into place. This would ensure that at election time citizens might have a real choice between candidates indisputable on ethical and moral grounds and that the candidates are professionally and technically prepared to manage the highly complex and interdependent issues faced by today's public leaders.

Rethinking and reforming governance at all levels

There is much discussion about reinventing government and rethinking the ways the international system is structured and how it operates. So far not much has taken place to indicate that one is moving beyond mere debates.

The process of rethinking governance should be accelerated and should lead to effective reforms. It should also embrace together national, continental or regional, and global governance which cannot any longer be treated separately. It is somewhat an illusion to redesign the United Nations without addressing the question of the reform of domestic institutions as well as the role and the structure of regional organizations. Governance must be treated in a holistic way.

A world constructed from the bottom

The main trend has for long been towards the centralisation and concentration of power. This trend is now slowly being reversed. Decentralization is the order of the day. However, this trend reversal still proceeds from the same approach, that is, top to bottom.

A world where everyone is in charge should be naturally constructed from bottom up and not through a decentralized process decided at the top. Individuals, families, associations, small communities, villages and towns, as well as regions have to have full responsibilities within clear frameworks for issues which are within their domain and which they can face by themselves. All should be educated to manage such issues. They should be prepared to deal with, and solve by themselves, tensions and conflicts which naturally arise among individuals and within communities.

A world of partners in common societal projects

Equal rights and self-determination of peoples constitute pillars of the present international order. These pillars appear somewhat in contradiction with the concept of minorities to be protected. The concept of minority is not quantitative, but qualitative. Sometimes "minorities" constitute the majority of the population in a given society. For example, women in many societies consider themselves as a minority.

Protection of minorities underlines and perpetuates inequalities. It humiliates the "weak" to whom protection is granted. It frustrates the "majority" which resents a kind of arm twisting. Minorities, feeling excluded, tend to live and develop apart. They do not feel concerned by the problems of the overall society to which they formally belong. Minorities are not always willing to participate and to make the needed sacrifices which the existence of this overall community implies.

A fresh approach to the treatment of minorities would certainly deflate tensions and contribute to diminishing the risk of conflict escalating into violence. Minorities should cease to be treated as minorities, but should be considered as equal but different partners in a common societal project.

Redefining the meaning and the nature of borders

Where entire communities are divided by existing frontiers, there is a need to rethink the concept of borders and to attempt to develop an approach to the border which will not partition or isolate. Borders should increasingly be conceived in an open way so as to allow communities who intend to share what they have in common to do so. Short of new approaches to borders, the pressure to change them will certainly continue to mount and constitute a major source of conflict in the coming century.

Triggering changes

Identifying key areas where new thinking and changes are imperative is not enough. Once new approaches are considered as sensible and practical enough, they should be transformed into reality. Here lies probably the main difficulty and the foremost challenge.

Resistance to change is paramount. Among many factors, it is rooted in vested interests, fear of losing power and privileges, as well as the difficulty in accepting the approaches of others. Institutions are built like fortresses which defend their territory and interests with a narrow and self-centred concept of a public good.

One does often incriminate lack of political will as a primary source of immobilism. Political will, however, seems to be more than anything a convenient explanation. In other words, good and firm leadership—while a central factor—does not provide the only answer to paralysis. Structures and processes have also to be fundamentally improved, and clear and limited priorities established in order to prompt the needed action.

Coping with violence in our societies and in the international system is probably the most prominent imperative underlying the elements of the agenda proposed here. Invariably, since the dawn of history, mankind has been striving to be civilized. If time has an arrow and proceeds in an irreversible direction towards more complexity, civilization for its part evolves in an uncertain way. Achieving one day a "higher degree" of civilization—whatever meaning this expression has—gives no insurance as regards the degree of civilization of tomorrow. To strive for civilization implies a constant and repeated effort, an effort reminiscent of Sisyphus.

LIST OF CONTRIBUTORS

Ayodele Aderinwale (Nigeria)—Programme Manager, Africa Leadership Forum, Ota, Ogun State
Ednan Agaev (Russia)—Ambassador to Colombia; former Director, Directorate of Analysis and Forecasting, Ministry of Foreign Affairs of the Russian Federation
Chief Emeka Anyakou (Nigeria)—Commonwealth Secretary-General; former Foreign Minister
Peter Anyang' Nyong'o (Kenya)—Member of Parliament (FORD-Kenya)
Eme Awa (Nigeria)—Professor; former Chairman, National Electoral Commission
Tunji Abayomi (Nigeria)—Legal Practitioner and Chairman, Founder's Council, Human Rights Africa
Chief Afe Babalola (Nigeria)—Legal Practitioner, FFPA, SAN
Babafemi Badejo (Nigeria)—Senior Political Adviser, United Nations Political Office for Somalia, Nairobi; former Senior Political Adviser to the Special Representative of the Secretary General, United Nations Operations in Somalia (UNOSOM); former Senior Lecturer, University of Lagos
Roloef F. (Pik) Botha (South Africa)—Minister of Mineral and Energy Affairs; former Foreign Minister
Muhammadu Buhari (Nigeria)—Major-General (rtd.); former Head of State and Commander-in-Chief of the Armed Forces
Prince Mangosuthu G. Buthelezi (South Africa)—MP, Minister of Home Affairs and President, Inkatha Freedom Party
Lord Callaghan of Cardiff (United Kingdom)—former Prime Minister
Jimmy Carter (United States)—former President
Joaquim Alberto Chissano (Mozambique)—President of the Republic of Mozambique
Pierre Claver Damiba (Burkina Faso)—former Assistant Administrator and Director, Regional Bureau for Africa, UNDP and former Executive Secretary, African Capacity Building Foundation
Olatunji Dare (Nigeria)—Chairman of the Editorial Board, The Guardian
Francis Mading Deng (Sudan)—Senior Fellow, The Brookings Institution, Washington, D.C.; former Minister of State for Foreign Affairs

Boubakar Diaby-Ouattara (Cote d'Ivoire)—Executive Secretary, Global Coalition for Africa

Colin Eglin (South Africa)—Member of Parliament and Chief Constitutional Negotiator of South Africa's Democratic Party; former Leader of the Opposition (Democratic Party) in the South African Parliament

Peter Eigen (Germany)—Chairman, Board of Directors, Transparency International, Berlin

Emmanuel A. Erskine (Ghana)—Lieutenant-General (rtd.); former Commander, United Nations Interim Force in Lebanon (UNIFIL)

Jean F. Freymond (Switzerland)—Director, Centre for Applied Studies in International Negotiations (CASIN), Geneva

Ibrahim Agboola Gambari (Nigeria)—Permanent Representative of Nigeria to the United Nations, New York; former Foreign Minister and Professor

Reginald Herbold Green (United Kingdom)—currently Senior Social Policy Advisor to the Mozambique Planning Commission and Professorial Fellow, The Institute of Development Studies at the University of Sussex, Brighton

François van Hoek (Netherlands)—former Director, European Center for Development Policy Management, Maastricht

Joan Holmes (United States)—President, The Hunger Project

Carol Lancaster (United States)—Deputy Administrator, United States Agency for International Development (USAID); Professor, Georgetown University

Tunji Lardner (Nigeria)—New York correspondent of West Africa magazine

Terencia Leon-Joseph (Peru)—former Administrative Assistant, InterAction Council and Africa Leadership Forum

Flora Lewis (United States)—Senior Columnist, The New York Times and the International Herald Tribune, Paris

Robert von Lucius (Germany)—Southern Africa Correspondent, Frankfurter Allgemeine Zeitung, based in Johannesburg

Mehri Madarshahi (Iran)—Senior Management Analyst, United Nations Secretariat

Mario Graça do Machungo (Mozambique)—former Prime Minister of Mozambique

Bona Malwal (Sudan)—Editor and Publisher, Sudan Democratic Gazette, Oxford; former Minister of Information

Ali A. Mazrui (Kenya)—Albert Schweitzer Professor in the Humanities and Director, Institute of Global Cultural Studies, State University of New York at Binghampton, N.Y.

Robert S. McNamara (United States)—former Secretary of Defense and former President, The World Bank

King Moshoeshoe II. (Lesotho)—King of Lesotho

Abul Maal A. Muhith (Bangladesh)—former Minister of Finance and Planning

Dragoljub Najman (Yugoslavia)—former Assistant Director General, UNESCO, and former Executive Secretary, InterAction Council, Paris

Magemeso Namungalu (Uganda)—former Editor-in-Chief, Uganda News Agency

Babacar Ndiaye (Senegal)—President, African Development Bank, Abidjan

Ad'Obe Obe (Nigeria)—former editor, Africa Forum and West Africa

Thomas R. Odhiambo (Kenya)—President, African Academy of Sciences and Director, The Research and Development Forum for Science-led Development in Africa (Randforum)

Onukaba Adinoyi Ojo (Nigeria)—Playwright; served with United Nations Operations in Somalia 1994/1995; former News Editor, Sunday Guardian, Lagos

Chief Jonathan Adio Obafemi Olopade (Nigeria)—businessman

Gabriel O. Olusanya (Nigeria)—Professor and Ambassador of Nigeria to France; former Director General, Nigerian Institute of International Affairs

Hans d'Orville (Germany)—former Executive Coordinator, InterAction Council; President, Africa Leadership Foundation, Inc.

Oyeleye Oyediran (Nigeria)—Professor and Chair of Political Science, University of Lagos

Per Pinstrup-Andersen (Denmark)—Director General, International Food Policy Research Institute, Washington, D.C.

Jeremy Pope (New Zealand)—Managing Director, Transparency International, Berlin; former Director, Legal and Constitutional Affairs Division, Commonwealth Secretariat, and Legal Counsel to its Secretary General

Jonathan Power (United Kingdom)—international affairs columnist

Sir Shridath Ramphal (Guyana)—former Commonwealth Secretary-General and Co-Chairman, Commission on International Governance

Yohei Sasakawa (Japan)—President, Sasakawa Foundation

Ellen Johnson Sirleaf (Liberia)—Assistant Administrator and Director, Regional Bureau for Africa, United Nations Development Programme

R.E. Ted Turner (United States)—Chairman of the Board, Turner Broadcasting Systems

Layashi Yaker (Algeria)—former Under-Secretary-General and Executive Secretary, United Nations Economic Commission for Africa

CONTRIBUTING ARTISTS

Werner Bartsch (Germany)
Thomas Florschütz (Germany)
Pina + Via Lewandowsky (Germany)
Elimo P. Njau (Kenya)
Bruce Onobrakpeya (Nigeria)
A.R. Penck (Germany)
Twins Seven-Seven (Nigeria)
Clemens Weiss (Germany)

A publication of
The Africa Leadership Foundation, Inc.
New York, New York

Tel: (212) 534-2355
Fax: (212) 534-0637